INJUSTICE

INJUSTICE

EXPOSING THE RACIAL AGENDA OF THE OBAMA JUSTICE DEPARTMENT

J. CHRISTIAN ADAMS

Since 1947
REGNERY
PUBLISHING, INC.
An Eagle Publishing Company • Washington, DC

Library of Congress Cataloging-in-Publication Data

Adams, J. Christian.
  Injustice / by J. Christian Adams.
    p. cm.
  ISBN 978-1-59698-277-2
  1. United States. Dept. of Justice--Corrupt practices. 2. Political corruption--United States. 3. United States--Politics and government--2009- 4. Presidents--United States--Election--2008. I. Title.
  KF5107.A712 2011
  364.1'324--dc23

                          2011034065

Published in the United States by
Regnery Publishing, Inc.
One Massachusetts Avenue, NW
Washington, DC 20001
www.regnery.com

Manufactured in the United States of America
10 9 8 7 6 5 4 3 2 1

Books are available in quantity for promotional or premium use. Write to Director of Special Sales, Regnery Publishing, Inc., One Massachusetts Avenue NW, Washington, DC 20001, for information on discounts and terms or call (202) 216-0600.

Distributed to the trade by:
Perseus Distribution
387 Park Avenue South
New York, NY 10016

To Jana,
who made this possible

For Abigail and Amelia,
who made it necessary

Contents

Introduction

For much of his life, Attorney General Eric H. Holder Jr. carried around something peculiar. While most people keep cash, family photos, and credit cards in their wallets, Holder revealed to a reporter in 1996 that he keeps with him an old clipping of a quote from Harlem preacher Reverend Samuel D. Proctor. Holder put the clipping in his wallet in 1971, when he was studying history at Columbia University, and kept it in wallet after wallet over the ensuing decades.

What were Proctor's words that Holder found so compelling?

Blackness is another issue entirely apart from class in America. No matter how affluent, educated and mobile [a black person] becomes, his race defines him more particularly than anything else. Black people have a

1

common cause that requires attending to, and this cause does not allow for the rigid class separation that is the luxury of American whites. There is a sense in which every black man is as far from liberation as the weakest one if his weakness is attributable to racial injustice.[1]

When asked to explain the passage, Holder replied, "It really says that … I am not the tall U.S. attorney, I am not the thin United States Attorney. I am the black United States attorney. And he was saying that no matter how successful you are, there's a common cause that bonds the black United States attorney with the black criminal or the black doctor with the black homeless person."[2]

Has anyone ever asked Holder what exactly is the "common cause" that binds the black attorney general and the black criminal? More important, what should the black attorney general do about this common cause? Should the black criminal feel empathy for the black attorney general, or more likely, do the favors only flow in one direction?

Holder's explanation of Proctor's quote offers some key insights into our attorney general's worldview. First, being "more particular" than anything else, skin color limits and defines Americans—in other words, race comes first for Holder. Second, despite Americans' widespread belief in trans-racial principles such as individual liberty and equal protection, blacks are expected to show solidarity with other blacks. And third, black law enforcement officers are expected to show this solidarity toward their racial compatriots, including black criminals.

It may seem shocking to hear these racialist views ascribed to America's top law enforcement officer. But to people who have worked inside the Civil Rights Division at the Department of Justice, these attitudes are perfectly familiar. In fact, Holder's revelation is small stuff compared to the racial bias and leftwing extremism that pervade that institution.[3]

The Civil Rights Division was set up in 1957 by the Eisenhower administration. Since then, as the DOJ website proudly proclaims, "The Division has grown dramatically in both size and scope," now employing almost four hundred lawyers and, with support staff, over eight hundred employees. It is responsible for enforcing a wide swath of laws, especially civil rights laws and voting laws.

The division provides a welcoming home for purveyors of fringe beliefs that are alien and repugnant to mainstream America—namely, that civil rights laws do not protect everyone equally, but only certain "oppressed" minorities. Not everyone who works there subscribes to these views, but nearly everyone who manages the place now does. As a result, the Civil Rights Division has squandered its moral authority. Having initially been infused with the spirit of the original civil rights movement and its emphasis on racial equality and color-blindness, the division is now home to the rotted industry of racial grievance.

Eric Holder clearly had big plans for the Civil Rights Division from the beginning of his tenure. At his confirmation hearings in January 2009, he called the division the "crown jewel" of the Justice Department, adding that he wanted to become attorney general in part to "restore" the division's "great traditions" that had supposedly eroded during the Bush administration.[4] Yet Holder's term has been marked by racially discriminatory law enforcement, politicized and ideological hiring, court-imposed sanctions on DOJ lawyers, and corrupt decisions to allow American voter rolls to overflow with deceased citizens and ineligible felons.

As shown by the still-murky details of Operation Fast and Furious—a secret operation run by the DOJ's Bureau of Alcohol, Tobacco, and Firearms that deliberately allowed guns to flow to

Mexican drug cartels—the DOJ is experiencing serious problems under Holder's leadership. Nevertheless, other DOJ divisions by and large don't suffer from the same toxic mix of employee malfeasance and racial bias that infects the Civil Rights Division. When I worked there, attorneys from other divisions would describe their competent, professionally run agencies and then ask me if my division was really as bad as its reputation. The answer was yes—and then some. As this book will show, the Civil Rights Division can best be described as a soap opera, within a cabal, surrounded by a racialist culture of dysfunction.

The DOJ's dismissal of the New Black Panther voter intimidation case—a case I brought and ultimately resigned over—gave the public a glimpse of the racially discriminatory worldview that characterizes this influential government agency. But the publicity surrounding that case was unusual. Until now, no one has fully conveyed to the American public exactly how deep the rot goes in the Civil Rights Division, and the many disgraceful scandals that have unfolded behind its closed doors.

People from outside the DOJ typically react in stunned disbelief when I explain the sheer unprofessionalism I saw there. The Obama administration promotes government lawyers who were subject to hundreds of thousands of dollars in court sanctions? You must be kidding, they tell me. Nearly a thousand employees from the nation's premier federal law enforcement agency get the day off for a retreat where employees perform juvenile skits? Impossible, they figure. A workplace where people openly protest arriving to work on time? Inconceivable. A government agency opposed to Christmas? No way.

Take picnics. Most Americans probably have fond memories of picnics on sunny summer days. It is a common, wholesome tradition, as American as July 4 fireworks, Thanksgiving football, and Memorial Day parades.

But don't mention picnics around attorney Charla Jackson of the Civil Rights Division's Housing and Civil Enforcement Section. She doesn't want to hear the word, because she believes it is racist. The word picnic, you see, is derived from an event familiar to white Americans, or so Jackson believes. Around a century ago, large numbers of white folks would supposedly gather at a park, almost always in a small, southern town. They brought lemonade, table-cloths, ham sandwiches, cold chicken, potato salad—and an important item in this alternative universe—lynching rope.

After a few servings of slaw topped off with a piece of cherry pie, the white folks with full bellies would get a hankering to go find—or in this case, "pick"—some not-so-white folks at random, presumably those within easy reach. Hence, the "pic" part of "picnic." The "ni" gives you a good sense where the second part of the word supposedly comes from. Once a victim was selected, he would be promptly dispatched with the lynching rope as the "picnickers" feasted on watermelon and staged sack races.

Naturally, no such event ever really happened at any picnic, much less comprised some sort of murderous American tradition. But it's widely known in the Housing Section that employees are banned from staging picnics, or at least using the term. Meanwhile, a quick perusal of the Oxford Dictionary would reveal just how wrong Jackson is. The word "picnic" derives from the French *pique-nique*, roughly meaning to peck at a worthless thing.

This sort of derangement might be funny if it weren't emanating from such a powerful government agency. The people who find a dastardly, racist subtext to an everyday picnic are the same people the DOJ empowers to sue landlords, mortgage lenders, and apartment complexes, and to decide legal matters pertaining to evidence, racial intent, and discrimination law. Indeed, it should be deeply disturbing to every American that U.S. businesses are at the mercy of racially paranoid attorneys who can bring discrimination lawsuits against them.

This problem is far from hypothetical; as a government attorney, Charla Jackson herself has brought multiple lawsuits against businesses for alleged racial discrimination, including against Adams Mark Hotels and Nara Bank. And the Housing Section where Jackson works has filed discrimination lawsuits against numerous American business, such as Dominos Pizza, AIG, Chevy Chase Bank, Cracker Barrel, Erie Insurance, Denny's, Nationwide Insurance, Marriott, Hard Times Café, Fleet Mortgage, Pulte Homes, and Nissan Motor Acceptance.

Business groups have failed to comprehend the ramifications. They have some basic understanding of the jurisdiction of the Civil Rights Division, but they mostly assume it is populated by professional, law-abiding attorneys. And such attorneys can in fact be found there, especially since the Bush administration hired many lawyers with professional litigation experience, as opposed to those hired under Holder, whose main qualification, as explained in chapter three, is often their experience working with a leftwing activist group.

But businesses and business associations that acquiesce to bullying by the Civil Rights Division are making an enormous mistake. They assume they can't beat the DOJ in litigation and that the attorneys bringing the cases are competent legal technicians. But if they realized how often these legal actions are actually frivolous, ideologically motivated acts of political warfare carried out by racial extremists, they might be more inclined to fight back by forming mutual defense associations or creating information clearing houses about tort litigation like those established by insurance companies.

The stakes are high, because the Civil Rights Division wields enormous jurisdiction over the American economy. The Disability

Rights Section, for example, zealously enforces the Americans with Disabilities Act and has brought movie theatres like AMC and Cinemark, Norwegian Cruise Lines, the USGA, Days Inn, and the International House of Pancakes practically to their knees. It sued the Virginia Bar for the unforgiveable crime of asking attorneys if they have been treated for a mental disorder. It even brought a case on behalf of *dead* disabled people in *United States v. Vasquez Funeral Home.*[5]

The division's attorneys know that most businesses they target, fearing adverse publicity and believing in the DOJ's legal supremacy, will buckle quickly on whatever face-saving terms they can muster, no matter how outrageous the lawsuit may be. Thus, business by business, some of America's most radical political activists are imposing their will on the American people—almost completely under the media's radar.

The assault on American business is damaging enough, but it is within the Voting Section of the Civil Rights Division that the far-left racialist mindset most afflicts American political life. I served as an attorney in the Voting Section for more than five years, litigating numerous cases to protect the rights of racial and language minorities. During that time, I saw from the inside how an agency that already employed a good number of leftist zealots quickly descended during the Obama administration into outright racial demagoguery.

The Voting Section has enormous power over the systems of government adopted by states, counties, and cities. Furthermore, where you vote, how you vote, and for whom you vote are all impacted by Voting Section bureaucrats. Every American voter is affected by these laws in one way or another. A brief review of the

Voting Section's authority will convey how crucial the section is for upholding the integrity of our voting system, and therefore of our entire constitutional republic.

Section 5 of the Voting Rights Act requires the federal government to approve every law affecting voting in nine states and parts of seven others. Even statewide laws that affect those other seven states are subject to approval or rejection by the federal government. The scope of Section 5 is vast. Because states are given the power to run their own elections in the Constitution, Section 5 rests at the farthest frontier of federal power.[6] Even the DOJ has called it a "substantial departure ... from ordinary concepts of our federal system," with then-Supreme Court Justice John Paul Stevens asserting that the section's "encroachment on state sovereignty is significant and undeniable."[7]

In jurisdictions subject to Section 5, if a county wants to move a polling place a block down the street, or change the hours of operation of a voter office, or alter the method of translating ballots into Spanish, or if a local government wants to adopt a redistricting plan, then the Voting Section must approve. If it finds that any of these changes could have even a hint of any negative effect on a racial minority, the DOJ will "object," which effectively blocks the change. Much of the front-line work on Section 5 submissions is actually done by college students, who call citizens in affected states, review statistical data, and ultimately recommend whether the federal government should block a proposed change in state or local law.

Another significant law enforced by the Voting Section is Section 2 of the Voting Rights Act. Under this section, the United States may sue a state, or any other sovereign body that has power over voting or elections, when a practice or device is used to discriminate.[8] The DOJ typically uses this broad authority to prosecute "vote dilution" cases that seek to replace an at-large system of election with a single member district plan. But Section 2 also prohibits discrimination against a "language minority group."[9] This effectively empowers the DOJ to file lawsuits if English-language ballots and election materials cannot be understood by certain groups of people who don't speak English.

Similarly, Section 203 of the Voting Rights Act imposes requirements to publish ballots and election materials in a foreign language in some, but not all, parts of America. Today, the largest metropolitan areas are required to print ballots in a foreign language: New York, Los Angeles, Houston, Miami, Boston, Tampa, San Francisco, Philadelphia, and Phoenix. DOJ bureaucrats enforce this constitutionally dubious law and oversee compliance, often far outside the purview of a federal court.

The Voting Section also is tasked with enforcing Section 11(b) of the Voting Rights Act. This is the anti-intimidation law used in the action against the New Black Panther Party in Philadelphia, as described in chapters four and five. It prohibits intimidation, threats, or coercion against voters, or attempts to do the same.

The Voting Section is further responsible for protecting the right to vote for overseas voters and, notably, military voters, who are banned from filing lawsuits themselves to obtain their ballot.

Additionally, the Voting Section monitors elections in many states under the Voting Rights Act. Known as "federal observer coverage," this power allows the DOJ to place federal eyes and ears inside the polls to collect evidence on the conduct of state and local elections. Even in places where it is not empowered to conduct "observer coverage," the DOJ routinely sends "attorney observers" who are not empowered to be inside the polling place without consent, though the states and local governments almost always agree to their presence when asked. If they understood this request is often the first indication they are going to be sued, they might not be so quick to approve it.

Finally, the Voting Section enforces the National Voter Registration Act of 1993,[10] widely known as "Motor Voter," as well as the Help America Vote Act of 2002, or "HAVA."[11] Among other mandates, these laws require states to adopt a centralized database of eligible voters. If states do not adequately keep up the required list by purging it of dead, duplicate, and ineligible voters, then the attorney general, through the Voting Section, may sue.

These voter lists have come under attack from leftwing extremists who denounce many voting regulations and requirements as being racist. It is no coincidence, then, that under Eric Holder's tenure as attorney general, the DOJ has undertaken absolutely no enforcement activity to remove dead and ineligible voters, as explained in chapter six. However, Holder has shown a keen interest in Section 7 of Motor Voter, which requires states to turn welfare agencies into voter registration offices and requires state officials to urge welfare recipients to register to vote.

In sum, the Voting Section has enormous power. Through multiple federal statutes, it can regulate or reject every aspect of elections in all or parts of sixteen states, require foreign language ballots, help (or ignore) military voters, sue to replace state election procedures including voter identification requirements or at large elections, require (or not) states to keep clean voter rolls, and send hither and thither swarms of federal officials to monitor state and local elections. When so much power is concentrated in one government office, who occupies that office is a substantial public concern.

Because of the expansive power concentrated in the Voting Section and across the Civil Rights Division, Americans have a right to expect that its management and leadership act impartially, especially in racial matters. But soon after President Obama's inauguration in January 2009, I discovered that would not be the case.

Immediately after he was sworn in as president, even while the rest of the country was still celebrating post-racial hope and change, Obama tapped Deputy Assistant Attorney General Loretta King to be the acting assistant attorney general—the head of the entire Civil Rights Division—before the Senate could confirm a nominee. Former Bush political appointees who worked with King have described to me how she proudly boasted that her career advanced primarily through race-based preferences. King, whose sordid history at the division is discussed throughout this book, was a Democratic Party loyalist who spoke openly to co-workers of quitting her job and running for elective office in Maryland.[12] The Bush Justice leadership knew she was a bumbling radical in their midst, but they couldn't do much about it except relegate her to tasks that minimized her ability to do damage.

The Bush administration's instincts about King were proven correct when Eric Holder took the reins at Justice. King accompanied the new attorney general to meet Voting Section employees in March 2009, not long after he was confirmed by the Senate. That day I met Holder as he passed through the throngs of excited employees. He gave me a limp handshake and avoided eye contact with me, making me wonder whether he was disengaged with everyone there, or just with some of us.

As a giddy King introduced Holder to us, she said something astonishing and unforgettable: "I can't tell you how exciting it is to go to work every day, and look up at the photos, and see that we now have two black men running the country." Most of the Voting Section, though not everyone, cheered her racially charged introduction. It was considered acceptable and even laudable, though if a manager at a state agency had gathered his workers to celebrate white men running the country, the very same Justice Department would probably sue him for employment discrimination.

Of course, America's election of its first black president was an historic event. But a racially charged address in front of the attorney general and the whole Voting Section rightfully would have been blasted on the front page of the *Washington Post* if it had occurred during a Republican administration. The press, however, didn't show any interest in the story, and we can reasonably guess that Holder declined to admonish King afterward—after all, we know what's in his wallet.

The end result when racial extremists dominate such a powerful division of federal law enforcement is, in a word, lawlessness.

Impervious to sanctions and penalties handed down by federal courts, the DOJ Civil Rights Division feels unconstrained by department regulations or even by federal law. We now face the Orwellian situation where government lawyers brazenly ignore and subvert the law they have sworn to uphold, and where a leading civil rights protection agency discriminates against some racial groups while it favors others. This is not only lawlessness, it is the most dangerous kind of lawlessness—for history shows that once a nation's laws cease to apply to the law enforcers, individual liberty does not survive for very long.

This injustice cannot stand. The stakes are too high to allow this wanton abuse of power to continue. It's time the American people found out exactly what is happening at the Department of Justice and who's allowing it to happen. The situation will not improve until the true extent of the racial fanaticism and corrupt dysfunction that pervades that department is made clear—and that's exactly what this book will do.

CHAPTER ONE

★ ★ ★

Payback Time in Mississippi

A Declaration of War

R ace has affected the American experience since the nation's earliest days. From the arrival of the first African slaves in the Virginia colony in the early 1600s, to the constitutional compromises of 1787, through the unsettled decades before Lincoln's election, through the bloody Civil War, to three constitutional amendments promoting racial equality and their dilution over the ensuing decades—race has been a central force in our history. Through much of the twentieth century, enforcement of racially discriminatory Jim Crow laws in parts of America meant race did not play an openly contentious role—the supporters of Jim Crow ruled the field. But resentment at the political and economic oppression of one group of Americans by another boiled below the surface.

In the 1960s, the modern civil rights movement pricked the conscience of America. In the face of bitter and sometimes violent resistance, its brave adherents paved the way for Congress's passage of the Civil Rights Act of 1964 and the Voting Rights Act of 1965, which together knocked down the walls of legal discrimination. After 189 years, Thomas Jefferson's prose of 1776—that all men are created equal—was transformed from an aspiration to a legal truth.

By that time the echoes of the whip and chain had grown faint, but America could not simply seal off its past and forget it. A quick return to normalcy was impossible in a nation that had never known normalcy about racial issues.

I am reminded of my experience some years ago conducting research in Jefferson County, along the Mississippi River in the southwest corner of Mississippi, where I spent many weeks at the Jefferson County Courthouse poring over circuit court files. Lacking a single hotel, Jefferson presented a bleak economic landscape that barely resembled the rest of America. In place of the familiar national restaurant chains, a cart in the parking lot of the no-name grocer served a variety of lunchtime options, including parts of pigs I never knew people ate. Driving around the county seat of Fayette, I saw shanty-style homes that seemed to date to the turn of the last century, complete with roof holes patched with cut vegetation. It was obvious that the long history of slavery and segregation echoes across time to disadvantage present generations, whose ancestors were prevented from accumulating wealth and passing down lessons of economic success to their children.

The civil rights movement struggled valiantly to rectify the injustices of Jim Crow that had created dire circumstances for so many black Americans. Dedicated to racial equality, race-blind justice, personal responsibility, and inter-racial goodwill, civil rights pioneers like Ida B. Wells, William Monroe Trotter, Martin Luther King, and Rosa Parks were truly giants who sacrificed to make America live up to its founding ideal that all men are created equal. The moral foundation of their cause rendered it unstoppable.

But somewhere along the way, the civil rights movement transformed into something wholly different. It abandoned its commitment to legal equality and inter-racial harmony, adopting instead the ignoble goals of racial entitlements, race-based preferences, and unequal enforcement of federal law. The quintessential civil rights group, the NAACP, is a thoroughly different creature today than the eminent organization that led the nation in fighting lynching and supporting legal equality—it is now almost indistinguishable from the galaxy of organizations that comprise the racial grievance industry.

The organizers of the historic Selma to Montgomery voting rights marches weren't motivated by anger toward whites or disdain for America's history. They had a singular, noble mission—eradicating laws that systematically denied blacks the right to vote. Equality was their aim, not vengeance. They drew upon the long American tradition of justice to strengthen their case. As those brave marchers crossed the Edmund Pettus Bridge on March 7, 1965, to start the long walk to Montgomery, Alabama, they were confronted by rows of police officers sent by Alabama's power brokers. Meeting at the base of the bridge, the two sides represented contrasting worldviews: one was armed with clubs and tear gas, the other had nothing except its moral authority. White and black marchers were attacked together that day, and both white and black civil rights activists were killed in Selma in the weeks surrounding the marches.

The Edmund Pettus Bridge has become a civil rights monument. Every March, activists commemorate the anniversary of the attack by recreating the march across the bridge. Notables come from all over the country to participate—Jesse Jackson, Barack Obama, Harry Reid, Al Sharpton, and Steny Hoyer have all made the pilgrimage.

The nation's premiere voting rights museum—the National Voting Rights Museum—now sits at the foot of the bridge. The museum is an inadvertent monument to the civil rights movement's degeneration. Its outlook is neatly captured in ten words that begin its timeline display of the civil rights movement. There, we find a replica of John Trumball's iconic depiction of the signing of the Declaration of Independence with the caption, "1776. The Declaration of Independence signed by wealthy white men."

The original civil rights giants would never have tolerated this historically false assertion. They were patriots, driven by love for their fellow countrymen and a burning desire to make America a better place for all its citizens. They repeatedly and vehemently rejected hatred. But the nasty caption captures the bitter spirit of much of the civil rights movement today and of numerous race-based activist groups around the country.

"Let us not seek to satisfy our thirst for freedom by drinking from the cup of bitterness and hatred," pleaded Dr. King from the steps of the Lincoln Memorial in August 1963.[1] This was a constant refrain in his speeches. Several years earlier, he had linked the same theme to Christian faith. Speaking of the command of Jesus to love your enemies, he preached:

> Far from being the pious injunction of a utopian dreamer, this command is an absolute necessity for the survival of our civilization. Yes, it is love that will save our world and our civilization, love even for enemies.... If I hit you and you hit me and I hit you back and you hit me back and go on, you see, that goes on ad infinitum. It just never ends. Somewhere somebody must have a little sense, and that's the strong person. The strong person is the person who can cut off the chain of hate, the chain of evil.[2]

That sentiment is irreconcilable with the bitter sense of racial grievance that is peddled today by the sullied descendents of the civil
rights movement. Under the Obama administration, adherents of
this radical movement have seized control of the Department of
Justice and especially its Civil Rights Division. From that powerful
position, they have enforced an explicitly race-based concept of
justice, as described throughout this book.

But before we discuss those transgressions, readers must understand that everything the DOJ is doing today is part of a larger war
between two camps: those who support a racialist future for America in which the law treats people differently according to their race,
and those who support a race-blind future.

From the 1970s through the 1990s, the racialist camp met hardly
any resistance as it displaced the traditional civil rights movement
and spread its tentacles throughout American society. Its adherents
bamboozled many Americans by appropriating Dr. King's language
of "equality," "civil rights," and "justice" even as they subverted the
meaning of those terms, transforming them into code words for a
callous system of racial spoils they are striving to impose on the
entire nation. Hundreds of activist groups sprung up around the
country dedicated to furthering this agenda and enshrining it in
local, state, and federal law.

During this period, there was no "war" to speak of between the
racialist and race-blind camps—the racialists simply moved from one
victory to another, constantly strengthening their position in government and using spurious accusations of racism to snuff out any
incipient signs of pushback. But that suddenly changed in 2003, when
the first shot was fired back by the other side. Having become accus-
tomed to advancing their agenda at will through any means necessary,
the racialists finally went too far, provoking the Department of Justice,
for the first time, to act to protect a disenfranchised white minority.

The entire conflict today between the Obama DOJ and proponents of race-neutral law enforcement is part of the war that began with that first act of resistance in 2003. And it all started not in the hallowed halls of Washington, but in a little-known, rural area of eastern Mississippi.

Named after the Choctaw for "stinking waters," Noxubee County is located along Mississippi's border with Alabama. Historically, the county has been sparsely populated, though its population jumped 42 percent in the 1870s thanks to an influx of black migrants attracted by the rich soil and thriving cotton industry. By 1880, the Census showed Noxubee to be 83 percent black and 17 percent white.[3]

Due to its unusual racial demographics, Noxubee became a focal point of the Ku Klux Klan, whose terror tactics included whipping freedmen for attempting to rent farmland, emasculating black men, whipping black women "servants" deemed too friendly with their male employers, and patrolling black areas of the country at night.[4] Meanwhile, the small white minority was terrified by the potential of organized violence similar to slave uprisings throughout history, whose details they knew intimately.

Until the 1960s, white officials retained power by committing myriad abuses designed to prevent blacks from registering to vote. One of the more common schemes was for registration offices to change their hours of operation during black voting registration drives or even to close down completely when blacks came to register. If persistent black citizens chanced upon an open office, they would face a gauntlet of impossible requirements. Civics questionnaires would appear asking absurd questions such as, "How many bubbles are in a bar of soap?" Character references, literacy exams, and constitutional exams most law students would fail were other tools used for the same purpose.

Today, Noxubee is about 70 percent black and 30 percent white. Corn and cattle farms dominate the pastoral landscape, punctuated by catfish ponds with huge paddlewheel aerators. Dogs sometimes trot along the road with a giant catfish in their mouths snatched from a pond, providing a welcome contrast to the multitude of dead dogs that litter the roads. Polling places are scattered in tin shacks and in old fire stations across far corners of the county, often close to rattlesnake-infested woods. Graded sandy dirt forms many, if not most, of the county's roads, which stretch for miles in straight lines across unspoiled countryside.

Just outside the county seat of Macon, up a winding road on a hillside, is the Oddfellows Cemetery, where almost two centuries of Noxubee history is memorialized through time-worn angel monuments, broken marble crosses, and grand statutory displays. Parts of the cemetery have fallen into disrepair, testaments to a long-vanished, wealthier time. At the top of the hill is a Civil War-era plot in which rows of unknown Union soldiers lie beside rows of their unknown Confederate counterparts. These 300 dead, all that Macon could handle, were brought from Shiloh packed in lime on a train that unloaded Macon's unsolicited share of bodies on their journey south. There is a sense of sadness here—only in death could the blue and the grey lie together in peace.

Noxubee has struggled economically since the mid-1900s, with its population dropping to around 12,000 today, a third of its 1900 level. Its 20 percent unemployment rate routinely leads Mississippi. A brick plant recently shut down, leaving a sawmill as one of the few industrial ventures providing well-paying jobs. Still, the county has its share of hard-working, industrious people, including a community of Mennonites who run successful farms and an even more successful restaurant called, simply, "The Bakery."

In 2003, this sleepy county became ground zero in a national political war thanks to the activities of one man: Ike Brown.

Hailing from Madison County, Mississippi, Ike Brown graduated from Jackson State University in 1977. He dropped out of law school after one year and moved to Noxubee County to work in political campaigns. He was an on and off member of the statewide executive committee of the Mississippi Democratic Party, worked as a jury consultant, and eventually became chairman of the county Democratic Party. These were curious offices for someone with Brown's history of legal problems; in 1984, he pleaded guilty to forgery charges relating to misconduct in the insurance industry, and he was convicted in federal court in 1995 of nine charges of aiding and abetting the filing of false income tax returns.

Bill Ready, a civil rights activist from Meridian, Mississippi, knew Brown and described his background to me: "Ike learned what he did from his daddy in Canton. Ike's daddy was a runner for the white power structure, and everything Ike did in Noxubee he learned from the whites in Madison County." Ready was literally a foot soldier in the civil rights movement. While synagogues were being dynamited and churches burned in Meridian, Ready, an attorney, represented blacks who fought back. Meridian blacks formed an armed self defense group that guarded Ready's home and once exchanged gunfire with attacking whites.[5] "We were at war," Ready says.

The tall and lanky Brown is always a swirl of energy working on some project or scheme, sometimes many at once. Quick in conversation and boasting an encyclopedic knowledge of history and of the Dallas Cowboys, he has undeniable charisma, even if it is unpolished and rash at times. With his intelligence and charm, he became a singular force in Noxubee politics. Yet his story, in many ways, is an American tragedy.

Consumed with animosity toward whites, Brown unleashed a toxic mix of raw political power and racial anger in an effort to switch the positions of historic oppressor and the historically oppressed in Noxubee. In due course, his racialist jeremiads found a receptive audience. Instead of causing revulsion, his anti-white rancor spawned a corrupt, Tammany Hall-style political machine. Throughout the county, Dr. King's dream of Christian love, equality, and integration gave way to a malicious campaign to exert racial payback.

One can understand the extent of Brown's racial animus by listening to several cassette tapes stored at the library at the University of Mississippi in Oxford.[6] Donated by Georgia State professor Colin Crawford, the tapes relate to Crawford's book *Uproar at Dancing Rabbit Creek*, which details a racially charged debate in the 1980s involving solid waste companies in Noxubee—a mostly black group wanted a dump built, while a white-led group opposed it.[7] Like most controversies in the county, Ike Brown was in the center of it, leading the largely black faction.

Armed with a tape recorder, Crawford captured Brown's true feelings about his white neighbors in Noxubee. Crawford's book never related Brown's most incendiary statements—but the United States did when it later put Brown on trial in Jackson, Mississippi, for discrimination against white voters. Brown is asked by Crawford on tape what was needed to improve race relations in the county. "Funerals," he replies. Audibly laughing, Brown continues, "Funerals will help it out. We had one, a supervisor, [who] died that was against [the waste dump]." Crawford asks which supervisor. Brown replies, "Ken Misso, Jr., yeah he died, and it opened a chance for a black to get elected. So it's good to have funerals sometimes."[8] Misso had passed away at the age of forty-seven, leaving behind two boys.

On tape, Brown explains with shocking honesty some of his race-based political tactics involving absentee ballots. Describing why his operatives in this scheme only collected the ballots of black voters, Brown says, "We got a precinct that is ninety five percent black, and you know it's pretty well gonna vote for the black candidate against the white, right, and why wouldn't you get all the absentees out of that precinct? Cause they're gonna be going your way anyway, right? You don't see any of us over there getting the absentee votes of white folks. It's cutting your own throat."[9]

Brown later observes, "When two blacks run against [each other], when black run against black, for example, there's a perception among black people to vote for the blackest candidate."[10] Brown always let Noxubee voters know who the "blackest" candidates were and which black candidates had assembled unacceptable biracial coalitions.

In the interviews, Brown characterizes his political operation as a racially motivated "machine" similar to other political machines across the country: "I have a history of electing blacks all over. So it's a natural white thing to keep blacks from getting in power. And that's what I'm doing—putting blacks in power.... People support the machine because they get something out of it.... And all of us should work together to spread power."[11]

At another point, Brown becomes angry when Crawford asks him why he holds today's whites in Noxubee, and presumably millions of other white Americans, responsible for the sins of their ancestors. Brown's voice rises and quickens as he answers, "But they *are* responsible! Well we just taking something back that we gave you. And then all hell breaks loose. That's what they call 'reverse discrimination.' In other words, *she* wouldn't be where *she was* if *her folks* hadn't done *what they did*!"[12]

Brown's ideology was expressed most concisely by one of his allies, Noxubee County Election Commissioner Russell Smart. At a public election commission meeting, Smart refused a citizen's request to remove a group of ineligible voters from the voter rolls. Smart later recalled that the citizen "said this is no different from the way, you know, whites used to treat blacks the way you all doing down here, you know. And I turned around and said, 'Well, maybe it's payback time.'"[13]

Payback time—it was an agenda Ike Brown dedicated his career to advancing. The "machine" of racial grievance would use every trick in the book to take back something improperly given to whites—namely, political power and wealth.

Although Brown's primary aim was to concentrate all power in the county in the hands of blacks, he did not hesitate to lob incendiary racial slurs even at fellow blacks who displeased him. For example, he nearly came to blows with black county supervisor William "Boo" Oliver when the board of supervisors was considering whether to fire two black clerks who appeared to have embezzled more than $40,000 from the county. Although Oliver wanted to fire the pair, Brown emphatically supported them at one board meeting and denounced Oliver as a "white man's nigger." Oliver, a burly farmer, leapt out of his chair, fists clenched against Brown, before the county attorney broke up the confrontation. When Oliver won the vote and the women were fired, Brown stormed out of the room yelling that Oliver had "sold out to the white folks."[14]

Turning racial demagoguery into an art form, Brown became an influential power broker in Noxubee. When he left town in March 1995 to serve a year-and-a-half stretch in an Alabama federal prison, he was feted by prominent local politicians. Brown even retained much of his political influence behind bars, penning political messages that were hung around town and published in the local newspaper. "Keep Hope Alive, Vote Black in '95" he exhorted. From jail, Brown also served as a political consultant to Larry Tate, a candidate for county supervisor. By prison telephone, Brown explained to Tate the importance of defeating white candidates and electing only blacks. "Since the county was predominately black, we need a black candidate," he told Tate, urging him to run against a white incumbent.

Brown was especially focused on the contest for Noxubee County sheriff. From prison he wrote:

> We are not free yet. As I am imprisoned, so could you, but in a different manner. They thought by getting rid of me they could fool you. Don't let them carry you back to the old days, when blacks were found dead in the jail, you couldn't even go in the courthouse, you weren't even respected, I help bring change to Noxubee County, and I will be back soon. You must win this one yourself. I am asking you to remember me by supporting these candidates who have pledge [*sic*] to keep the dream alive.[15]

After his release from prison, Brown returned to Noxubee County. Local and state politicians threw him a welcome home party with an enormous food order that citizens told me was paid for by the Noxubee County sheriff's office, leaving county jail inmates short of food for days.

★　★　★

Back in Noxubee, Ike Brown resumed his campaign to secure black domination of the county's power structure. In the Democratic

Party primary elections of 2003, however, his zeal crossed all bounds of decency and legality. Brown resorted to such shameless corruption and coercion that he joined the likes of Bull Conner, George Wallace, and Lester Mattox on the wrong side of civil rights history. At the same time, his shocking campaign of vote fraud—the likes of which, most Americans believe, is rarely seen outside third world nations—sparked a national war over civil rights that continues to this very day.

Noxubee County's August 2003 Democratic primary, whose winners were sure to take office due to the reluctance of the county's black majority to vote Republican, had all the local offices on the ballot—county supervisor, county prosecuting attorney, board of education, circuit clerk court, and the office that most concerned Brown, county sheriff. Sheriffs wield enormous power in rural Mississippi—they control the jails and the treatment of prisoners, and collect and present evidence in criminal cases. They played a starring role in civil rights history, especially during the Freedom Summer campaign of 1964, when their deputies scooped up civil rights workers crossing through their counties. The most famous such case was the murder of civil rights workers James Chaney, Michael Schwerner, and Andy Goodman in Neshoba County, just southwest of Noxubee. The gruesome killings were committed by Klansmen who were abetted by Deputy Sheriff Cecil Price and, most likely, by Sheriff Lawrence Rainey. The case was a major impetus for passage of the Voting Rights Act the following year.

Intimately familiar with this history, Brown made the re-election of a black sheriff, Albert Walker, over a white candidate, Tiny Heard, a no-holds-barred affair. He made no secret of his mission, telling black voters at the polls, "You've got to put blacks in office, because we don't want … white people over us anymore."[16]

One of the first things he did to game the election system was to appoint a nearly all-black force of poll workers to work on election day. Brown knew black poll workers were more likely to follow his commands than were whites, who generally opposed his racialist agenda. Although Brown had repeatedly attempted to remove whites as poll workers in the past, by 2003 he had risen to become chairman of the Noxubee Democratic Party, giving him the power to deploy an almost all-black poll worker force.

Although courts have cited the importance of compiling a racially diverse poll worker force,[17] in the 2003 primary in Noxubee, only seven whites served among 110 poll workers. The county's largest three towns—Brooksville, Macon, and Shuqualak—did not have a single white poll worker. In a runoff election two weeks later, Brown selected seventy-six poll workers, including just two whites. None of the white candidates running in the original primary or the runoff were contacted for names of potential poll workers.

When the Mississippi Democratic Party challenged Brown's racially lopsided poll worker force, Brown told State Chairman Rickey Cole, "In Noxubee County, we hire who we want to."[18] Furthermore, Brown preposterously insisted he could not find healthy white volunteers to work at the polls—though the party had no problem finding white poll workers until Brown became its chairman. Brown's excuse is particularly absurd in light of the story a black Noxubee resident named Doris Wilborn later told in court. According to Wilborn, she received a letter one day informing her she had been appointed to be a poll worker. She had never sought the job and Brown had never asked her, but she was magically appointed anyway despite suffering from diabetes and having had several heart attacks, triple bypass surgery, and a knee replacement.[19]

Controlling the poll workers was crucial for Brown because Mississippi invests them with powers he needed to exploit, such as the power to check in voters on election day. Because Mississippi does not require people to show photo IDs to vote, an honest poll worker who personally knows the voters is the only safeguard against a voter falsely claiming to be someone else. In Noxubee, a witness overheard Brown instructing people outside the polls to vote under false names.[20]

Poll workers were also crucial for allowing another kind of political operative to help fix the election results for Brown. When most Americans vote, they enter an orderly line that streams to well-functioning check-in tables. They vote privately, and then a cheerful octogenarian often gives them an "I Voted" sticker. But voting in Noxubee County is entirely different. The fire stations, community centers, and schools used as voting precincts are clogged with mobs of noisy loiterers, both inside and outside the polling places. Historically, among these crowds you would find crooked operatives known as "assistors."

Assistors were often Brown loyalists who accosted black voters either outside or inside a polling place and imposed "assistance" to ensure they voted for Brown's preferred black candidates. Sometimes they lingered around the polling site, snagged approaching voters, and marked the ballot themselves without any input from the voter. Other times, the assistors arrived unannounced at voters' homes to drive them to the polls, coaching the voters on the ride.

This practice was a corrupt implementation of Section 208 of the Voting Rights Act, which gives disabled or illiterate voters the right to assistance by anyone of their choice, save for a boss or union representative. The assistors traditionally controlled hundreds of votes in Noxubee elections—this was a substantial sum, considering only around 5,000 votes were recorded in a typical election. Their activities were ignored by Brown's poll workers, who were responsible for policing voting sites.

One of Brown's activists helping to pump up the election day vote was Patsy Roby, who became one of Noxubee's key political operatives despite her lack of any defined career. An imposingly large woman, Roby is pugnacious and confident. In a deposition, she described her career as "getting a check"—in other words, collecting welfare—though two rooms of her house were occupied by enormous flat screen TVs. Further explaining her personal history, she said she "done did everything. I done stole, broke in, robbed, done did a whole lot of stuff. I just got a record. I done did a lot of things." Asked about her participation in Noxubee elections, she testified that she could not remember what she did. One thing she could remember doing, however, was smoking crack.[21] One of Roby's criminal convictions involved burglarizing a store by sending children to crawl through a hole in a building to steal jackets.

Roby and other assistors would lead voters to the registration table, tell them, "Give 'em your name," and then instruct them, "Tell 'em you need assistance!" After they accompanied a voter to the booth, observers would often hear them guide the voter in selecting candidates, telling them, "This one, this one, that one" as they went down the ballot. In other instances, the assistors simply seized the pencil and assumed the role of the voter. Because assistors could only vote one person at a time, they had to implement an assembly line process during busy parts of election day, keeping their flock of voters waiting in line outside while inside they hurriedly worked through a voter's ballot.

Poll workers were key to one other major part of Brown's voter fraud operation—the manipulation of absentee ballots. Under the law, three poll workers are supposed to review the ballots for compliance with form and signature requirements. If the signatures on the envelope and absentee ballot application do not match, the poll workers are obligated to vote to reject the application. Because Brown's agents trolled the county collecting absentee ballots—some illegally—it was critical to have poll workers who would approve dubious absentee ballots without question or hesitation.

The treatment of absentee ballots in Noxubee's 2003 Democratic primary was thoroughly lawless and systematically corrupt, aided by lax state laws allowing circuit court clerks to mail out absentee ballots without first receiving an application for them. Over 21 percent of all ballots cast in the primary were absentee; the normal rate in Mississippi is between 3 and 6 percent. Predictably, in precincts that had the largest numbers of absentee ballots, the black candidates did the best. In the contest between black sheriff Albert Walker and white candidate Tiny Heard, the absentee ballots ran for Walker over Heard by a count of around 1,046 to 155.

These lopsided counts for black candidates were no accident. White citizens requesting absentee ballots from the circuit clerk were forced to send in a written form that they had to create themselves. When white voters noticed they weren't getting their ballots after sending in their forms, the circuit court clerk informed them they could request a ballot by phone—as all the black citizens had been doing for days.[22]

In his mania to engineer black electoral victories across the board, Ike Brown even disenfranchised black voters. Exploiting their access to voting lists, Brown's operatives visited black voters who had requested absentee ballots on the day the ballot arrived in the mail. Sometimes the operatives snatched the ballot out of the mailbox before the voter knew it arrived. Other times, ballots were sent to black residents who hadn't even requested them, and a Brown-paid notary would conveniently appear to "help" the resident fill it out. One ballot was sent to a voter who hadn't lived in the county for years; it arrived at her abandoned house, which was covered in kudzu and had a tree growing through the roof. The resident of the abandoned house voted in multiple elections even though she had moved out of the county.[23]

The swarms of notaries who scoured the county were Brown's agents—he paid the registration and bonding fees for at least forty-three notaries leading up to the 2003 elections. He submitted the applications in bulk to the Mississippi Secretary of State, always using a check drawn on his company, RMB Enterprises, Inc. The unusual pattern set off alarms inside the Secretary of State's office in Jackson. Normally only financial institutions sent in large bundles of notary registrations, but Brown's company was in the scrap metal and political consulting business—a strange pairing indeed, and one in little need of dozens of notaries. Brown paid at least $1,425 to create these teams of notaries, and probably much more. Naturally, every notary Brown added to his squad was black. He sought to obtain financial help for this project from the state Democratic Party, but they refused to participate.

One of Brown's notaries was Gwendolyn Spann. Brown trained Spann to harvest absentee ballots, and the Noxubee circuit court clerk armed Spann with rolls of postage stamps to use to mail back completed absentee ballots, presumably paid for by the county's taxpayers. The circuit clerk's office also gave Spann regular, real-time lists of voters who had requested absentee ballots by phone. Violating Mississippi law, Brown promised to pay Spann according to the number of absentee ballots she harvested.[24]

Carrie Kate Windham, a member of the county Democratic executive committee, was another member of Brown's notary team. Windham called the circuit clerk and requested absentee ballots be sent to voters who had not requested them. Just as a ballot would arrive in the mailbox, Carrie Kate would knock on the front door. One of the voters for whom Windam requested an absentee ballot was Macon resident Susie Wood. "I don't know how my name got to be where they could come to the mailbox," Wood testified in court, unaware that Windham played the role of election day concierge. Wood said she didn't pick any candidates herself, but instead, "I have Carrie Kate Windham to pick out the best one for me."

Wood testified that in every election, Windham visited her house the day the ballot arrived, and Windham voted the ballot for her, her husband, and her daughter. During her testimony, the judge asked Wood, "And every time you voted at home, would anybody bring you the ballot other than Ms. Windham?" Wood responded, "[Unless] it come through the mail, and then Carrie would come over and fill them out." The judge, perhaps representing the perspective of most of America, asked another question of Wood: "Let me ask you, was there any reason why you couldn't mark the person's name if you wanted to?" Wood answered, "No, sir, it wasn't no reason that I couldn't."[25]

Carrie Kate Windham also went to the home of Macon residents Nikki Halbert and her mother, Pauline Grissom. When Halbert resisted Windham's attempt to influence her vote, Windham took their ballots without even putting them in an envelope, as required by law. When later presented a copy of her purported ballot envelope containing her signature, Halbert told a federal court that the signature was not hers. More outlandish, on Halbert's absentee ballot application, the signature line contained the signed letters "C-A," which were then scratched out and the name "Nikki Halbert" was signed in the same handwriting.[26] Apparently Windham, probably tired from falsifying so many signatures, inadvertently signed her real name.

Immediately after providing this testimony to the federal court in Jackson, Halbert was targeted by the Brown machine. Brown and Carrie Kate Windham's sister, co-defendant Dorothy Clanton, loudly discussed Halbert's testimony outside the courtroom. Brown was heard on the phone saying, "Go get Carrie Kate." When Halbert returned home the night of her testimony, she was visited by Carrie Kate Windham and Brown confederate Catherine Johnson. Confronting Halbert about her testimony, Windham warned her, "We black people need to stick together." Windham then instructed Halbert to go back to court "and tell them that you probably didn't understand what you was being asked." The two women badgered Halbert for over an hour to get her to change her testimony.[27] Halbert did return to federal court, but testified about Johnson and Windham's efforts to suborn her perjury. To this day, no one has been prosecuted for either the forgeries or the suborning of perjury in federal court.

Windham visited seventy homes to notarize ballots for the 2003 election—and she was just one member of Ike Brown's gang of notaries that harvested hundreds of ballots. (Remember, only 5,000 total votes were cast in the election.) On election night, Windham and other notaries were posted inside the precinct polling places where they could quash any complaints about the ballots they had notarized.

After the roaming notaries mailed back the illegally gathered absentee ballots to the circuit clerk, often with postage stamps provided by the circuit clerk court, the ballots faced one final hurdle—campaign representatives acting as poll observers, who could challenge the ballots' validity. But the poll observers' challenges were decided upon by Ike Brown's trios of poll workers, who outright ignored most challenges. When white poll observers insisted that the law be followed and each challenge be voted on by the poll workers, Democratic Party official Dorothy Clanton yelled back, "Well, today we're not going by state law. We're going by my law."

Recognizing the fix was in, white poll observers in that precinct simply stopped making challenges.[28]

At one precinct, poll workers ignored the legal requirement to read aloud the names of absentee voters before opening their ballot envelopes. When white poll watchers protested, a uniformed Deputy Sheriff John Clanton shut them down. "Don't you listen" to them, he instructed the poll workers, exercising a power the law did not provide. "You know what you are supposed to do. You know how you've been told to do it. You open those ballots now."[29] As we've seen, the re-election of Clanton's boss, Sheriff Walker, was one of Ike Brown's primary election day goals.

At another precinct, Brown himself ordered ballots that were being contested to be fed directly into the optical scanning machine without being ruled on, thus irretrievably mixing potentially illegal votes with legal ones. "Pick up those absentee ballots that are on that table and bring them over here and put them in that machine right now," he ordered poll workers.[30]

A hot argument erupted at still another precinct when Brown illegally refused to allow a white observer for a campaign to be present at every table where absentee ballots were being counted. When Libby Abrams, a poll observer for sheriff candidate Tiny Heard, complained to Brown, Brown's response could have described what was happening all across the county that night: "This isn't Mississippi state law you're dealing with. This is Ike Brown's law."[31] Eventually a circuit court found that at least thirty-three of the absentee ballot envelopes were defective under state law, including a finding that some of the signatures on the ballot envelopes failed to match the signatures on the absentee ballot applications. Because thirty-three defective absentee ballots would not be enough to reverse the outcome, however, a new election was not ordered.

Amazingly, all this corruption was still not enough for Brown. The night before the election, he loaded the absentee ballots into the trunk of his car and took them to his house. There, he examined the absentee ballots for defects, placing yellow sticky notes on ballots explaining why poll workers should reject them. This was an act of brazen illegality, since only the poll workers, not Brown, were entitled to examine the ballots. But from inside his home, Brown ordered that certain ballots be discarded because this signature drifted a whisker below a line or that signature failed to cross the sealed flap. All the while, *every* ballot that Brown condemned was cast by a white voter.[32]

Finally, no vote fraud operation would be complete without hundreds of unaccounted for ballots. A review after the 2003 Noxubee primary found that 367 regular paper ballots were unaccounted for at just one precinct in the town of Shuqualak. In Brooksville, 181 ballots were unaccounted for. Tiny Heard, who of course lost the sheriff race to Albert Walker, complained to the circuit court clerk about the circumstances. "This one is sure screwed up," was the clerk's only response.[33]

Brown's machinations in 2003 may have been unique in scope, but they were not unprecedented in Noxubee. Voter fraud was so widespread in the county that it had already been the subject of multiple court challenges. One such lawsuit, brought by Macon resident Mary Allsup, involved an election in which Allsup, who is white, faced Earnestine George, who is black, for election commissioner. A black voter named Earline Moore testified that Carrie Kate Windham came as a notary to her house when Moore voted an absentee ballot. Moore told Windham she did not want to vote for Allsup or George, and did not want to vote in that particular contest at all. Windham managed Moore's ballot as she did Nikki Halbert's. When the absentee ballot envelope was opened in court, it revealed that a vote had been cast for George despite Moore's instructions not to vote for either candidate. Enough fraudulent votes were cast that a court ultimately overturned George's election.[34]

Aside from outright fraud, Ike Brown resorted to intimidation to manufacture the 2003 election outcome. Before the primary, he published the names of 174 voters—all of them white—in the *Macon Beacon*, the local newspaper. Brown indicated these individuals' votes would be subject to challenge because, allegedly, they were secret Republican sympathizers. Even if this were true, they would still be legally entitled to vote since the election was an open primary, but the crass move had the intended effect; one woman from the list, Kari Hardy, later said she was too afraid to vote, while another insisted that a male relative accompany her to the polls to guard her personal safety.[35]

Brown also targeted white elected officials for smear campaigns, insinuating they were growing marijuana on their property. He took out a newspaper advertisement accusing the last remaining white county supervisor, Eddie Coleman, of perpetuating slavery by engaging in racially discriminatory road paving—even though privately, Brown admitted that Coleman did a better job paving roads than any other supervisor on the board. Eventually, in a dramatic move to get rid of Coleman, Brown engineered the revocation of the supervisors' authority over road maintenance, so that Coleman could no longer claim credit for well-maintained roads during his re-election campaigns.

Black residents were not immune to Brown's thuggish tactics. When state representative Reecy Dickson heard that a black constituent was supporting Tiny Heard for sheriff, Dickson drove to the woman's house and pounded on the door. The woman, who thought the incumbent black sheriff was weak on crime, answered her door and heard Dickson snap at her, "I just came to tell you that we don't need a white sheriff in Noxubee County."[36]

Brown undertook a similar act of intimidation against Debra Rice, another black supporter of Heard. When Brown heard Rice was campaigning for Heard, he went to Rice's home and upbraided her for supporting a white for sheriff. Rice chased Brown off her property, yelling that she "had the right to vote for who the fuck I want to vote for." She called him later that day and told him, "What you just did when you came to my house, that was wrong, I have my rights to vote for who I want to vote for."[37]

Brown's allies continued this campaign of racial intimidation during election day. When Aldine Cotton, a black voter, came to vote an absentee ballot in the circuit clerk's office, Circuit Court Clerk Carl Mickens, a black man who was running for reelection against a white candidate, gave Cotton her ballot. After she voted and gave her ballot envelope to Mickens, he angrily growled at her, "You didn't vote for me. You voted for the white folks."[38]

Brown, it might be argued, would later become involved in even more outrageous acts of intimidation. In 2005, in an effort to wipe out white representation on the Macon city council, Brown suggested that Kendrick Slaughter, a black police officer and former deputy for the Noxubee County sheriff, falsely claim he lived with his sister to make him eligible to run for the Macon city council. Slaughter wanted to run against a black incumbent and a white challenger in a different race, but Brown warned him he risked "[splitting] the black votes between the black and let the white one win." Slaughter, however, refused Brown's entreaties.

Two months later, Slaughter was driving on Highway 45 through Noxubee County when he was pulled over by Deputy Terry Grasseree. Ike Brown's infamous muscle man, Grasseree later testified he went to polling places on election day "to break up arguments." Grasseree, who served alongside Brown on the Noxubee Democratic Executive Committee, was nicknamed "the big dog," a name referenced on a sign hung in the county jail— "Better watch out for the big dog, he ain't been fed yet."

After stopping Slaughter, Grasseree told him, "The sheriff needs to see you." When Slaughter told Grasseree it would have to wait, Grasseree became enraged. He pounded on the hood of Slaughter's car, screaming, "Mother fucker, I'll pull you out of this truck and kill you." After being told by Grasseree, "You better get out of here before I kill you," Slaughter drove off. But minutes later, Grasseree drove up behind him and slammed into the back of Slaughter's truck. Slaughter then drove to the courthouse, figuring he'd be safer among the usual crowd there. Once Slaughter exited his truck, Grasseree arrested him, handcuffed him, and said, "You are going to go with me to the jail and talk. I don't want you to say a mother fucking thing in my jail."[39]

The outrageous act of intimidation provoked an unusual event— a federal judge enjoined the state criminal prosecution of Slaughter. Further, the United States asked for an order to prevent witnesses from being harassed and intimidated. Slaughter himself filed an action in federal court over the arrest.

Slaughter wasn't the only Noxubee police officer arrested for political reasons. Ernest Eichelberger was a Mississippi State Trooper who ran against Sheriff Walker in 1999. Eichelberger was black but was supported by many whites, which landed him on the wrong side of Ike Brown. Walker ultimately won the contest, which was so infested with absentee ballot irregularities that a circuit court judge ordered a new election to be held.[40] However, Brown declined to schedule a new primary election, allegedly because Eichelberger never asked him to do it.

Since he had fallen afoul of Brown, it was unsurprising that the Noxubee police later arrested Eichelberger on a laughably trumped up charge. One day, Eichelberger had to photocopy evidence from a drunk-driving breathalyzer record book needed to prosecute a drunk driver. Because there was no working photocopy machine at the sheriff's office, where the book was kept, he took the book outside the office to make copies—and was charged with removing government property. Recognizing the spurious nature of the charges, Ricky Walker, the county attorney targeted by Brown, refused to prosecute Eichelberger. Sheriff Albert Walker was unwilling to dismiss the charges against his old foe, so they languished for years without resolution.

The lawless campaign against Eichelberger did not end there. In July 2005, when the Department of Justice was looking into Ike Brown's corrupt operations, the United States filed the names of 110 potential witnesses with a federal court. Along with Slaughter, Eichelberger was listed as a potential witness. After this event, a mysterious entry appeared on the court file detailing the charge against Eichelberger: next to "Disposition," someone wrote the word "guilty." Although Eichelberger was never even prosecuted, he was magically convicted in his file, and that bogus conviction was entered into the centralized state criminal conviction records. The FBI later investigated the phony entry, but the case went nowhere. Although the counterfeit "guilty" notation has since been removed from Eichelberger's court file, the charges against him are still pending today.

A final noteworthy target of Ike Brown was county prosecuting attorney Roderick Walker, one of Noxubee's last remaining white officials.

In Mississippi, county prosecuting attorneys manage felony arraignments and bring misdemeanor cases to trial. The office holds enormous power in managing the long docket of criminal cases and in deciding how much jail time to include in plea deals. During the 2003 primary, Brown aimed to replace Walker with a black attorney, but he encountered a problem: Mississippi law requires the county prosecuting attorney to be a county resident, and Noxubee County didn't have a single black lawyer. The county was home to just three attorneys, and all were white.

So Brown decided to import a black attorney named Winston Thompson. Thompson was a member of the Mississippi Bar but lived in Jackson, over 110 miles away, so Brown and state representative Reecy Dickson helped him find an apartment in Macon. But the entire effort was a ruse; Thompson later admitted he never spent a single night in the phony residence, which didn't even have a bed or any furniture. Nevertheless, after Thompson was "established" in his apartment, he changed his voter registration to Noxubee County and filed his candidate declaration form to run against Roderick Walker. The form made it clear that Thompson's candidacy was illegitimate; it listed business telephone numbers in far-off Jackson and failed to include his apartment number and zip code (perhaps because he didn't know them) or his home phone number (because his fake Macon home had no phone). The prospective new county attorney never even changed his address with the Mississippi Bar Association.

Alerted to this pathetic scam, Roderick Walker prepared a petition seeking to have Thompson knocked off the ballot. But the body to hear Walker's petition was the Noxubee Democratic Party headed by Ike Brown, who turned the hearing into a racially charged clown show.

Late on a Friday afternoon, a handwritten note on a torn out piece of paper was delivered to Walker's law office. It served as the official notice that a hearing on Walker's petition was scheduled for the next business day—in Ike Brown's living room. The courtroom would have been available for the hearing, but Brown scheduled it in his living room because, as he later said, "I wanted to do it." Walker tried to obtain the names of the people who would rule on his petition, but Brown refused to provide them. He also rejected a request from a local newspaper reporter to attend the hearing.

When the hearing convened, Brown sought to exclude two white members of the Democratic Party executive committee. When longtime committee member Robert Cunningham entered Brown's open garage area on his way to the hearing, Brown called the local sheriff. Soon afterward, Brown's thuggish enforcer, Noxubee County deputy Terry Grasseree, appeared. Brown eventually relented and allowed the white committee members into his house, but he banished them to his kitchen.

Thus, the only members of the committee sitting in judgment of Roderick Walker's petition were black. They filled Brown's living room, sitting on chairs and couches, while Walker had to sit on the short brick fireplace hearth. Brown had not informed Winston Thompson, the man whose candidacy hung in the balance, about the hearing, having simply assured Thompson that "we believe you live here and can run." Eventually the "hearing" got underway as a TV set blared in the room. Having failed to provide copies of Walker's petition to any of the committee members, Brown stopped

Walker from distributing copies himself, claiming the petition had various procedural defects. He then abruptly suspended the hearing.

Walker, an attorney for twenty-five years, raced back to his office to repair the defects that the law school dropout had alleged were in his petition. By the time he returned with an amended petition, Brown had adjourned the meeting, effectively rejecting Walker's case.[41] Though denied justice, Walker was later vindicated after he filed a successful lawsuit to have Thompson's candidacy declared illegal.

Although Brown failed to remove Walker in 2003, he continued to scheme against him after the election, as he freely admitted to *USA Today*. The paper reported in 2006, "[Ike Brown] chuckles when noting that Noxubee has only one white official elected countywide: prosecutor Ricky Walker. 'If I could find a black lawyer who lives in the county, we'd get him, too,' Brown says with a sly grin."[42]

It is clear why Ike Brown resorted to corruption and intimidation in the 2003 elections and indeed throughout his political career—to further an agenda of black racial solidarity at the expense of Noxubee County's white minority. But this brings up an important question: Why did he think he could get away with it? After all, he was violating numerous state and federal regulations. The answer to this question will be deeply unsettling to anyone who believes America is, and should be, a nation of laws.

First, Brown presumed that the law didn't apply to him because he was black and his victims were white. Sadly, Brown probably came to this conclusion with the support of the entire national racial grievance industry. Indeed, perhaps the most unsettling part of the lawlessness that consumed Noxubee was the extent of collusion by others, including individuals and institutions that should have been leading the fight *against* Brown's corrupt machine. The NAACP should have made the egregious civil rights violations in Noxubee into a major issue. But they didn't—because they were on Ike Brown's side. The head of the Mississippi NAACP, while addressing a 2005 election rally in Macon, announced that black candidates had "taken Shuqualak, the county, and Brooksville and now it [is] time to take the city of Macon." He then mockingly asked whites in the crowd, "Are you feeling uncomfortable yet?"[43]

Incredibly, elected officials, Democratic Party officials, armed sheriff deputies, and dozens of poll workers were all accessories to Brown's scheme. Perhaps most disturbingly, as described in chapter two, Department of Justice lawyers were also complicit in Brown's operation. When Brown heard that Mississippi's Secretary of State was concerned that he might try to stop whites from voting in 2003, Brown told the *Clarion-Ledger* newspaper, "I didn't know that white voters were covered under the Voting Rights Act."[44] I can testify from personal experience that this same sentiment is widespread in the DOJ Civil Rights Division.

Another reason Brown thought he would escape justice is because he was allies with Sheriff Albert Walker. In fact, Walker's deputies assisted Brown's scheme, chauffeuring him around the county on election day, ordering poll workers to count illegal votes, and threatening political opponents with arrest for campaigning on the courthouse steps. Brown sometimes appropriated the sheriff's office as his own, even using the sheriff's fax machine for personal or political business. With Brown as his crucial benefactor, Walker never took any position contrary to Brown's interests, even allowing Brown to break the law.

Walker's 2003 opponent, Tiny Heard, entered the contest with the goal of restoring law and order in Noxubee County. Heard told me the story of Katie Lee Ramsey, a black Noxubee resident who pleaded with Heard to run for sheriff. Ramsey frequently stopped by Heard's barbeque stand and recounted how Walker refused to stop her neighbors from threatening her—they were Walker supporters, so he had no interest in enforcing the law against them. "They're going to kill me one day, you just wait," she told Heard. The threats against Ramsey finally stopped in August 2004, after she was bludgeoned to death in her home with hammer blows to the head. To this day, the sheriff has failed to solve the murder. In fact, the sheriff's office has lost the evidence in the case.[45]

Lawlessness still pervades Noxubee County today, as the local authorities continue to view law enforcement through the prism of race. Multiple citizens tell me of ongoing dog-fighting rings among the county's black community. They say to increase the pit bulls' aggression, small pet dogs are stolen and thrown into cages with them, where the little dogs are torn to pieces. The fights reportedly take place deep in the country in old farm structures, heavily splattered in dog blood, with lookouts lining the road approaching the site. The sheriff is allegedly aware of the crimes but does nothing to stop them.

Brown's lawlessness should have been stopped by a grand jury indictment and trial. But this didn't happen because the jury list, which is the voter list, was controlled by Brown himself, who made a side living as a jury consultant to tort lawyers and criminal defense attorneys. His close association with Circuit Court Clerk Carl Mickens gave him access to the data and any developments regarding the use of the list. Simply put, prosecutors in Noxubee would not attempt to indict Brown because they knew the local grand jury would never do it. And even if an indictment were obtained, no jury would ever have convicted him; it was impossible to empanel a jury in Noxubee that would not have at least one dissenter allied with Ike Brown.

In some states, criminal charges for election fraud could be brought through a statewide grand jury on a motion of the state attorney general. This was unlikely in Mississippi, where Democratic Attorney General Jim Hood received 77 percent of the vote in Noxubee County in 2003. But the bigger problem is that Mississippi's statewide grand jury has a very limited jurisdiction largely confined to drug crimes. The Noxubee County grand jury has sometimes refused to issue a single felony indictment during a court term.

As a result, for years Ike Brown operated above the law. Routinely terrorized by Brown's political machine, Noxubee's white minority was left with no legal recourse—that is, until one lawyer at the Department of Justice defied his colleagues and set out to impose the rule of law.

CHAPTER TWO

* * *

One Small Step for Justice

I t's hard to say which is worse: Ike Brown's fraud, intimidation, corruption, and disenfranchisement of white voters, or the fact that prior to 2003, one of Brown's most valuable allies was the United States Department of Justice.

Under the 1965 Voting Rights Act, Noxubee was designated as a county where the federal government could send registers and election observers. This means the discrimination and oppression of black citizens was so extreme before 1965 that the federal government allowed for special measures to facilitate black political participation. Thanks to the Voting Rights Act, state and county officials who had colluded against blacks were removed from the voter registration process in Noxubee, and the federal government essentially assumed local circuit court clerk powers and served as the new means to register to vote. Federal officials would typically sit in the post office with ledger books to enroll voters, and these voters could not be removed from the rolls by local officials.

The Department of Justice had a heavy presence in Noxubee from 1965 through 2003, dispatching federal election observers there more than twenty times. Every time, the observers were tasked with protecting the voting rights of black citizens. This brought the DOJ into close cooperation with Ike Brown. How close? Macon resident Mary Allsup told me when she was on the Noxubee County Election Commission during the Clinton era, Ike Brown opposed her attempt to move voters who were in the wrong voting district into the correct district. Incredibly, DOJ voting section lawyer Nancy Sardeson took Brown's side, warning Allsup that the DOJ would not tolerate moving voters into their appropriate districts. Whatever Brown wanted, the DOJ wanted.

Allsup told me another story illustrating the same point. After the results were settled in one election, Brown left the courtroom along with a group of federal election observers. They filed down the courthouse steps, where DOJ lawyer Sardeson approached Brown to say goodbye. Sardeson has had a checkered legal career— she was sanctioned by the federal court in a Georgia redistricting case, and was eventually suspended from the practice of law for appropriating assets of an estate she administered.[1] Sardeson's handwritten meeting notes at DOJ were once obtained by an opposing party in a South Carolina redistricting lawsuit. The notes revealed she regularly referred to the South Carolina legislators she was communicating with as "white boys."

As Allsup watched from an upstairs courthouse window, Sardeson embraced Brown in a long, intimate hug. This was a brazen display of bias by a federal election observer toward a citizen politically engaged in the area she was monitoring. The embrace delivered a stinging message to opponents of Brown's anti-white crusade—you can't count on the federal government to protect you.

Brown was so close to the DOJ that he once was feted as a dinner guest at the home of the DOJ Voting Section chief, who is the DOJ's top election official. Indeed, federal observers were sometimes sent to Noxubee County due to information provided to the DOJ by Brown himself.

Brown encountered such a cooperative attitude from the DOJ for a simple reason—the department, particularly the Civil Rights Division and its Voting Section, is infected by racial grievance. Although the Voting Section in theory is dedicated to race-neutral equal protection as mandated in the Voting Rights Act, in fact, as we shall see, some of its attorneys are full supporters of Brown's racialist agenda who refused to take a stand against "payback time."

Just after the Noxubee Democrats' 2003 primary, the DOJ Voting Section received a "congressional"—it was a letter from Mississippi Senator Thad Cochran that included complaints by white citizens and white candidates about the corruption and lawlessness that had subsumed the primary. Despite myriad credible reports of severe voting rights violations, Voting Section lawyers almost unanimously elected to ignore the letter; investigating the disenfranchisement of white voters was simply not what they had signed up to do.

But one attorney had a different view—Chris Coates, then a Special Litigation Counsel inside the Voting Section. Unlike his colleagues, Coates believed in race-neutral law enforcement—that civil rights violations should be prosecuted the same way regardless of the race of the alleged perpetrator or the alleged victim. Coates recommended sending monitors to observe the Noxubee runoff elections slated to be held a few days later. But his recommendation immediately sparked opposition from within the Voting Section. Current Obama administration Voting Section chief Christopher Herren wrote a detailed memorandum arguing against sending monitors to Noxubee to protect white voters. Instead of basing his analysis on the facts or the law, Herren offered the purely political argument that sending monitors would upset civil rights groups. The move was also opposed by Voting Section chief Joseph Rich.

A lone voice for action in the Voting Section, Coates seemed poised to be overruled until he received a phone call from Hans von Spakovsky, a Counsel to the Assistant Attorney General for Civil Rights. That call would change the course of history in Noxubee County.

Von Spakovsky had learned of Coates' recommendation and took the matter to his boss, Deputy Assistant Attorney General Bradley Schlozman. The pair was angered and amazed that Joe Rich and Chris Herren would resist sending monitors to Noxubee. In an interview, Schlozman later told me, "I always had the impression Joe Rich was partisan in his enforcement of the Voting Rights Act, but what he did—or, should I say, didn't do—in Noxubee County caused me to lose complete confidence in his management. From then on, our relationship was one of total friction."

The DOJ's political leadership reversed Rich's position within days, sparking a fateful phone call in which von Spakovsky told Coates, "Notwithstanding the Section Chief's recommendation not to go, you all are going down to Mississippi to monitor the runoff in Noxubee County." The call marked an historic moment—the first time the DOJ would use the Voting Rights Act to protect white voters. It was inarguably the right move for race-neutral law enforcement, but it infuriated the racialists both inside and outside the Justice Department who viewed—and still view—civil rights laws as being inapplicable to white victims. Coates later testified under oath that Robert Kengle, a deputy chief of the Voting Section, exclaimed to him, "Can you believe we are going to Mississippi to protect white voters?"

Kengle has denied making that statement, insisting he merely did not want to prioritize the Ike Brown case over other discrimination cases in which minorities were the alleged victims.[2] This was a common, hair-splitting explanation offered by Civil Rights Division radicals when they were forced publicly to explain why they opposed the Ike Brown investigation. Coates told me he heard a similar refrain from Voting Section deputy chief Gilda Daniels, who argued, "I know that Ike Brown is crooked, everybody knows that, but the resources of the Division should not be used this way."[3]

DOJ radicals have used these dissembling arguments to claim, preposterously, that the Bush DOJ was "politicized," and that the protection of whites dominated the Civil Rights Division's agenda during the Bush years. In fact, the Bush DOJ initiated hundreds of cases to protect racial minorities, versus just a handful to protect whites. But for some critics, even a few cases is too much protection for white voters.

Other Voting Section attorneys including Herren were well aware of Ike Brown's antics even before the 2003 elections, yet refused to take any steps to stop them. Some—perhaps even most—did not outright support Brown's behavior, but none had the wherewithal or courage to do anything about it until Coates came forward. The whites of Noxubee County were left to fend for themselves while the system broke down all around them.

It's important to understand that when critics such as current Attorney General Holder accuse the Bush Civil Rights Division of "politicization," they are using a code word to denounce decisions like the one to send federal observers to Noxubee County. Such critics refer to their own agenda of race-based law enforcement as "traditional civil rights work," while they accuse the opposing camp, which supports race-neutral law enforcement, of "politicizing" law enforcement. Thus, when you hear Eric Holder or his top DOJ officials speak of their efforts to "change" the Civil Rights Division, to "restore its proud traditions," and to "get back to doing what it has traditionally done," what they really mean is abandoning the Bush administration's race-neutral commitment to equality and returning to a race-centric approach. The reason they resort to these euphemisms is because an overwhelming majority of Americans, both black and white, deeply believe in race-neutral law enforcement.

When Coates arrived in Noxubee County in August 2003 to monitor the runoff elections, he was stationed at a polling place where he and other DOJ monitors observed the same kind of outlandish corruption and intimidation that had occurred in the first primary. Astonishingly, Noxubee's culture of lawlessness was so entrenched that the Ike Brown political machine could not turn it off, even though they knew these federal monitors, unlike monitors stationed there in the past, were there to monitor *them*.

Coates and other DOJ attorneys prepared, as is customary, a post-election coverage memo detailing their observations. Based on these findings and the prior complaints, the DOJ opened an investigation into Brown's activities. At first, Coates could not find anyone in the Voting Section willing to work on the case with him—a testament to the widespread opposition to the investigation among Voting Section radicals. Eventually, he found two willing confederates. The first was a bright, no-nonsense Harvard Law School graduate named Karen Ditzler. The second was perhaps the finest paralegal in the United States, Joann Sazama, who was assigned to the matter soon after joining the Voting Section and would prove crucial to organizing and advancing the case. Later, after I joined the Voting Section, I was assigned to work the case as well.

It was a good thing Sazama was up to the task, because she ended up having to do the job of the DOJ's in-house historian. The historian is often a key assistant in Voting Section cases, conducting background historical research and interviewing knowledgeable local citizens. Peyton McCrary has been the historian for decades, providing me with valuable assistance on cases I worked helping black victims of discrimination. But as Coates testified before the Civil Rights Commission, McCrary "flatly refused" to work on the Ike Brown investigation because he was opposed to bringing the case.[4] Eventually, late in the case, McCrary did travel to Noxubee County, but for the most part Sazama had to do his job. Coates viewed McCrary's lack of cooperation as a kind of insubordination— behavior I would encounter a few years later while working the New Black Panther Party voter intimidation case.

McCrary, of course, was not alone. Coates testified to the Civil Rights Commission that an attorney who accompanied him to monitor the Noxubee runoff elections told Coates he was opposed to bringing any civil rights cases against blacks in Mississippi until such time as blacks in the state had achieved socioeconomic parity with whites—a crude corruption of voting rights law.[5]

Coates encountered this hostility within the Voting Section time and again. Nobody is hated like a heretic, and Coates had committed high heresy for proposing an investigation of black lawbreakers. He was an unlikely person to be demonized in this way; a former ACLU lawyer, Coates spent his entire career working with the liberal left on civil rights cases. He argued a major Section 2 Voting Rights Act case before the United States Supreme Court to help black victims of discrimination. He brought civil rights cases to protect blacks for three decades before bringing the Ike Brown case. Black elected officials throughout the South are in power today because Coates brought lawsuits to change the systems of election.

But with his involvement in the Ike Brown case, suddenly none of that mattered anymore. Many Voting Section attorneys stopped talking to Coates. He had met Peyton McCrary for lunch at least once a week for many years, but that tradition quickly ended. A Voting Section lawyer who entered the United States as an illegal alien, Luz Lopez-Ortiz, referred to Coates in a DOJ email as a "Klansman." For militants like Lopez-Ortiz, enforcing the law equally was tantamount to joining a group of racist terrorists.

Soon after I joined the Voting Section, I got a glimpse of the hostility Coates was facing courtesy of Voting Section attorney Avner Shapiro, my assigned mentor. A bright, fun, and charming guy, Shapiro treated me to many pleasant conversations about growing up in Margaret Thatcher's London, the British economic malaise of the early 1980s, places to go in London, and fantastic books he had read. But throughout these exchanges, he would sprinkle a running commentary about the rightful priorities of the Voting Section, and in particular, his opposition to the Ike Brown case to which I was assigned. I was amazed at how conversant he was in all the arguments that might be available to the defendants, including implausible, highly legalistic ones. He constantly reminded me that I could refuse to work on a case if I was philosophically opposed to it, and at some point, the friendly discussions evolved into hostile badgering.

I mentioned Shapiro's hectoring to Coates. Unaware of the long history of hostility Coates had faced over the case, I struck a nerve. Coates keeps an even keel in almost every circumstance, but I saw a flash of deep anger on his face. He said he wanted to speak to Shapiro or the section chief to put an end to the behavior, but I begged him off, not wanting to rock the boat in my new job.

Coates later testified to the Civil Rights Commission that in arguing against bringing the Ike Brown case, Shapiro had once told him,
"I didn't come to work in the Civil Rights Division at the Department
of Justice to sue black people."[6] The sentiment was common enough
at the Voting Section, and it certainly reflected Shapiro's views as I
knew them. He would eventually leave the Voting Section, but as we
will see in later chapters, his wife Julie Fernandes would prove
extremely effective under the Obama administration in helping to
ensure that DOJ lawyers would no longer have the unpleasant task
of suing black people.

Despite his ostracism from his colleagues, Coates pressed forward with the Ike Brown case. After observing the Brown machine
in action during the runoff elections, Coates and Ditzler prepared a
memorandum recommending an investigation commence against
Brown, the Noxubee County Democratic Executive Committee, and
the Noxubee County Election Commission. Following normal procedure, the memo was forwarded to the Voting Section chief, who
is typically tasked with reviewing recommendations and passing
them up to the political appointees, usually to the Deputy Assistant
Attorney General. Unfortunately, the section chief who received
Coates' memo was the same one who sought to squash the original
election coverage—Joseph Rich.

Rich was a problematic employee, having been reprimanded for
insubordination and having had a detailed misconduct memorandum placed in his DOJ personnel file. He earned that reprimand for
ignoring repeated orders to stop allowing a female Voting Section
employee to work remotely in New York City instead of in the office
in Washington.

He was also a militant leftist who hired attorneys for blatantly political and ideological reasons. He told one job applicant who had worked for a prominent Republican attorney, "It's obvious [that] you're a conservative, too. Why would I hire a right-winger to work in the Voting Section? This must be some sort of joke. You must be coming in as a mole to undermine me."[7] (When the DOJ Inspector General denounced the Bush Civil Rights Division for supposedly favoring conservative job applicants, the investigators mysteriously declined to comment on Rich's hiring practices.) Coates told me about one particularly spiteful episode involving Rich; while complaining to Coates that a Voting Section attorney had previously worked for Reagan Civil Rights Division head Brad Reynolds, Rich blurted out that the attorney was suffering from AIDS—a private piece of information that only Rich—somehow—knew.

After Rich received Coates' memo, Rich reviewed it and then forwarded it to Hans von Spakovsky and Bradley Schlozman for approval. But by the time it reached its recipients, something strange had happened: its most important part—Coates' recommendation to investigate Ike Brown, the Noxubee Democratic Executive Committee, and the county Election Commission—had vanished. Rich had simply erased the recommendation out of the memo. The ruse was only discovered when Coates and von Spakovsky discussed the case after running into each other at a DOJ social event. After that, Rich was ordered to restore Coates' recommendation and resubmit the memo.

Rich was again reprimanded for insubordination, this time through an adverse annual review that detailed his dishonest deletion of the recommendation to investigate Ike Brown. After losing an appeal of the review, he eventually retired from the DOJ and now works with Robert Kengle at the leftwing "civil rights" group the Lawyers Committee from Civil Rights Under Law. After Rich left the DOJ, national media outlets such as the *Los Angeles Times* and *New York Times* bafflingly relied on him as an authoritative, credible source for stories alleging rightwing bias in the Bush DOJ.[8] Naturally, the press failed to divulge that their source was twice reprimanded for misconduct. That, as they say, wouldn't fit the narrative.

Rich's insubordination demonstrates the difficult time Republicans will have controlling the entrenched career ranks in the Civil Rights Division even if they retake the White House. The division's section chiefs are mostly radicals who will not necessarily follow orders or policies that conflict with their ideology. After all, the prospect of advancing their agenda is what attracted many of them to the Civil Rights Division in the first place.

Based on Coates' unadulterated memo and recommendation to investigate Ike Brown, his superiors eventually approved a decision to file a lawsuit against Brown. But even after the suit was filed in February 2005 in federal court in the Southern District of Mississippi, the investigation into Brown's behavior continued. By this time, the Bush administration had hired numerous attorneys dedicated to race-neutral law enforcement. A good example was Mississippi attorney Joshua Rogers, who was added to the Ike Brown case. Brought to the Civil Rights Division under the prestigious Attorney General's Honors Program, Rogers was refreshingly non-ideological, dedicated simply to enforcing the law as written. He brought vital skills and experience to the case, arriving fresh from a clerkship with the Mississippi Supreme Court. He understood Mississippi and its people, spoke their language, and could connect with both the black and white communities.

Around this time, the national media took an interest in the man-bites-dog story of the DOJ suing a black political operative. Predictably, they fit the tale into their pre-existing narrative of Bush administration hostility to civil rights. Under the headline "United States sues black activist," MSNBC attributed the lawsuit not to Brown's voter fraud, intimidation, or total disregard of the law, but to his political success. Brown was, according to the report, "both loved and hated for his ability to turn out black voters and get his candidates into office. That success has also landed him at the heart of a federal lawsuit that's about to turn the Voting Rights Act on its head."[9] The article quoted Jon Greenbaum, a former Voting Section attorney who was thereafter employed by a leftwing "civil rights" group, questioning the case's merits. Although Greenbaum had privately told Coates he supported race-neutral enforcement of the law, when the media came calling, he was a reflexive leftwing lap-dog. Similarly, the *Washington Post* wasn't so much interested in Ike Brown's illegal discrimination, but in "signs of the Bush administration's commitment to minority issues."[10]

Despite the negative press, the members of the DOJ Noxubee team soldiered on, spending many long weeks in Noxubee County cold knocking on doors, interviewing witnesses, and conducting depositions. One of the problems we encountered was that the defendants' lawyers were friends with many of our DOJ coworkers, and these colleagues would aggressively mine us for information about case strategy. Along the same lines, one of the defendants' attorneys liked to casually mention to us that he was speaking with Voting Section employees—about other matters, of course. Clearly, there was an information pipeline running straight out of the DOJ to the defendants' legal team.

The legal process leading up to the trial exhibited some of the same slack compliance with the rules that characterized Noxubee's elections. For starters, defendant Ike Brown never filed initial disclosures, something that is supposed to happen at the beginning of every federal case. Like the handwritten hearing "notice" he provided to Roderick Walker, Brown submitted a scrawled-out list of possible witnesses. He was eventually sanctioned $500 by the federal judge but never produced initial disclosures.

Brown also failed to provide a pretrial order with a trial witness list to the United States. Listing witnesses and stipulations, a pretrial order is the agreed-upon ground rules that govern any trial in federal court. At a pretrial conference, the defendants said they needed to fix some typographical errors in their pretrial order, but instead they substantively changed the agreed-upon pretrial order and added new witnesses. This led to a stunning moment at trial when the judge experienced firsthand the kind of legal malfeasance that so many white citizens of Noxubee County had long endured. I had the uncomfortable task of informing United States District Court Judge Tom Lee that the defendants and their lawyer, Wilbur Colom, had played games with the pretrial order.

> **Adams**: Well, Your Honor, this—we may address this after the witness steps down, but I believe that you have competing pretrial orders with different stipulations and unfortunately Mr. Colom's came in a few days before New Year's. We had given you one long before that.
>
> **Judge Lee**: Are you telling me that those—that I announced as stipulations are not, in fact, stipulations? I have never tried a case without a pretrial order, and it's not up to each side to present their own pretrial order. If there were a difference, it would go to the magistrate judge for resolution of it. I have never heard of this.

Adams: We concur, Your Honor, and that's why two weeks before the pretrial conference we submitted a pretrial order. On the day of the pretrial conference we delivered it. Mr. Colom indicated to you that he had some technical corrections, some typographical ones, which became substantive additions a few weeks later.

Judge Lee: He did mention typographical errors. I recall that.

Adams: Substantive additions were made to that pretrial order by counsel for the defendants, and we consequently now have two competing pretrial orders.

Judge Lee: That's ridiculous that I'm trying a case and learning today that we don't have an established pretrial order. When we take a recess I want y'all to get together and get that harmonized and if there are differences, they need to be resolved and if not, we'll proceed—this is just outrageous.[11]

Even in a federal courtroom, Ike Brown didn't play by the rules.

In January 2007, the trial of Brown, the Noxubee Democratic Executive Committee, and the Noxubee Election Commission was held in U.S. District Court in Jackson, Mississippi. Colom made an opening statement casting the defendants as the victims of centuries of racial oppression. The case wasn't about white victims, he indicated, "rather this case began in 1865 when the freed slaves were first given the right to vote in Noxubee County, Mississippi, the right that turned out to be nothing more than a mirage." Subtly invoking the theme of payback time, Colom continued, "Generations of blacks in the county were subject to a sadistic form of rule by a tiny group of whites. This system of apartheid, much like the one that plagued South Africa, did not come completely to [an] end in

Noxubee County until the mid-1990s. Indeed, majority rule came to South Africa before it came to Noxubee County. A white minority of 30 percent ruled the black majority with an iron fist."[12]

His inflammatory racial appeal, of course, was intended to divert attention from the real matter before the court: Ike Brown's racially motivated discrimination against whites. The statement, which was accompanied by a PowerPoint presentation of photographs from the 1960s civil rights movement, was interrupted by Judge Lee. Perhaps grasping the disingenuous nature of the opening statement, the judge asked, "Excuse me Mr. Colom, are these photos from Noxubee County or are they just portraying the times?" Naturally, the photos had nothing to do with Noxubee—Brown was simply trying to wrap his behavior in the noble banner of the civil rights movement.

In *United States v. Ike Brown*, the court heard forty-one witnesses for the United States and twelve for the defendants. Many of Brown's witnesses were last-second additions who had not been previously disclosed to us, as the rules require. The court allowed them to testify, but only after a grueling and bizarre pseudo-deposition by the United States over a weekend trial break. Ike Brown marched all his previously unknown witnesses into a small room at the Noxubee County Courthouse, where they were questioned under oath. All the new witnesses testified uniformly that nothing ever went wrong in Noxubee elections. Notably, one of the new witnesses, Chester Turner, had invoked the Fifth Amendment in a prior lawsuit involving his own absentee ballot fraud in Noxubee County.[13]

After the trial concluded, the Noxubee County NAACP sponsored a "pre-victory celebration" for Ike Brown's lawyer. Civil rights history had turned inside out—a once great civil rights group was celebrating a man for defending someone about to be found liable for egregious civil rights violations. Worse still, Colom's insidious opening statement from the trial would be lionized at the gathering. An NAACP advertisement for the event stated, "There will be a pre-victory celebration and reception in honor of Attorney Wilbur Colom for his outstanding performance representing the Noxubee County Democratic Executive Committee. A video presentation of Attorney Colom [sic] opening statements will be shown. Noxubee County lets [sic] show our gratitude. Sponsor: Noxubee County Branch NAACP."[14]

When the trial concluded, Wilbur Colom demanded that the Noxubee County Board of Supervisors pay his $179,000 legal bill for defending Ike Brown, even though Colom had said during the case he was working for free. Of course the county, one of America's poorest, declined to pay, after which Colom threatened a lawsuit.[15] Incidentally, Colom's bill contained a curious item—line entry 114 showed two hours of work, billed for $250, for reviewing a court clerk's half-page note indicating that a motion that had been referred to one judge would now be decided by a different judge.

On June 29, 2007, Judge Lee ruled that Ike Brown was liable for violating the Voting Rights Act. "No one could reasonably argue that an election official's racially motivated decision to count the votes of black voters while rejecting those of white voters is discrimination that can be countenanced under any view of Section 2 [of the Voting Rights Act]," the court found. "In purpose and in effect, that is what has occurred in this case."[16] The ruling was an historic victory for equal rights and race-neutral law enforcement. As such, some DOJ radicals to this day try to limit the scope of the decision by falsely claiming the Court entered a limited ruling, only finding Brown liable for his intent, or state of mind. Thus, even in victory, many in the DOJ were ashamed to have sued a black political operative—and those people are now running the Civil Rights Division.

Calling Brown's racialist manipulation of absentee ballots "the most serious charge" in the case,[17] Judge Lee explained that a voter fraud operation of the massive scope attributed to Brown was hard to believe—but that after reviewing the evidence, he found that the incredible operation did, in fact, exist. He described in precise detail Brown's comprehensive system of voting corruption, reaching the unsettling conclusion that elections across an entire American county were infested with racially motivated absentee ballot fraud: "While the Government's theory in this regard, that Brown and his associates and allies orchestrated such a scheme, may seem improbable, having thoroughly reviewed and considered the evidence, the court has come to the firm and definite conclusion that there is substance to the Government's position."[18] The opinion, one of the most comprehensive descriptions of the mechanics of vote fraud ever published, should be required reading by students of politics, law, and constitutional government.

Judge Lee offered some advice to the state Democratic Party: "[Brown's] actions are properly to be condemned, and in the court's view, the State Democratic Party was remiss in failing to take action to rectify his abuses."[19] Sadly, the Mississippi Democratic Party ignored Lee's counsel and refused to remove Brown from the state executive committee even after he was found to have engaged in blatant discrimination.

With Judge Lee's finding, the DOJ had to decide what remedy could compensate for Brown's racially motivated lawlessness. Chris Coates believed Brown's lawlessness was so extreme and unapologetic that the only solution was to remove Brown's power, along with that of the Noxubee County Democratic Executive Committee, to run primary elections. At the time, a Democratic Party primary scheduled for August 2007 was just weeks away, so the United States submitted a request to the Court asking for the elections to be postponed until a remedy could be imposed. Ike Brown vehemently opposed a delay, knowing if the elections were held before the remedy was imposed, then his slate of candidates, including incumbent Sheriff Albert Walker, would be almost guaranteed to serve another four years.

As a gesture of good faith, Brown promised the Court he would have nothing to do with the upcoming election, vowing he would spend election day at home "watching television." But Judge Lee proved unwilling to delay the election. Brown then reneged on his promise and spent election day traversing the county, ordering poll workers to disregard ballot challenges, and presiding over an outrageous repeat of the 2003 election.

This time, however, the county was swarming with federal observers who recorded every instance of lawlessness. After promising not to touch a single ballot, Brown was photographed by DOJ officials handling hundreds of absentee ballots in the courtroom at the county courthouse. He managed the distribution of absentee ballots, as he always had, and was assisted by his operatives among the poll worker force, which was largely the same workforce as in the 2003 election. Brown appeared at one polling place, the Earl Nash precinct, and told a federal observer, "I don't care what the court says; I'm still legally responsible for running this election"—a decisive repudiation of his days-old vow that he would have nothing to do with the election.

When the polls closed, officials throughout the county once again disregarded Mississippi law to examine each absentee ballot to see if the signatures matched. Requests were denied from poll watchers for white candidates to review absentee ballots. In one precinct, as whites were trying to verify that ballots were properly examined, poll worker Samantha Dixon hung up her cell phone and yelled, "Ike says shut it down!" All the absentee ballots were then blasted through for counting without any review, just as they had in 2003.[20] The same thing happened in the Earl Nash precinct, where poll worker Mildred Reed received a call from Brown instructing her to hurry the absentee ballot review.[21]

In Shuqualak, federal observers heard poll official Velma Jenkins announce that mismatched signatures cannot be a basis for challenging absentee ballots, even though Mississippi law was explicit that they could be. Jenkins, who was also Mayor of Shuqualak, proceeded to review the absentee ballots without the input of poll workers—another legal violation. At the Earl Nash precinct, poll official Catherine Johnson, the same woman who suborned perjury from Nikki Halbert at the trial in Jackson, announced she was the only person who needed to rule on whether an absentee ballot should be counted. When three poll workers exercised their power to review and vote on absentee ballot challenges, Johnson insisted she "had veto power" over their decision. Realizing the lawless situation, the poll workers ceased their challenges.[22]

The most startling event on election day was the hundreds of recorded instances of illegal voting assistance. At the Macon Fire Station, about fifteen "assistors" stationed themselves inside the polls and approached voters as they entered. Federal observers documented vans of voters arriving, assistors descending upon them when they attempted to vote, and assistors even casting the vote themselves without the voters' input. Similar behavior occurred throughout the county. At the Vo-Tech precinct, federal observers recorded assistors instructing voters to "choose him" or "choose him." The voters reportedly offered no resistance. The "assistance" was astonishingly pervasive—at the fire station, 188 black voters were "assisted," while in the town of Shuqualak, assistors helped 138 of the 348 black voters.[23]

Some assistors became belligerent toward the federal observers, with one assistor, a woman named Teresa Green, instructing voters to tell the observers they could not watch them vote. Poll official Octavia Stowers told federal observers she "wished that you would take your ass to the Courthouse and stand around." At another polling place, Noxubee County Democratic Executive Committee member Billy Dixon said of the federal observers, "I don't care who they are. Tell them to get out of here." And it's no wonder Dixon wanted them gone; records showed that some voters were voting twice—right in front of federal observers.[24]

In fact, all these instances of illegal assistance were conducted in plain sight of dozens of federal officials who memorialized every utterance and submitted sworn affidavits to Judge Lee after the election. This situation demonstrated that illegal assistance has become a stunningly ingrained practice—and as we shall see in chapter six, it is not confined to Noxubee. Simply put, many people simply regard illegal assistance as a normal part of elections. But it is a dangerous normalcy that violates voters' rights and converts entire regions into spigots of illegal votes.

Voters who surrender their vote to assistors do so for a variety of reasons. From my experience, the main dynamic is that the assistors care far more about the election than do the voters who give up their rights. Another reason is that the assistors are often politically connected operatives who can give or withhold access to scarce jobs or public assistance. In such instances, the "offer" of assistance becomes an offer the voter cannot refuse.

Regardless of the reasons, the sight of hundreds of black citizens surrendering their right to vote is something I will never forget. It is an insult to the civil rights pioneers who risked everything to secure that right. The civil rights movement fought to guarantee the right of everyone to fully participate in the political process, not to ensure a particular outcome.

Judge Lee held further hearings on this new wave of election fraud, featuring witness after witness presenting mountains of evidence. Curiously, as the systematic and prolonged violation of voting rights in Noxubee became indisputably clear, the mainstream media lost interest in the story. Only reporters from three Mississippi papers, the *Jackson Clarion Ledger*, *Macon Beacon*, and *Columbus Commercial Dispatch*, attended the new hearings and reported on Brown's most recent behavior.

And yet, in the end, the Ike Brown lawsuit was testimony to the power of a free press. Our paralegal Joann Sazama first discovered much of the evidence against Brown in the local Noxubee County weekly, the *Macon Beacon*. Published by Scott Boyd, the *Beacon* had been fearlessly and relentlessly covering Brown's antics for years. While the national media was primarily interested in questioning the Bush administration's decision to bring the case in the first place, the *Beacon* diligently memorialized crucial political events and reported the straight facts.

Brown's outlandish behavior left Judge Lee with few options. He could simply order Brown to obey the law, a traditional limited remedy in these circumstances, but it was doubtful Brown would comply in light of his blatant lawlessness and his broken promise to Judge Lee that he would be home watching TV on election day. So Lee ultimately accepted the United States' proposal to appoint a special election administrator to run the Noxubee Democratic primary elections. Taking over state law functions is an extraordinary remedy, no doubt. But the court seemed swayed by the testimony of Professor Ted Arrington, the expert for the United States, who argued that Noxubee's Democratic primary simply could not be legitimately run under the authority of Ike Brown and the other defendants.

Judge Lee appointed former Mississippi Supreme Court Justice Ruben V. Anderson as the administrator of Noxubee's Democratic primaries. Anderson is virtually a one-man civil rights institution, having served as counsel to the NAACP from 1967 to 1975 and later becoming the state's first black Supreme Court Justice. It was a good choice—a man who represented the original moral principles of the civil rights movement replaced a man who debased those principles. Anderson administered Democratic primaries in 2009, resulting in a much improved process free of racial discrimination.

The Fifth Circuit U.S. Court of Appeals eventually upheld Lee's verdict. As a result, Anderson continues to run Noxubee's Democratic primaries today, and his work has been exemplary. Nevertheless, a single voting administrator can only do so much.

Francis Grund, the nineteenth-century French commentator on America, once said, "Change the domestic habits of the Americans, their religious devotion, and their high respect for morality, and it will not be necessary to change a single letter of the Constitution in order to vary the whole form of their government."[25] If morality, decency, and the rule of law are replaced by angry grievance and the rule of men, then election administrators cannot be expected by themselves to ensure legitimate elections. Ultimately, free and fair elections rely on enough people believing in free and fair elections. And it is extremely difficult to guarantee free and fair elections when powerful figures both locally and nationally accept racial payback as a system of governance.

America will confront this issue much more often in the near future. Ike Brown repeatedly asserted to the DOJ team that the state of Mississippi is trending toward a black and Hispanic majority. He seemed to relish the prospect, viewing it as an opportunity to get racial payback on a much bigger scale. As our nation becomes more racially diverse, Noxubee County offers a stark warning of a future, balkanized America in which the law is just another tool to manipulate in a zero-sum competition for racial spoils. However, the DOJ's victory in the Ike Brown case, and its affirmance by the appeals court, was a step in a better direction, warning future Ike Browns that justice remains blind, and that racial discrimination in any form will be prosecuted.

Race-neutral law enforcement is not only good policy, it's required by the Fourteen and Fifteenth Amendments to the Constitution. Enacted after the Civil War, these amendments were meant to remedy not only violence and discrimination against black freedmen, but against all Americans regardless of race. In the aftermath of the Civil War, Senator Oliver Morton spoke of the need to end persecution of "the loyal men, both white and black, [who were subject to] a thousand annoyances, [and] the insecurity of life and property."[26] Similarly, Senator Joseph Fowler observed, "It cannot be affirmed that the white race do not require relief.... It is not for the right of any race, color, or condition that we should legislate; it is for the family of man.... Let it embrace all, not a part. Let it protect the white man as well as the colored."[27] Senator William Stewart spoke of "a large mass of people black and white, who were loyal to this Government, who were oppressed by this unjust refusal on the part of the Democratic Party and those in operation with them, who were denied their civil rights, to whom there was no protection."[28]

The desire to enshrine equal justice for all races is evident in the congressional debates over the Fifteenth Amendment, especially the reaction to Michigan Senator Jacob Howard's proposal to narrow the amendment's language to protect only freed blacks.[29] This was an attempt to retain the states' power to disenfranchise other races, such as Asians or Indians. Republican senators aggressively attacked the Howard proposal and the amendment failed, 35 to 16.[30]

Congressman William Lawrence, while debating the Civil Rights Act of 1866, described the universal aspirations of his congressional colleagues after they had endured the cataclysm of the Civil War: "This bill is not made for any class or creed, or race or color, but the great future that awaits us will, if it become a law, protect every citizen, including the millions of people of foreign birth who will flock to our shores to become citizens and to find here a land of liberty and law."[31] With the rage and sorrow of their recent past, those congressional leaders established legal principles designed to prevent any race from securing unfair electoral advantages. That it took almost a century for America to realize their vision only serves to show how revolutionary their legislation was.

Unfortunately, the Obama administration has halted and reversed our progress toward race-neutral law enforcement. In light of the ruling in *United States v. Ike Brown*, the DOJ should be using the Section 5 preclearance process of the Voting Rights Act to protect white victims of voting discrimination. But the Obama administration has refused this course of action. In other words, blacks and Hispanics are protected by Section 5, but a white minority is not. This is true even in places like Noxubee where a federal court affirmed that whites had, in fact, been victimized. Attorney General Eric Holder and his political appointees overseeing the Voting Section seem to wrongly believe they have the power to write race-blind protections out of the constitutional and statutory framework of the Voting Rights Act.

This policy has allowed blatant discrimination against whites to continue, even in Noxubee. During the county's 2011 redistricting process for county supervisor seats, the districts were drawn so as to ensure that no white candidate could be competitive except in a single area around Macon. The right of a racial minority to elect a candidate of choice is enshrined in Section 2 of the Voting Rights Act, subject to a variety of legal elements, but this right was ignored as the county adopted a plan recommended by a paid redistricting consultant that deliberately diluted the white vote. Who was this redistricting consultant? Why, none other than Ike Brown.

In any normal case where a racial minority was victimized so blatantly, the DOJ would have interposed an objection under Section 5 in no time—especially if a person found liable of discrimination was driving the redistricting process and the victims were previously found by a federal court to have been subject to discrimination. But because Brown is black and his victims are white, the DOJ did next to nothing; it purported to look into the matter, but its investigation was a farce. Although it is standard procedure in this circumstance for the DOJ to contact the potential victims and seek their input, I spoke with every prominent white Noxubee political figure, and only one of them had received a call. It did not even come from the Section 5 unit, but from my old colleague on the Ike Brown case, Joshua Rogers, who was trying to establish grounds for an objection even though he knew his political bosses opposed it. DOJ sources told me there was simply no interest in objecting to the Ike Brown redistricting plan. After all, in the view of the Holder DOJ, whites aren't protected by Section 5 of the Voting Rights Act.

I testified to the U.S. Civil Rights Commission in July 2010 that the DOJ's disinterest in the Noxubee redistricting plan represented an unequal application of Section 5. Tellingly, not a single DOJ official denied it—they couldn't deny it, because they knew the DOJ does not conduct Section 5 reviews to protect any white minorities. If this does not change, the Supreme Court may well strike down Section 5 based on its unconstitutional application.

The DOJ did grab one fig leaf. Although Ike Brown's attempts to ban people from voting had been included in the case against him, he made a new submission seeking permission for him to bar Republicans from voting in his primary in May 2010. In my testimony to the Civil Rights Commission, I predicted the DOJ would not use Section 5 to block this discriminatory effort. After I began drawing wider attention to this issue in articles I wrote for *Pajamas Media*,[32] the DOJ convened a meeting to discuss Ike Brown's submission. Voting Section chief Chris Herren hit upon the clever solution of asking Judge Lee to extend the remedy against Brown by extending Ruben Andersen's tenure as the primaries' administrator. The request also sought to prevent Brown from making any further submissions, since those might embarrass the Obama administration.

The request was essentially a ploy to buy Holder time—since it was unlikely Lee would rule on the motion anytime soon, the DOJ could point to the motion as proof that the Civil Rights Division cared about white voters, even though everyone knew the judge was extremely unlikely to grant the motion. And in April 2011, as expected, Judge Lee denied the DOJ request to extend the remedy. Nevertheless, DOJ radicals and the left-leaning media continued to trumpet the DOJ's mere submission of the hopeless motion as evidence that the DOJ had tried to protect white voters. The court did rule that Brown could not make any further submission while

Ruben Andersen ran the elections, which spared the administration some further possible embarrassment.

Civil rights attorney Bill Ready was more cynical about the events in Noxubee County, sensing there were grave limits on America's ability to deal with people like Ike Brown absent a better educated populace. He reflected on his long career in civil rights starting as a young attorney in Meridian, Mississippi, in the 1950s. "We just opened the door, the law just opened the door," he told me. "What walks through is the unanswered question." In Noxubee, Ike Brown and his henchmen walked through the door opened by Ready and other civil rights leaders who put their lives on the line. Ready added, "I don't think Brown is immoral, he's just amoral. Nobody there thinks they are doing anything wrong. They just think they are doing everything the whites did to them."[33] You can't describe payback time any better.

Ike Brown's illegal actions may have been exceptional, but the ideology that motivated them is depressingly familiar. He is, in fact, the face of much of today's civil rights industry: intolerant, venomous, and dedicated to a quasi-religious crusade to enrich and empower specific racial interest groups. Civil rights laws are no longer great moral levelers, providing equal opportunity and breaking down legal barriers. Instead, Ike Brown and his allies at the DOJ view civil rights laws as a system for redistributing wealth and power along racial lines. Visits to the deep South are seen by some Voting Section employees as expeditions to alien territory. Anyone who questions this simplistic worldview must be a racist, if not an outright Klansman.

The entrenchment of this ideology at the DOJ, which I witnessed firsthand, is a dangerous development. In arguing against taking action against Ike Brown, some DOJ lawyers even defended the corrupt activities of the voting assistors, arguing they were a natural part of the South's emergence from Jim Crow. And thanks to that perverse view, the DOJ continually turned a blind eye to forced assistance until the Ike Brown case.

This argument captures the rotted evolution of the civil rights movement—any malfeasance that can be connected to Jim Crow, no matter how tenuously, should be excused. If hundreds of black voters are robbed of their vote while Patsy Roby marks their ballots, we should avert our gaze because the deed helps blacks get elected. If Nikki Halbert has her vote stolen by the forgery of Carrie Kate Windham, we should temper our outrage, since the deed helps elect a black sheriff. If masses of voters surrender their hard-won rights to the notary's knock at the door, why complain? The machine will elect black candidates to office, and the dreams of oppressed forefathers provide absolution for the notary's crimes.

In effect, the precise institution designed to protect our rights is populated by people who believe some of us aren't worthy of protection. The DOJ already had its share of leftwing radicals during the Bush administration, but their skullduggery was counterbalanced by the professionalism of newly hired, non-ideological attorneys and by the political leadership. Later, under the Obama administration, I saw what happens when every part of the bureaucratic machinery resists doing the right thing—that is, protecting *all* Americans from racial discrimination.

As explained in the next chapter, the DOJ is now staffed with far more extremists than ever before. The prospect that these are the precise individuals who will be enforcing election laws in the 2012 elections should keep every law-abiding American awake at night.

CHAPTER THREE

★ ★ ★

Personnel Is Policy

L itigation was brought against Ike Brown largely thanks to the efforts of one Department of Justice employee and the support he received from DOJ political appointees. This bears out an old axiom: personnel is policy. And you have to hand it to Barack Obama—he understands this perfectly.

It was clear from the Obama administration's first days that the DOJ would be a main focus of the "change" Obama had vowed to bring to America. During his long campaign, Obama and his close allies had continually assailed the department for allegedly failing to enforce civil rights laws. The Voting Section, where I was working at the time, was a frequent target of Obama's broadsides. In fact, Obama took the rare step of attacking individual Voting Section employees, making it clear he wanted specific heads to roll.

For example, On December 14, 2007, when John Tanner announced he was resigning as Voting Section chief to do a detail, Obama pounced on one of his frequent targets. "It is unacceptable that the Administration is simply shuffling deck chairs by moving Mr. Tanner," he lectured. "I called on him to be fired."[1] Then-Senator Obama had been hounding Tanner for months, having shot off a letter to the DOJ on October 19 demanding his dismissal. Tanner, you see, had the audacity to overrule DOJ lawyers who found that a photo ID requirement for voting in Georgia would discriminate against blacks. Leftwing activists claim virtually any photographic ID requirement for voting is racist, and Tanner's apostasy on this issue was clearly intolerable—even though the Georgia law was eventually upheld by every appellate state and federal court that reviewed it.[2] Obama's demand may have marked the first time a presidential candidate has called for a specific civil servant to be fired.

Candidate Obama also pursued his vendetta against Voting Section personnel by putting a hold on the nomination of Hans von Spakovsky to the Federal Election Commission (FEC). Von Spakovsky was a former DOJ Voting Section lawyer who had angered leftwingers by refusing to support objections to the Georgia photo ID requirement or to a Texas congressional redistricting plan that activists had denounced as racist. After disgruntled DOJ attorneys leaked internal memoranda castigating von Spakovsky, Obama impeded his nomination to the FEC, where von Spakovsky was already serving through a recess appointment. Ed Blum of the American Enterprise Institute wrote at the time about the electoral calculations behind Obama's move against von Spakovsky: "When you're ten points behind in the polls, less than two months away from the first presidential primaries, and African American Democrats are divided between you and the front-runner, what is the easiest way to narrow that gap? Apparently, if you're Sen. Barack Obama (D-Ill), you play the race card."[3]

In other words, Obama followed the Machiavellian playbook set out by Saul Alinsky, the Godfather of radical community organizing: "Rule 12: Pick the target, freeze it, personalize it, and polarize it."[4] And indeed, Obama's hold ultimately sank von Spakovsky's nomination to the FEC. Coincidentally or not, a few months after he acted against von Spakovsky, the little-known Obama won the Iowa caucuses.

Americans would naturally presume that the attorneys and political appointees who work in the Civil Rights Division, particularly its Voting Section, would be straight shooters, unbiased and competent. The legal profession at large presumes that DOJ attorneys are beyond reproach. In most parts of the department, they are—but not in the Civil Rights Division. As presaged by Obama's attacks on Tanner and von Spakovsky, the Obama administration has fought to thoroughly remake the division's personnel, staffing it with radical leftwing activists dedicated to exploiting civil rights laws to further their agenda of racial grievance. Working in the shadows and largely escaping media scrutiny, these extremists are re-shaping our fundamental system of governance, particularly our voting system.

The problem dates back to the Clinton administration, which packed the Civil Rights Division with radical lawyers and staffers. Determined to maintain their chokehold on the division after Clinton's presidency ended, leftwing activists in the DOJ issued desperate pleas as soon as George W. Bush was elected—get us resumes from leftists, quick! William Yeomans, then a senior Civil Rights Division official who later served as legislative counsel to Senator Ted Kennedy, spearheaded a hiring blitz that lasted up until Bush took the presidential oath. As a result, the division became a refuge for some of the most militant leftists in the entire federal government.

The situation changed dramatically once Bush appointees took control of hiring. While many new lawyers in the Civil Rights Division still came from liberal activist groups, the Bush DOJ also hired numerous attorneys with real-world litigation experience in private practice. These attorneys—highly experienced lawyers used to juggling huge caseloads and multiple pressing deadlines—had a realistic view of what constitutes relevant and persuasive evidence. In contrast, the hires from the insular world of leftist nonprofits—which the press often refers to, inaccurately, as "civil rights organizations"—tended to have little or no real-world litigation experience, although during investigations they were often skilled at identifying the local dynamics within racial communities. The influx of experienced attorneys under Bush was a crucial correction to the abundance of lawyers who had spent their whole careers in the Civil Rights Division, breeding stagnation and process worship.

The Bush hires resulted in a diverse staff with a mix of skill sets—and that was a problem for Barack Obama. As part of its concerted attack on the Bush Civil Rights Division, the Obama campaign—along with former leftist DOJ lawyers, various leftwing groups, Democratic senators, and liberal media outlets—relentlessly accused the Bush administration of packing the division with personnel dedicated to undermining civil rights laws.

Leftwing activists in the DOJ's Office of Professional Responsibility (OPR) joined in the attack, issuing a critical report on Bush-era DOJ hiring policies that completely omitted evidence provided to the office showing the large number of liberal attorneys hired and promoted by the Bush DOJ.[5] Notably, the OPR attorney who prepared the final report, Tamara Kessler, was later rebuked by the Office of the Deputy Attorney General for concocting a shoddy, overturned legal assault on John Yoo and Judge James Bybee regarding terrorist interrogation policies.[6]

Upon President Obama's inauguration on January 20, 2009, the Left's charges of biased hiring at the DOJ were quickly revealed as the most splendid hypocrisy. From the very beginning, the Obama administration flooded the Civil Rights Division with dozens of new attorneys hired for their ideological views and their affiliation with liberal activist groups.

The hiring frenzy was a godsend for struggling leftwing organizations, which were laying off their own attorneys as the sluggish economy depressed the groups' fundraising. For example, just two days after Obama's inauguration, the ACLU announced it was laying off a tenth of its employees. But thanks to Obama's election, many of the newly jobless ACLU staffers landed plum jobs in the federal government. Meanwhile, perhaps sensing that the ACLU's influence would rise under the Obama administration, donors soon returned to the organization; indeed, fifteen months after the layoffs, an ACLU press release trumpeted, "ACLU Announces Historic Fundraising Success, Exceeding Goal And Building Civil Liberties Infrastructure In Battleground States."[7] The missive did not explain what civil rights fundraising has to do with "battleground states," considering the ACLU Foundation that conducts litigation is a 501(c)(3) nonprofit that is legally prohibited from engaging in partisan political activities. But no explanation was needed—everyone knows today's "civil rights movement" has little to do with civil rights and lots to do with fighting for partisan advantage, particularly in election law.

To lay the groundwork for transforming Civil Rights Division personnel, Acting Assistant Attorney General Loretta King redrafted the division's hiring guidelines and distributed them to all section chiefs. Overseen by new Attorney General Eric Holder, the revised rules ensured that only committed leftists would be hired, jettison-ing the ideological balance that characterized hiring under previous Attorney General Michael Mukasey and his Bush-era predecessors.

This was accomplished in two phases. First, King stacked the hiring committees across the division with leftwing Obama loyalists. Second, she implemented a stealthy ideological litmus test by adopt-ing the following clause as a hiring criterion: "Commitment to civil rights (e.g., extracurricular activities, volunteer work, internships)."[8] Of course, King's appointees to the hiring committees interpreted this "commitment to civil rights" as a commitment to leftwing activ-ism, just as King intended.

While King's memos present "commitment to civil rights" as merely one of many considerations for hiring at DOJ, in practice it is the dominant criterion. Under Eric Holder, if a candidate has not worked for a leftist activist group or otherwise demonstrated some affinity for the Left's causes, he or she will not be hired at the Civil Rights Division—period. King and other political appointees would habitually reject ideal attorney job applicants with near-perfect academic records and extensive litigation experience merely because they had no background with a leftwing activist group. Hiring com-mittee members told me that during committee meetings, King would simply tut-tut "no civil rights experience" and move on to the next applicant.

Harboring big plans for the Civil Rights Division, the Obama administration decided to expand the agency despite the ballooning federal deficit. "The President has asked Congress to increase the Division's funding by 11.3 percent … which includes the addition of 62 new positions," announced Assistant Attorney General Tom Perez in an official email in February 2010.He added, "Already for the current fiscal year, the Division received funding for 102 new staff positions, which we are now working to fill."[9] Perez, who was confirmed by the Senate to his post in October 2009, then engaged in the sort of political puffery that is now routine at the DOJ, though it was unheard of during the Bush administration. "The President's mention of the Civil Rights Division in his State of the Union address lets us know he believes civil rights enforcement is a top priority," he declared. "His continued willingness to invest in the Division backs up that belief with action."[10] It was also backed up with 162 million taxpayer dollars.

As a result of the extra funding and the hiring blitz, a slew of new employees from activist groups settled into the Civil Rights Division from 2009 through 2011. Although many of them had nothing to do when they arrived, they were instrumental to the administration's plans, as described by Perez, to "transform" the division. Some of the incoming hires were so militant that they distrusted the leftwing lawyers hired from activist groups during the Bush years. But this was par for the course at a time when the derangement toward all things Bush was taking on bizarre extremes.

It should be disturbing to every American that the Obama administration has made the Voting Section, which rushed to fill fourteen civil rights analyst positions after Obama's election, a key target of its politicized hiring campaign. Because the mere perception of corruption or bias in our voting system can undermine confidence in our entire republican form of government, the Voting Section, perhaps more than any other DOJ agency, must go to the farthest possible lengths to guarantee Americans of its probity and objectivity. It is now utterly impossible for the agency to give such a guarantee, considering the political activists recently employed there.

Perhaps the section's most radical new hire was Anna M. Baldwin. A Harvard alum, she came to the DOJ from the law firm of Jenner Block, where she practiced with current Associate Attorney General Tom Perrelli. Baldwin was a militant gay activist at Harvard, serving as a leader of the "Queer Resistance Front." In one incident, she led a mob that harassed Jewish and Republican students attending a "Conservative Coming Out" dinner. As the *Harvard Crimson* reported, "Bullhorn in hand, Anna M. Baldwin '00 led about 30 poster-toting protestors, who chanted 'Shame! Shame! Shame!' as dinner guests made their way in to the event."[11] On another occasion, Baldwin condemned the defunding of a campus show, barking to the *Crimson* that "cultural diversity isn't just about a food fair. [The funders] thought this was just a bunch of sexual crap." What could have given the funders that idea? Perhaps it was the show's name—*Clitty Clitty Bang Bang*.[12]

Daniel Freeman was another Voting Section hire under Obama. This former clerk on the Ninth Circuit Court of Appeals was named the pro-bono attorney of the year by the American-Arab Anti-Discrimination Committee and was a Liman Fellow at New York Civil Liberties Union, where he zealously attacked the FBI's counterintelligence operations. Another attorney, Bradley Heard, came to the Voting Section from the Advancement Project, a group dedicated to blocking efforts to purge voter rolls of ineligible voters and felons. Having fought to prevent Michigan Secretary of State Terri Lynn Land from purging voter rolls before the 2008 election, he also vigorously denounced Georgia's voter ID law as well as the state's secretary of state, Cathy Cox.

Voting Section lawyer Elizabeth Westfall also emerged from the Advancement Project, where she challenged Florida laws designed to ensure electoral integrity. Before she was hired, she described the Advancement Project's activities: "In 2008, Advancement Project worked in nine battleground states, including Virginia, where there was significant voter registration and populations of voters of color."[13] Westfall did not reveal why a purported civil rights organization was so interested in "battleground" states. She also donated thousands of dollars to Democratic politicians including Barack Obama, Hillary Clinton, and John Kerry.[14]

Before coming to the Voting Section, attorney Catherine Meza represented Unidad Latina en Acción, an illegal alien rights group that agitated for the right of illegal aliens to receive government services confidentially. She also sat on the board of Advocates for Children of New York, which serves primarily to hector the New York public schools into expanding taxpayer-funded services for minorities, such as providing bilingual education materials.

Obama attorney hire Elise Shore was the Regional Counsel for the Mexican American Legal Defense Fund, which litigates to break down America's borders for illegal aliens. Based on Shore's complaint, the DOJ objected in 2009 to a Georgia citizenship verification law, though the law still took effect after Georgia Secretary of State Brian Kemp sued the DOJ. The law required those registering to vote to prove they are eligible citizens of the United States. For good measure, Shore donated $1,000 to the Obama campaign.[15]

Meredith Bell-Platts was hired as deputy chief of the Voting Section after she left the ACLU Voting Rights Project. There, she had pursued a range of partisan litigation, including an attempt to stop Michigan from removing ineligible voters prior to the 2008 election. Bell-Platts was also involved in litigation just before the 2008 election that effectively opened the floodgates in Ohio for same-day voter registration and simultaneous voting—policies that are notoriously prone to fraud and abuse.

Bryan Sells was also hired from the ACLU Voting Rights Project. Sources have told me that before coming to the Voting Section, Sells incited a boycott and march on Martin, South Dakota, to protest the firing of a local Native American sheriff. Although protestors decried the sheriff's dismissal as racist, in fact the sheriff had quietly resigned after being indicted eighteen times for criminal conduct. The boycott made front page news around the state and inflamed racial tensions, though its underlying rationale was eventually disproven in court.

Other non-attorney hires in the Voting Section passed the ideological litmus test through work with leftwing activist groups like the NAACP, the illegal alien advocacy organization Casa Cornelia Law, the SEIU, the Stanford Immigrant Rights Project, AFSCME, the Lawyers' Committee for Civil Rights Under Law, the American Constitution Society, the Asian and Pacific Islander American Health Forum, the Urban Institute, the Asian American Justice Center, the "No Human Is Illegal" campaign, the League of United Latin American Citizens, the Refugee Rights Clinic in Cape Town, South Africa, and various anti-police organizations.

Service with these groups now serves as an ideological admissions ticket to high paying jobs in the Holder DOJ, an especially valuable benefit for activists from financially struggling organizations. This litmus test is applied so strictly that under Holder, *the Voting Section has not hired a single conservative or even a single non-leftist*. Even the *New York Times*, in a May 2011 article repeating the false myth of politicized hiring at the Bush DOJ, noticed that hiring under Obama was fantastically biased—though of course, that's not quite how the paper reported it. According to the *Times'* analysis of hiring in the Voting Section and two other DOJ sections,

> about 90 percent of the Obama-era hires listed civil rights backgrounds on their résumés, up from about 38 percent of the Bush group hires.... At the same time, there was a

change in the political leanings of organizations listed on the résumés, where discernible. Nearly a quarter of the hires of the Bush group had conservative credentials like membership in the Federalist Society or the Republican National Lawyers Association, while only 7 percent had liberal ones. By contrast, during the first two Obama years, none of the new hires listed conservative organizations, while more than 60 percent had liberal credentials. They consisted overwhelmingly of prior employment or internships with a traditional civil rights group, like the NAACP Legal Defense and Educational Fund.[16]

The DOJ's ideological hiring practices and worshipful fealty to "diversity" sometimes degenerate into farce—seeking new Voting Section employees, the department actually placed advertisements that specified, "The department encourages applicants who suffer from 'mental retardation' and 'mental illness.'"[17] It is, of course, impossible to know whether any of the new employees described above applied in response to this particular appeal.

Jokes aside, the corruption of the Voting Section is a serious issue. The bottom line is this: in the Voting Section, lawyers whose main career experience was in subverting voting laws will be standing watch over America's voting system during the 2012 presidential election.

The DOJ's politicized hiring process extends beyond the Voting Section to the ten other sections of the Civil Rights Division. In one typical example, Tom Perez hired Aaron Schuham from Americans United for Separation of Church and State (AUSCS). Founded in 1947 as a rabidly anti-Catholic organization, AUSCS is one of America's most militantly atheist and anti-religious organizations, even participating in a campaign to stop state troopers from erecting highway crosses to memorialize fellow officers killed in the line of duty. Schuham's background is bad enough, but what's worse is the job the DOJ assigned to him within the Employment Litigation Section—protecting Americans' religious liberties.

Or consider line attorney Seth Rosenthal, who came to the Civil Rights Division's Criminal Section after working for the Southern Center for Human Rights, an Atlanta organization dedicated to ending the death penalty and freeing murderers from death row. Rosenthal distinguished himself during the case of John Allen Muhammad and Lee Boyd Malvo, the Washington, D.C. "beltway snipers" arrested for killing ten people. Facing the choice of trying the duo either in Virginia or Maryland first, then-Attorney General John Ashcroft opted for Virginia, where the jury was more likely to return a guilty verdict and a death sentence. In response, Rosenthal fired off a haughty email to the number two man in the DOJ, Deputy Attorney General Larry Thompson, denouncing Ashcroft's "bloodlust" for choosing Virginia—a choice widely supported by Americans who don't work at the Civil Rights Division.

Rosenthal's superiors cancelled his bonuses and warned him he would be fired for another outburst, yet his outrage at the potential execution of mass murderers was unsurprising considering his background. When Rosenthal later left the Civil Rights Division, he went through the revolving door with leftwing groups and ended up with the Alliance for Justice, a George Soros and Barbara Streisand-funded group that partners with EarthJustice and the Feminist Majority to oppose pro-business judicial nominees.

This revolving door is just one example of how the far left influences the DOJ. Leftist foundations, litigators, and organizations have established permanent non-profit structures, often based on racial or ethnic solidarity, designed to affect the American economy, legal rules, and government policy, including through aggressive contact with the staff of the Civil Rights Division. Project Vote, DEMOS, the Prisoners' Legal Service Project, the Asian American Legal Defense Fund (AALDF), the Mexican American Legal Defense Fund (MALDEF), the NAACP Legal Defense Fund, the Advancement Project, the National Association of Latino Elected and Appointed Officials (NALEO), the League of Women Voters, the Asian Pacific American Legal Center, and Common Cause are just some of the groups that attempt to influence DOJ policy. The organizations are also adept at shaking down big business and corporate foundations for millions of dollars in contributions by threatening boycotts, protests, or otherwise ginning up adverse publicity.

Hundreds of activists man permanent stations, full time, at these groups. They bring litigation, pressure the DOJ to pursue cases they can't or won't take on themselves, lobby the Civil Rights Division to object to voting changes and to sue corporations, and generally bully the division into advancing their racialist agenda, In short, they endeavor to make the DOJ's Civil Rights shop an arm of their own organizations. And in the Obama Justice Department, that is exactly what has happened.

Former Voting Section chief Chris Coates has been on the inside of the "civil rights" industry since the mid-1970s. He described to me how these groups have become a well-funded apparatus for extracting partisan political advantage rather than working for race-neutral equal protection. "When you enforce only some voting laws and ignore others, it results in using the Justice Department to obtain a partisan advantage," he explained. "When you seek to restore the voting rights of felons, but fail to ensure the voting rolls are not polluted with ineligible voters, it results in a partisan advantage."

The Civil Rights Division and these activist groups have become fungible employers. During Democratic administrations, the groups' employees jump to federal jobs inside the Civil Rights Division, then move back to their organizations when Republicans take control. In either capacity, they work to advance the same goals and ideology. Even while drawing federal paychecks, they view themselves as partisan crusaders, not as law enforcement officials. Defendants are usually racists, they presume, particularly in the South. They believe American minorities are systematically oppressed, and thus the DOJ's proper task is to impose a remedy on racist companies, people, and government bodies, notwithstanding the law or facts.

The DOJ's aggressive hiring of leftwing activists is tantamount to providing a taxpayer subsidy to their movement. After one crop of lawyers and staffers is taken off the groups' payrolls and moved to the DOJ, the groups can hire a new crop of young employees. While working for Justice, these attorneys routinely make from $130,000 to $160,000 a year, even though many of them have never tried a case.

Moreover, radicals running the Civil Rights Division have concocted an ingenious way to further enrich activist groups: forced funding through judicial consent decrees. The division's Housing Section, for example, sued AIG Federal Savings Bank for allegedly forcing blacks to pay disproportionately high interest rates and fees.[18] Settlement was unusually easy because the plaintiff—the United States government—had an ownership interest in the defendant, stemming from the recent bailout binge. Strangely, the terms of the settlement focused on pumping cash toward outside liberal activist groups. Specifically, the Holder-approved settlement required the defendants to set aside a cool million for a "qualified organization to provide credit counseling, financial literacy, and other related educational programs targeted at African-American borrowers."[19] And of course, the Civil Rights Division is empowered to approve which "qualified organization" will be the beneficiary of the slush fund.

This is the sort of shakedown that helped fund the now-defunct ACORN group before its excesses and corruption sparked public outrage and the government cut off its subsidies. And the AIG settlement was no isolated incident; Civil Rights Division radicals created another money pot for their political allies in the settlement of *United States v. Sterling*, a housing discrimination case.[20] This kind of blatant corruption is prohibited in other DOJ divisions—but not in Civil Rights. As Robert Driscoll, a former DOJ political appointee during the Bush years, noted, "The practice of the Civil Rights Division steering settlement funds to favored advocacy groups is at odds with both civil rights laws and common sense.... Allowing the Civil Rights Division to steer a defendant's money to its ideological allies is offensive."[21] And most Americans would agree—if they knew it was happening.

The ascendency of leftwing activists has resulted not only in political bias in the Civil Rights Division, but in startling unprofessionalism as well. For example, for several months beginning in January 2010, a rash of stolen wallets and pilfered cash was reported inside the secure offices of the Civil Rights Division's Housing and Voting Sections. Sending out notices after each crime, Voting Section chief Chris Herren essentially copied and pasted the same email, changing just a few words. "It appears that there was another theft of money from a wallet in the Voting Section today," read one notice, followed shortly thereafter by another proclaiming, "It appears that there was *yet* another theft of money from a wallet in the Voting Section today." The appearance of an outright criminal inside the Civil Rights Division surely fulfilled Tom Perez's vow to transform the agency, though not in the way he had implied.

The tight connection between leftwing groups and the DOJ is a long-standing problem that habitually results in scandal, as shown by one particularly embarrassing incident from the late 1990s and early 2000s. In Louisiana, the parish of East Baton Rouge consolidated with the city of Baton Rouge. Although the DOJ approved the move, activists feared it would reduce black political control of Baton Rouge city. When local activist Darrell Glasper filed a voting rights case to try to stop the consolidation, he gained the passionate support of then-DOJ Voting Section attorney Deanne Ross.

Known inside the Voting Section as an eccentric who would appear in federal court and at depositions wearing short skirts, high heels, and bobby socks, Ross persuaded the Civil Rights Division to intervene on Glasper's behalf, and she and Glasper began working closely together in Louisiana. According to multiple DOJ sources, after Glasper's wife caught Glasper and Ross in questionable circumstances, the wife complained about Ross to DOJ overseers. Although Ross denied any wrongdoing, she was pulled out of Louisiana and taken off the case.[22] She left the DOJ shortly thereafter.

Perplexed by the unexplained and sudden departure of the zealous Ross, opposing counsel served discovery requests to determine why she was yanked from the case—they had every right to do so, considering the actual circumstances of her departure. Fortunately for Ross, the Civil Rights Division desperately resisted counsel's discovery and kept the truth concealed.[23]

The Civil Rights Division became much more professional and reliable during the Bush administration, but it was clear that trend would end with Obama's election, even before he took office. For example, during the Bush years, any political display inside the Voting Section was rightfully discouraged as being inappropriate for a federal agency. But on November 17, 2008, just two weeks after

Obama's election, a giddy Voting Section employee sent an email to the entire section informing us that change was indeed coming to our offices. She wrote,

> After our recent Ethics Training, I left with a few more questions than I got answers.... I was unclear as to when candidates or their campaigns are sufficiently considered over or "history" because I love to decorate my office with election related items.... The US Office of Special Counsel issued a statement which clearly spells out what we are permitted to display and when.... The last sentence is most helpful and reads: "Even though Senators McCain and Obama will still be Presidential Candidates until January 6, 2009, *we do not believe that wearing their campaign t-shirts or displaying their pictures after Election Day is activity directed at the success of their candidacies.* Accordingly, the Hatch Act does not prohibit a federal employee from doing so, even while on duty or in the federal workplace.

Needless to say, the employee was not asking about this issue because she wanted to hang campaign signs for the losing Republican candidate.

The cheerleading for Obama became so blatant that after Obama filed for reelection in 2011, orders were sent to remove Obama posters from office walls inside the Voting Section. Nevertheless, despite these orders the posters remained in place.

The posting of campaign material was small potatoes compared to more overt political activities that were openly supported by the Civil Rights Division leadership. For instance, in 2009 the division strongly promoted to its employees the NAACP Legal Defense Fund's annual conference in Warrenton, Virginia. In previous years, employees could go to the conference on their own time and on their own nickel. But in 2009, DOJ employees could attend without taking leave because it would count as approved training; the DOJ even assigned an employee to handle registrations in a central DOJ location.

Predictably, the conference agenda had little if any connection to DOJ business. The first night featured a session taught by Cassandra Butts, the Deputy White House Counsel, on "How to be proactively involved in the process of shaping the federal judiciary"—a topic that had nothing to do with being a DOJ lawyer but everything to do with being a leftwing activist. The next day, Harvard professor Charles Ogletree taught "Advocating for Racial Justice in a 'Post Racial' World." Also on the agenda was "Advancing Civil Rights in the Current Supreme Court." And in case anyone was tempted to view Obama's election as a reason to tone down the volume on racial issues, they would be set straight by the session "Post-Racial America?: Progress and the Continuing Salience of Race in the Struggle for Minority Voting Rights." Around the same time, the Holder DOJ was hiring Charles Ogletree's daughter Rashida to work as an attorney in the Civil Rights Division.

Nobody in the Civil Rights Division seems to have asked whether it was an appropriate use of government time to attend training sessions on furthering the NAACP's agenda—no one asked because the question of appropriateness would never occur to most of its employees. After all, the division in many ways is the taxpayer-funded wing of the same racial grievance industry in which the NAACP is a charter member.

★   ★   ★

The DOJ's politicization under Obama and its collusion with leftwing activist groups is also evident in the department's handling of Freedom of Information Act (FOIA) requests.

During the Bush era, DOJ leaders quickly fulfilled FOIA requests. For instance, in 2006 Charlie Savage, then at the *Boston Globe*, requested all the resumes of the recently hired attorneys in the Bush Civil Rights Division. The DOJ leadership produced the materials within days, well ahead of the legal deadline—they acted so fast, in fact, that some colleagues and I complained they were rushing. Suspecting we were being set up for a leftwing smear campaign, we urged DOJ officials to protect our privacy while fully complying with the requests. But our concerns were ignored and the information was rushed out anyway, resulting in a slew of slanderous media stories, some attacking us in extremely personal ways, followed by curious questions from our family members about why we were in the news. There was a particularly merciless leftist blogosphere attack on a pair of attorneys who happened to be two of the hardest working and most dedicated lawyers in the entire Voting Section.

Around June 2010, *Pajamas Media*, a news and opinion website for which I write, requested from the DOJ the same information about Obama attorney hires that Charlie Savage had requested about Bush hires. After the request was ignored for several months, *Pajamas Media* renewed the request on October 13. After more stalling, *Pajamas Media* filed litigation to force the DOJ to fulfill the FOIA request, as it is legally required to do. After many months the DOJ finally turned over the resumes of 130 new lawyers, but it redacted key portions of the resumes, including the lawyers' prior political activities and group memberships.

The resumes reveal that in almost every instance, the new hires were deeply steeped in leftwing activism. In light of the many leftwing radicals the Holder DOJ has hired, it's easy to guess why DOJ officials want to conceal their new attorneys' resumes. But the stonewalling is also part of a pervasive pattern of partisan obstructionism of FOIA requests; the Holder Civil Rights Division provides fast, favored access for leftwing organizations and for friendly media outlets like National Public Radio, while Republican or conservative-leaning requestors often have to wait nearly a year for a reply, if any is forthcoming at all.[24]

In February 2011, I obtained DOJ logs that clearly showed the Civil Rights Division's systematic bias in fulfilling FOIA requests. Consider the following list of right-leaning FOIA requestors and the long waits they faced:

- Michael Rosman of the Center for Individual Rights. Six-month wait.
- *Washington Post* blogger Jennifer Rubin, who was seeking records relating to employees, like Charlie Savage did. No reply at all.
- Congressman Frank Wolf. Five-month wait.
- Jed Babbin, then-editor at *Human Events*. Six-month wait.
- Jerry Seper of the *Washington Times*. Six-month wait.
- Jim Boulet of the English First Foundation. No reply at all.
- Jenny Small of Judicial Watch. Five-month wait.
- Republican Pennsylvania state representative Stephen Barrar. Four-month wait.

- Jason Torchinsky, a former DOJ lawyer who now works for the GOP. No reply at all.
- Ben Conery of the *Washington Times*. Five-month wait.

Now, contrast those delays with the efficient service enjoyed by left-leaning FOIA requestors:

- Gerry Hebert, partisan liberal and former career Voting Section lawyer who testified against Republican now-Senator Jeff Sessions when he was nominated to the federal judiciary. Same-day service.
- Kristen Clarke of the NAACP Legal Defense Fund. Same-day service.
- Ari Shapiro of National Public Radio. Five-day service.
- Nicholas Espiritu of the Mexican American Legal Defense Fund. Next-day service.
- Eugene Lee of the Asian Pacific American Legal Center. Three-day service.
- Edward DuBose, president of Georgia NAACP. Same-day service.
- Raul Arroyo-Mendoza of the Advancement Project. Same-day service.
- Nina Perales of the Mexican American Legal Defense Fund. Two-day service.
- Tova Wang of Demos. Three-day service.
- Mark Posner and Robert Kengle of the Lawyers Committee for Civil Rights Under Law. Same-day service.
- Brian Sells, formerly of the ACLU and now of the DOJ Voting Section. One-day service.

- Natalie Landreth of the Native American Rights Fund. Same-day service.
- Fred McBride, ACLU redistricting coordinator. Same-day service.
- Jenigh Garrett, formerly of the NAACP Legal Defense Fund and now of the DOJ Voting Section. Same-day service.
- Joaquin Avila, well-known election law professor who advocates for the rights of illegal aliens to vote in U.S. elections. Next-day service.

The liberals enjoyed this speedy favoritism even when they filed intricate requests. Take Ari Shapiro of NPR. On February 23, 2009, Shapiro sent a letter to the DOJ requesting "copies of all of the consent decree settlements that the civil rights division submitted to a court during the following two month period. January 19-February 19, 2009 and January 19-February 19, 2008." This was a complex request, requiring discussions with all the various component sections. It was certainly more complicated than the *Pajamas Media* request for resumes—all of which are housed in one central location at 1425 New York Avenue in Washington, D.C. Shapiro's request sought expedited service, and with a five-day turnaround time, he got it.

The NAACP's Kristen Clarke made particularly revealing requests, such as the one she sent by email late on the afternoon of June 17, 2009. Hunting for whatever Louisiana was telling the DOJ about a submission under Section 5, she asked for "any information provided by the State of Louisiana in connection with Submission No. 2008-3512 between January 1, 2009 and this request." She wanted to know Louisiana's official views, particularly since the NAACP was so engaged in the matter. As Clarke reminded Justice, the "NAACP Legal Defense Fund submitted a Comment Letter in connection with this submission." At 6:59 a.m. on June 19, Clarke got just what she wanted, by email no less.

This pattern of bias backs up reports I've heard from DOJ sources alleging that political appointee Julie Fernandes exploits FOIA requests to benefit Obama's leftwing allies. Specifically, sources say she instructs Voting Section staffers to inform leftwing groups about specific data from DOJ files that they might find useful in advancing their agenda. The operation functions like clockwork: after receiving a tip from a DOJ employee, an activist group files a FOIA request for the information, and cooperative DOJ employees then produce the documents within days.

Another baleful effect of the ideological hiring policy at the Civil Rights Division has been the sanction and fining of division lawyers. It should be noted that these penalties are part of a long, little noticed pattern. Although the Civil Rights Division has become particularly politicized under Holder's tenure, the division has always attracted its share of leftwing crusaders, even under Republican administrations. These rogue lawyers regularly break ethical and legal barriers, for which they frequently face legal penalties. A notable exception was the George W. Bush administration—although the Civil Rights Division hosted a fair number of leftwing renegades under Bush, DOJ leadership largely suppressed their excesses. As a result, during Bush's presidency, not a single Civil Rights Division attorney faced any court-imposed sanctions or fines.

The same cannot be said for the division's employees before and after Bush, that is, under Presidents Clinton and Obama. Perhaps the most disturbing aspect of this history of lawlessness is that many of the sanctioned lawyers still work at the DOJ, and some have even been promoted to management positions.

During the Clinton administration, Voting Section lawyers cost the American taxpayers $1,147,228 in *Hays v. State of Louisiana*. In that case, a federal court imposed sanctions after finding that "the Justice Department impermissibly encouraged—nay, mandated—racial gerrymandering."[25] The court noted that, in drawing the redistricting plans, the Louisiana legislature "succumbed to the illegitimate preclearance demands" of the Voting Section.[26] Simply put, the Voting Section illegally forced Louisiana to draw election districts to generate the election of black officials based on their race.

The bill for Civil Rights Division misbehavior was even higher in the Employment Litigation Section case of *United States v. City of Torrance*, in which the DOJ alleged that the city of Torrance, California, discriminated against minority applicants to the police force and fire service. The evidence for the DOJ's charge was so weak that a federal court made the rare finding that DOJ lawyers had violated Rule 11, which prohibits attorneys from filing frivolous lawsuits; the court found that the lawyers failed to allege any specific unlawful hiring practices, failed to turn over documents that could prove the case, and engaged in needless discovery designed to harass the city. Depositions from the Civil Rights Division lawyers reflected the same sloppy bias, asking inane questions such as "Is it important to be a good listener?" and "When I say common sense, what does that mean to you?"[27]

For this nonsense and more, the federal court sanctioned the Employment Section lawyers at Justice a bundle of money. The Ninth Circuit Court of Appeals upheld the sanctions, holding that the Civil Rights Division "continued to pursue the claim ... long after it became apparent that the case lacked merit."[28] The bill for the American taxpayer? $1,714,727. Were the responsible attorneys fired or even reprimanded? Of course not. In fact, one lawyer named on the court docket, Elizabeth Hack, has since been promoted to the post of Special Litigation Counsel inside the Civil Rights Division, while another sanctioned lawyer, Marissa Chun, was appointed by the Obama administration as a deputy associate attorney general.

The bill in another Clinton-era case, *Johnson v. Miller*, was a touch smaller—only $594,000—but the Civil Rights Division misconduct was even more egregious. In that case, the Voting Section fought to impose an illegal, racially gerrymandered legislative redistricting plan on the state of Georgia. In attempting to create as many black-controlled legislative districts as possible, Voting Section lawyers became sleazy advocates for leftist groups and, according to the court, may have committed perjury.

A federal court found that in the Georgia case, the DOJ had climbed into bed with the ACLU, which was "in constant contact with the DOJ line attorneys."[29] Pronouncing the communications between the DOJ and the ACLU "disturbing," the court declared, "It is obvious from a review of the materials that [the ACLU attorneys'] relationship with the DOJ Voting Section was informal and familiar; the dynamics were that of peers working together, not of an advocate submitting proposals to higher authorities."[30] After a Voting Section lawyer professed that she could not remember details about the relationship, the court found her "professed amnesia" to be "less than credible."[31] That's how federal judges call someone a liar—and this liar was an attorney for the United States Department of Justice.

The court concluded its denunciation of the Voting Section's misconduct by noting, "The considerable influence of ACLU advocacy on the voting rights decisions of the United States Attorney General is an embarrassment. It is surprising that the Department of Justice was so blind to this impropriety."[32] Instead of immediately acting to root out its lawless attorneys, the DOJ appealed to the Supreme Court, which affirmed the lower court's findings.[33]

Notably, one of the sanctioned lawyers in the *Johnson* case was then-Voting Section supervisor Loretta King.[34] After a federal court denounced her misconduct in *Johnson*, King was bafflingly promoted to a permanent position as a deputy assistant attorney general, a move that secured her position as a career senior manager at the Civil Rights Division across both Republican and Democrat administrations. With the advent of the Obama administration, King was pushed to the forefront, implementing the Civil Rights Division's partisan hiring policy and, as we will see in chapters four and five, helping to engineer the dismissal of the voter intimidation case against the New Black Panther Party.

This was by no means the full extent of court-imposed sanctions on Civil Rights Division attorneys under the Clinton administration. The Voting Section was forced to pay $95,000 in *Scott v. Department of Justice*,[35] and taxpayers were hit for $150,333 in fees and expenses as a penalty against Housing Section lawyers in *United States v. Tucson Estates Property Owners Association, Inc.*[36]

In *United States v. Jones*, the Voting Section was sanctioned $86,626 for bringing a frivolous case in Alabama. The DOJ brought the suit under Section 2 of the Voting Rights Act to block over fifty white voters from participating in an election in a majority black district. The appeals court ruled that the lawsuit was filed "without conducting a proper investigation of its truth [and was] unconscionable.... Hopefully, we will not again be faced with reviewing a case as carelessly instigated as this one."[37] The 11th Circuit Court of Appeals did not mince words in its scolding of DOJ lawyers including then-Voting Section attorney Gerald Hebert, who would later become a vociferous critic of the Bush DOJ:

A properly conducted investigation would have quickly revealed that there was no basis for the claim that the Defendants were guilty of purposeful discrimination against black voters.... Unfortunately, we cannot restore the reputation of the persons wrongfully branded by the United States as public officials who deliberately deprived their fellow citizens of their voting rights. We also lack the power to remedy the damage done to race relations in Dallas County by the *unfounded accusations* of purposeful discrimination made by the United States.

We can only hope that in the future the decision makers in the United States Department of Justice will be more sensitive to the impact on racial harmony that can result from the filing of a claim of purposeful discrimination.[38] (emphasis added)

Following President Obama's election, after avoiding court sanctions for the eight years of the Bush presidency, Loretta King was back in trouble with a federal judge in *United States v. Sturdevant*.[39] This related to a housing discrimination case brought by King along with then-Housing Section chief Steven Rosenbaum. According to Hans von Spakovsky, a former attorney at the Civil Rights Division, "As usual, the [Civil Rights Division] made broad accusations of discriminatory conduct when it filed its complaint, but when it was asked to provide specific examples or actual evidence of such discrimination, it failed to do so."[40] This was an obvious case of the leadership in the Housing Section, particularly Rosenbaum, lawlessly failing to comply with the rules of discovery. The defendants targeted by King and Rosenbaum gave the United States interrogatories to answer, demanding to know the facts supporting the charges against them. Rosenbaum refused to answer, and court sanctions followed.

Overall, the Civil Rights Division has been sanctioned $4,107,595 for bringing frivolous cases or engaging in misconduct, none of which was assessed during the Bush administration. This holds a crucial lesson for U.S. businesses: when the Civil Rights Division sues you, don't assume it has a good case. Businesses typically presume they can't win against these lawsuits, but millions of dollars in misconduct fines say otherwise.

Much of the misconduct by Civil Rights Division attorneys doesn't even involve monetary penalties. In one almost comical example, a federal court reprimanded a Housing Section attorney for habitually missing court deadlines. His excuse was that instead of writing down deadlines, he kept his court docket in his head. The Office of Professional Responsibility, the DOJ's internal ethics watchdog, recommended a 30-day suspension of the lawyer. But without authority and in violation of DOJ guidelines, Loretta King reduced the punishment to a few days. In light of this leniency, it was unsurprising that a few years later, the attorney's defective "mental court docket" caused him to miss more court deadlines. Needless to say, the twice offending lawyer kept his job.

There is a fundamental difference between the enforcement of civil rights laws under Republican and Democratic administrations: Republicans feel constrained by an objective reading of the facts in each case and by legal precedents, while Democrats, in order to fight America's supposed structural racism, are willing to contort the confines of the law to push legal precedent toward expanding federal power.

To the Obama administration, the Civil Rights Division is not a law enforcement agency; it is instead the leader of a continuing struggle harkening back to the freedom riders and Selma marches. America has changed little, if any, since the days of Jim Crow, Obama officials believe. And if you oppose their philosophy or methods, to them, you cannot be acting in good faith. You are the successor of racist cops who swung batons and unleashed dogs, the malicious descendent of Bull Connor and George Wallace.

For these crusaders, politics is a bitter, all-consuming struggle against a pernicious enemy—and that enemy is the American system of justice.

CHAPTER FOUR

★ ★ ★

See No Evil

The New Black Panthers' Travesty of Justice

On the day of Obama's election, two members of the New Black Panther Party, King Samir Shabazz and Jerry Jackson, patrolled in front of a polling place in Philadelphia, Pennsylvania. As Shabazz brandished a nightstick, the pair yelled at nearby whites that they would be ruled by a black man after the elections. This blatant act of voter intimidation, caught on camera and quickly posted on the internet, deeply disturbed many Americans, who assume this sort of thing only happens in dysfunctional foreign countries.

The incident would provoke a political firestorm, ultimately leading to my resignation from the Department of Justice. Despite a public outcry, the media largely tried to dismiss the event as an isolated incident, certainly nothing that would impinge on Obama's carefully constructed image as a "post-racial" healer of the race divide. But very few Americans knew that the previous year, Obama had watched and even participated as the New Black Panthers staged an ostentatious public display of support for his candidacy.

On March 4, 2007, then-Senator Barack Obama spoke at a large gathering in Selma, Alabama, a month after he had declared his candidacy for president. With Hillary Clinton leading the Democratic polls, Obama's candidacy was widely dismissed as a long-shot. He could not even count on the support of black voters, who had no interest in wasting their political capital on a losing candidate as many had with Jesse Jackson and others in the past. In fact, Obama's chances were worse than Jackson's in some ways, particularly because Hillary had secured the early support of civil rights legends like Congressman John Lewis and other prominent black politicians.

But Obama had a bigger problem, one that was referenced in an interview he gave with Steve Kroft of *60 Minutes* shortly before Obama's appearance in Selma. Aware of Obama's upbringing in Indonesia and Hawaii, and his time spent in Hawaii's elite Punahou Academy, Kroft observed, "There are African-Americans who don't think that you're black enough, who don't think that you have had the required experience."[1]

Securing overwhelming black support was crucial to Obama's hopes of winning the Democratic primaries the following year. He might fare well enough in early caucus states like Iowa and Nevada with the help of skillful, experienced operatives who could drum up support among the committed Democratic base. But he would need solid black backing to win the open primary in South Carolina, with its black-majority electorate. A victory there would give him momentum moving into the crucial Super Tuesday contests.

But as of March 2007, Obama had not rallied wide black support. So he went to Selma, Alabama, a city with deep meaning in civil

An exhibit at the National Voting Rights Museum in Selma, Alabama, describes America's founders. *Photo by J. Christian Adams.*

Ike Brown (L) celebrates the re-election of Noxubee County sheriff Albert Walker (R) after Walker's re-election becomes certain. *Photo by Scott Boyd.*

Department of Justice attorney Don Palmer (L) chats with Ike Brown (R) in the Noxubee County Courthouse in August 2007. *Photo by J. Christian Adams.*

A mural in downtown Macon, Mississippi, shows how the legacy of slavery still animates public sentiment in Noxubee County.
Photo by J. Christian Adams.

The Brooksville, Mississippi home of Lucille Bland, who continued to vote in Noxubee County elections from this registered address even though she no longer lived in the county. *Photo by J. Christian Adams.*

Noxubee County sheriff deputies John "Boogerman" Clanton (L) and Terry "Big Dog" Grasseree (Center) arrest Kendrick Slaughter (R) on July 15, 2005, days after Slaughter was named as a witness for the United States against Ike Brown. *Photo by Scott Boyd.*

(Left to Right) Joshua Rogers, Christopher Coates, and me, the three attorneys who tried to the case against Ike Brown in Jackson, Mississippi. *Photo by J. Christian Adams.*

The office of a DOJ Voting Section attorney who will be responsible for enforcing federal election law in 2012. The photo was taken in May 2011, after a Hatch Act memo was circulated ordering such displays to be removed. *Photo credit confidential.*

The office of a DOJ Voting Section analyst who reviews submissions under Section 5 of the Voting Rights Act. The photo was taken in May 2011. *Photo credit confidential.*

Members of the New Black Panthers march in Jasper, Texas, in July 1998. Then-party leader Khalid Abdul Muhammed is in the middle of the photo, wearing sunglasses and no hat. *Photo courtesy of Jana Birchum/Contributor/ Getty Images.*

New Black Panther Party leader Malik Zulu Shabazz speaks in Harlem. *Photo courtesy of NY Daily News via Getty Images.*

Then-candidate Obama stakes his claim to Selma, Alabama, at Brown Chapel on March 4, 2007. *Photo courtesy of Scott Olson/Getty Images.*

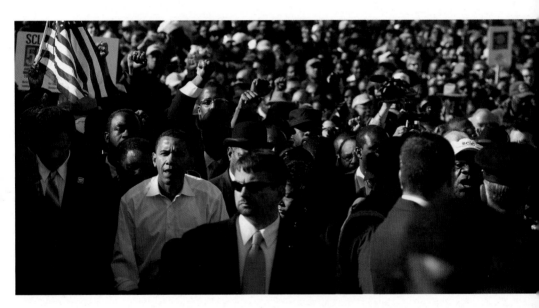

Malik Zulu Shabazz and other New Black Panthers give a black power salute behind Obama during the 2007 commemoration of the Selma-to-Montgomery march. *Photo courtesy of Scott Olson/Getty Images.*

rights lore thanks to the iconic Selma-to-Montgomery voting rights marches of 1965. Obama's goal was to launch himself to the black community as a credible, winning, and most important, authentically black candidate—and he sought to do that by grafting his budding campaign onto the classic civil rights storyline. Fittingly, he timed his visit to coincide with Bloody Sunday jubilee weekend, the annual commemoration of the 1965 marches culminating in the event's re-enactment on the Edmund Pettus Bridge.

On March 4, Obama arrived to address the congregation at Brown Chapel A.M.E. Church, the staging point of the original marches. He was welcomed from the pulpit by Congressman John Lewis and by Alabama State Senator Bobby Singleton. Singleton, whose wife would later plead guilty to voter fraud charges, welcomed Obama "on behalf of the 140 members of the Alabama legislature, particularly on behalf of the twenty six members of the Alabama black legislature."[2]

Several other speakers advanced to the pulpit to greet Obama. Then, a woman stepped forward and uttered a shocking welcome address. "My name is Pastor Estella Shabazz.... My husband, he's stuck outside, he couldn't get through the crowd, I bring greetings from him also, who is the National Spokesman of the New Black Panther Party, along with the Chief of the New Black Panther Party is outside also, they are also here in support of Senator Barack Obama."[3]

An aspiring president, one might imagine, would not appreciate a public pledge of support by a far-left hate group, one that even the leftwing Southern Poverty Law Center denounces as a "virulently racist and anti-Semitic organization whose leaders have encouraged violence against whites, Jews and law enforcement officers." The SPLC file on the Panthers contains many quotes from Panther leaders denouncing "no good Jew[s]" and "white, dirty, cracker whore bitches," and openly advocating the mass murder of both Jews and whites.[4] Yet video of Shabazz's remarks shows no discomfort on Obama's part; to the contrary, when Shabazz finishes speaking, Obama breaks out in a wide grin.

Obama took to the pulpit and hit all the necessary notes. To establish his racial bona fides, he began by invoking a dear friend of his in Chicago. "I must send greetings from Dr. Jeremiah A. Wright Jr. but I got a letter giving me encouragement and saying how proud he was that I had announced and encouraging me to stay true to my ideals and my values and not to be fearful." Later in his campaign, of course, Obama would distance himself from Wright and his "God-damn America" diatribes. But at this point, in front of this crowd, Obama's long-standing relationship with his mentor was politically useful.

If an upper-middle-class childhood in Hawaii didn't lend itself to adequate racial suffering, Obama reminded the congregation about the plight of his father at the hands of the British. "My Grandfather was a cook to the British in Kenya. Grew up in a small village and all his life, that's all he was—a cook and a house boy. And that's what they called him, even when he was 60 years old. They called him a house boy. They wouldn't call him by his last name. Sound familiar?"[5] Of course it sounded familiar to everyone in Brown Chapel. It wasn't a question. It was a bloody shirt.

Obama continued, "Yet something happened back here in Selma, Alabama.... [It] sent a shout across oceans so that my grandfather began to imagine something different for his son. His son, who grew up herding goats in a small village in Africa, could suddenly set his sights a little higher and believe that maybe a black man in this world had a chance." His father got his chance, Obama said, when the Kennedy White House organized an "airlift" that brought groups of Africans to the United States for an education.[6]

The story was touching, though largely inaccurate. Obama's attempt to link his family with the Kennedys is undermined by the fact that when his father came to the United States, the president was Dwight Eisenhower, not Kennedy. And by the time the Selma march took place in 1965, Obama's father, then on his third wife, had already been chased out of Harvard University and had his scholarship cut off for personal reasons including being a suspected polygamist.[7] At the time of the Selma marches, his father had already left America and been back in Kenya for eight months.

But the facts weren't important. What mattered was Obama inserting himself into civil rights history—and he wasn't subtle about doing so. "So don't tell me I don't have a claim on Selma, Alabama," he intoned on the heels of his highly embellished story. "Don't tell me I'm not coming home to Selma, Alabama."[8]

Playing to the crowd, Obama attacked the Bush Justice Department's race-neutral enforcement of civil rights laws. "The single most significant concern that this Justice Department under this administration has had with respect to discrimination has to do with affirmative action. That they have basically spent all their time worrying about colleges and universities around the country that are giving a little break to young African Americans and Hispanics to make sure that they can go to college, too."[9]

Obama was referring to a DOJ action against Southern Illinois University. However, his characterization of the case was disingenuous; in fact, the university was handing out scholarships to people only of particular races, excluding whites. What Obama called a "little break" was actually the provision of racially discriminatory taxpayer-funded scholarships.[10] Needless to say, his casual assertion that the Bush DOJ "spent all their time" fighting such cases was grossly inaccurate, but such fables can mesmerize many—and they certainly hit their mark with his audience in Selma.

Recapitulating the famous attacks on the Selma marchers of 1965, Obama assured his listeners that he was a trustworthy traveler in their continuing cause. "When you see heads gashed open and eyes burning and children lying hurt on the side of the road, when you are John Lewis and you've been beaten within an inch of your life on Sunday, how do you wake up Monday and keep on marching? Be strong and have courage, for I am with you wherever you go."[11] That last sentence was a curious use of the first person, part of a biblical statement (Genesis 28:15) made by God that Obama uttered without attribution.

Obama recited his entire speech in a dialect much different from his normal speaking voice. He also invoked religious imagery that is almost wholly absent from his presidential addresses. Then-NPR correspondent Juan Williams reported from Selma, "Senator Obama used the occasion [of his speech in Brown Chapel] to tie himself to the history of the civil rights movement and speak about how though some may question whether he's authentically black because his father was from Africa, he feels that he is in fact deeply tied, wouldn't exist without what happened here in Selma in 1965." He described the Selma trip as an effort by Obama "to really fight back against any suggestion he is not a black candidate and not in line with the grand traditions of the civil rights struggle."[12]

Time has not been kind to Obama's speech, which is tainted by a tinge of artificiality. Nevertheless, the crowd at Brown Chapel greeted it with deafening applause. Obama soaked in the acclaim as Congressman Artur Davis rushed to hoist his hand in the air.

Obama made his way from the chapel to a huge crowd waiting outside. Obama and other notables, including Hillary Clinton and Al Sharpton, addressed the crowd from a portable podium at the top of the chapel's entryway stairs. The speakers were all people one would expect to hear at this kind of high-profile event, with one exception: New Black Panther Party chief Malik Zulu Shabazz, a future defendant in a DOJ voter intimidation lawsuit. When he spoke, he was flanked at the podium by several Panthers in full Panther battle regalia—black fatigues, beret, insignia, and boots. One of them was Panther "Field Marshal" Najee Muhammad, who is seen in a Panther video called "Training Day" in which he encourages blacks in DeKalb County, Georgia, to don ski masks, lie in wait behind shrubs, and kill police officers with AK-47s. Following that exhortation he mocks the hypothetical victims' grieving widows.[13]

When the speeches ended, the crowd began the memorial walk to Edmund Pettus Bridge. For the duration of that one-mile trek, video reveals that the uniformed New Black Panther members shadowed close behind Obama, who showed no aversion to their presence.

Juan Williams reported excitedly from the scene, "It's an incredible scene, Debbie. You got Bill Clinton and Hillary Clinton linking arms in front of the march to the left-hand side; and on the right-hand side, Barack Obama, John Lewis. You got some from the New Black Panther Party behind them. And of course you got lots of young people—college students—just energized by this 42nd recreation of the powerful march across the bridge on the way to Montgomery."[14] When the marchers descended the far side of the bridge, Malik Zulu Shabazz and five other uniformed Panthers were captured by *Life* magazine raising their fists in a black power salute over Obama's head.

Somehow, the fact that the future President of the United States shared a podium with leaders of the New Black Panthers, marched with them, and received a public, formal greeting from their party has vanished from the history of Obama's campaign. Apart from Williams' single dispatch, no other media outlets ever reported it.

Yet the video and photographic evidence has been in plain sight for years, gathering dust in a box at the National Voting Rights Museum.

Obama did not publicly acknowledge the Panthers' tributes, but he made no effort to shoo them away, either. Malik Zulu Shabazz told a reporter he spoke with Obama that day in Selma, though he did not provide details about the conversation.[15] In the end, nobody knows what Obama thought about the Panthers' demonstration of support for him, because the media never asked him about it.

It is possible Obama found the Panthers deeply embarrassing. Perhaps in his conversation with Shabazz he told the Panther leader to stay away from him, but Shabazz marched right behind him anyway. Or perhaps Obama was indifferent to the Panthers, viewing them as a weird sideshow and not fully understanding exactly who these people were.

But we cannot dismiss the disturbing possibility that the Panthers' presence in Selma and on the podium outside Brown Chapel, as well as their positioning behind Obama during the march, was collaborative and deliberate. It is plausible that the Obama campaign acquiesced to the overtures of people like Malik Zulu Shabazz. The images of Obama and the Panthers together were useful to Obama, providing signs of his racial "authenticity" for important voting segments. And after all, it's clear that *some* elements in the Obama campaign sympathized with the Panthers; in March 2008, the official Obama campaign website posted the Panthers' endorsement of Obama, then quickly removed it when it drew negative attention.[16]

One can only imagine the media firestorm that would have erupted if a Republican presidential candidate had marched next to a racist hate group. And in fact, when then-candidate George W. Bush spoke at Bob Jones University on February 2, 2000, the media outcry was riotous. Over the ensuing five weeks, the *New York Times* printed no fewer than twenty-one critical articles on the speech under headlines such as "Right Wing Baggage Puts Drag on Bush Caravan."[17] Keep in mind that Bob Jones' primary sin was to ban interracial dating—an undesirable policy to be sure, but hardly comparable to the Panthers' exhortations to racial murder. Even after the university ended its interracial dating ban the month following Bush's visit, the media continued to denounce Bush relentlessly over the incident.

The media took a much different approach toward events in Selma. Throughout Obama's campaign, not a single reporter asked him about his interaction with the Panthers. It was such a well-kept secret that after Obama's election, when I was working with other DOJ lawyers on the Panther voter intimidation case, *we* didn't even know about it. And after the Obama administration squashed the voter intimidation case against the Panthers, we still didn't know about it, and neither did the American people. Only in February 2011, after I had left the DOJ, did I stumble across the Williams story.[18]

Incidentally, after the Obama administration had dismissed the voter intimidation case against the Panthers, I testified about the dismissal to the U.S. Commission on Civil Rights. Shortly after that appearance I was attacked by none other than Juan Williams, who accused me on Fox News of trying to "politicize" the case.[19] Williams declined to mention that he had personally seen Obama march with some of the very defendants whom his administration had just let off the hook.

Many people wrongly assume that the New Black Panthers are related to the 1960s-era Black Panthers of Huey Newton fame. To the contrary, they are completely distinct organizations that are actually involved in a long-running trademark dispute over the newer group's name. They are also separated by doctrine; the 1960s Panthers were black-power militants, but they worked with whites and had a human services component (albeit a socialist one). The group's new iteration, in contrast, is a venomously anti-Semitic, anti-white, and quasi-Islamic race hate group. Bobby Seale, a founder of the original Black Panther Party, denounces the new Panthers as "little black racists without the power to implement overt racism."[20]

Founded by Aaron Michaels in the early 1990s, the New Black Panther Party came to national prominence in the later half of the decade after Khalid Abdul Muhammad became its national chairman. Muhammad, a former assistant to Nation of Islam leader Louis Farrakhan, accomplished the rare feat of getting expelled from the Nation of Islam for being too radical. An internet video of an old speech by Muhammad shows him in typical ghoulish form, calling for the mass murder of all white South Africans:

> I say if they don't get out of town, we kill the men, we kill the women, we kill the children, we kill the babies, we kill the blind, we kill the cripple, we kill the crazy, we kill the faggots, we kill the lesbians, I say goddamit, we kill 'em all. You say, "Well why kill 'em all? Why kill the women? First, why kill the babies? They're just little innocent blue-eyed babies." Because goddamit they're gonna grow up one day to rule your babies. Kill 'em now.[21]

The Panthers earned a reputation for intimidating Asian-owned businesses in black neighborhoods. New York was one city where Asian merchants were plagued by Panther shakedowns and racist threats. As detailed in a 2001 article in *Washington City Paper*, Malik Zulu Shabazz, who would soon assume leadership of the Panthers following Muhammad's sudden death, undertook a similar, mafia-style extortion racket against Asian businesses in Washington, D.C.

The article captures one exchange between Shabazz, who was leading a group of Panthers, and an Asian business owner. Shabazz tells the businessman, "There are many of your kind here that are taking wagon-loads of money out of our community and giving nothing back." The man responds simply, "I'm working here, and I'm trying to make a living." Shabazz then becomes incensed. "Then we'll be back and boycott this place," he warns. "We're going to grind that cash register to a halt. To a halt. Mark my word." On his way out of the store, Shabazz ominously instructs a Panther, "Put them on our list."[22]

Frank Han's A-1 Grocery in D.C. also made "the list" following an altercation between the store's Asian owner and a young, black girl he accused of shoplifting. The Panthers spearheaded a week of boycotts, and the shop's outside wall was spraypainted with the message, "Burn them down, Shut them down, Black Power!" Shabazz told the *Washington Post* the store was "part of a citywide problem with Asian merchants and their African-American customers." After a week of these demonstrations, a pipe bomb exploded at the store's entrance.[23]

Asians, however, do not top the rankings of Panther demonology. That spot is reserved for Jews, whom Panther Field Marshal Najee Muhammad has called "the hook-nosed, bagel-eating, lox-eating, imposter, perpetrating-a-fraud, johnny-come-lately, just crawled out of the caves and hills of Europe" people.[24] The Anti-Defamation League has compiled an impressive online dossier on the Panthers' history of virulent anti-Semitism. For example, in March 2011 Malik Zulu Shabazz began a campaign encouraging blacks to boycott

Jewish institutions, declaring, "It's good to expose the manipulation … the abuses of the Zionists and the Jews on how they have
manipulated our community and [sic] sucking our resources. What
you gonna do about it? They still have their hands in our economy.
They still are making money off of us. What ever happened to the
spirit of 'shut 'em down'? Why don't we shut some people down?"[25]

Shabazz's documented history of anti-Semitism stretches back
decades. At a 1994 rally at Howard University, Shabazz, then a law
student, led an auditorium of nearly a thousand people in an anti-
Semitic chant. "Who is it that controls the media and Hollywood?"
he screamed.

"The Jews!" roared back the crowd.

"Who controls the federal reserve?" Shabazz cried.

"The Jews!"

"Who caught and killed Nat Turner?"

"The Jews! The Jews!" screamed back the crowd.

Richard Cohen at the *Washington Post* wrote a thoughtful piece
about the rally reminding readers that large-scale evil usually has
small-scale beginnings. "Washington had a little Nuremburg rally
last week…. '[T]he Jews, the Jews' was shouted by an audience of
about 1,000 people, at least half of them students…. They were led
in responsive anti-Semitism by a law student named Malik Zulu
Shabazz, a man we can only hope was born too late for his real calling: a pogrom."[26] Cohen also blasted the *Post* for downplaying the
event, identifying the racial double-standard that has become even
more ingrained, both in the media and in government, since he
wrote about it seventeen years ago:

> But maybe the saddest aspect of the … controversy is the
> degree to which the media apply a double standard when
> the bigots happen to be black. You can only imagine what

would have happened had a white university had itself a hate night. Page one could not have contained the story. Yet Howard's sordid evening was played in next day's *Post* at the bottom of the Metro page (with not a mention of Jew-baiting in either the headline or first paragraph) and a follow-up story was tucked within Metro. The reason for this, I think, is a certain institutional tone deafness to the authentic sounds of antisemitism and an addled version of multiculturalism, including the wrongheaded belief that since blacks are victims, they cannot also be victimizers.[27]

Cohen could have just as easily been admonishing today's officials in the DOJ Civil Rights Division.

The media often dismisses the Panthers as a "fringe" group, but it is mistaken to think the Panthers merely consist of a few isolated nuts. For starters, the group has a knack for conjuring crowds in urban settings. For example, on November 3, 2007, Shabazz held a rally at the federal courthouse in Charleston, West Virginia, that attracted around a thousand people and drew the support of the Southern Christian Leadership Conference and the Reverend Al Sharpton.[28] Later that month, Shabazz addressed a large lunchtime crowd in downtown Washington, D.C., at an Al Sharpton rally ostensibly aimed against hate crimes. Shabazz led hundreds of federal workers and other seemingly mainstream D.C. residents in chants of "Black Power!" replete with raised black power fists.[29]

The Panthers like to inject themselves into racially inflammatory situations, whether it is the gruesome dragging death of a black man in Jasper, Texas, or false accusations by a black woman of being gang raped by white Duke lacrosse players in Durham, North Carolina. And wherever they go, the Panthers attract a sizeable crowd of supporters. The party's Trenton chapter conjured dozens of people, including women and children, for a music video called "Bang Out" that advocates the murder of whites.[30]

Malik Zulu Shabazz regularly cites widespread support for the Panthers in the mainstream black community and among judges and elected officials. There are many indications this is no empty boast. In studying the Panthers, a producer of a National Geographic documentary on the group commented, "Beside talking with New Black Panther Party members, we reached out to scholars, activists and community leaders who both agreed and disagreed strongly with the New Black Panther Party's 'new' philosophies. Some people see them as simply a hate group, and others as a true agent of change leading the struggle to truly achieve racial equality."[31]

Michael V. Roberts, one of the nation's most successful black entrepreneurs, has attended Panther-sponsored events. Roberts, who owns TV stations, condo developments, a cabinetry company, real estate ventures, hotels across the country, and the Roberts Orpheum Theatre in St. Louis,[32] appeared at the National Black Power Convention hosted by the New Black Panther Party in Atlanta in May 2010. The announcement for the convention said, "With a mood that is more anti-black than at any recent time, it is imperative that we organize our forces, pool our resources and prepare for war!"[33] Roberts primarily speaks about entrepreneurial empowerment at these gatherings, but adds an imprimatur of respectability to these black separatist events.

The conference featured other notable speakers ranging from the well-known black studies professor Leonard Jefferies to Imam Siraj Wahhaj, an unindicted co-conspirator in the 1993 World Trade Center bombing. Louis Farrakhan sent a video message to the gathering thanking Shabazz and declaring, "May Allah be pleased with him and his organizational effort to bring the New Black Panther Party where it is today."[34]

The New Black Panther Party also served as "security" for Congresswoman Cynthia McKinney during her 2006 Democratic Party primary contest. When a reporter asked McKinney to what she attributed her loss, New Black Panther Chief of Staff Hashim Nzinga, who was part of her security detail, answered, "Why do you think she lost? You wanna know what led to the loss? Israel. The Zionists. You. Put on your yarmulke and celebrate."[35]

Perhaps most indicative of mainstream support for the Panthers, when Estella Shabazz welcomed Barack Obama at Selma's Brown Chapel on behalf of the Panthers, her remarks were not met with shocked gasps or pointed objections, but instead elicited a warm round of applause from the audience.[36] If the Panthers are an irrelevant "fringe group" as the media often claims, then a lot of people have not yet received the message.

Just before the November 4, 2008, presidential election, the New Black Panther Party announced a nationwide deployment of Panthers at the polls. The message was delivered jointly by Urhuru Shakur, head of the Atlanta Panther chapter, and by Field Marshall Najee Muhammad, the man who had appeared in the cop-killing Panther video and who, along with other Panthers, had shared the podium with Obama outside Brown Chapel. The two took turns reading a statement from party head Malik Zulu Shabazz. "We will not allow some racists and other angry whites, who are upset over an impending Barack Obama presidential victory, to intimidate blacks at the polls," Muhammad declared. "We must organize to counter and neutralize these threats using all means at our disposal.

This is a great time for our people, and we must ensure that peace prevails for our people."

The Philadelphia chapter of the New Black Panther Party is headed by King Samir Shabazz (no relation to Malik Zulu Shabazz), a former drug dealer now known on the streets of Philadelphia for spewing anti-white invective through a bullhorn at passersby around City Hall; ironically, he sometimes stakes out a spot near a sculpture of Robert Indiana's iconic "LOVE" lettering in John F. Kennedy Park. The week before the 2008 election, a *Philadelphia Daily News* article called him "one of the most recognizable black militants in a city known … for its vocal black-extremism community." In the article, Shabazz declares, "I'm about the total destruction of white people" and "the only thing the cracker understands is violence." He says his musical tastes focus on "revolutionary, cracker-killing-hip-hop."[37]

A few years earlier, Shabazz had appeared on the cover of *Philadelphia Weekly*. "If police ain't fuckin' with me, I ain't doing something right," he says in the accompanying article. "When the cops is knocking on your door, *now* you're doing something right." A teacher of arms training and guerilla warfare at Panther meetings, he describes his aspiration for a world where whites live in squalor and poverty under the rule of blacks. But ultimately, Shabazz says, "I won't be completely happy until I see our people free and Whitey dead."[38]

In accordance with Malik Zulu's order, on election day 2008, King Samir Shabazz patrolled in front of a polling place at the Guild House retirement community in Philadelphia. He was accompanied by fellow Panther Jerry Jackson, a man who adorned the entrance to his nearby home with a sign saying "Coloreds Only—No Whites Allowed."[39] Both men were dressed in black battle fatigues and Shabazz was armed with a nightstick.

When black poll watchers for the Republican Party arrived, the Panthers called them "race traitors." This led to the first complaints reaching Philadelphia Republican Party headquarters, which sent additional resources to the polling site and dispatched a videographer to record evidence.

When armed, uniformed thugs from a known hate group are patrolling a voting place and hurling racist abuse at people, that is a self-evident act of voting intimidation. You don't need a law degree to recognize that. But as soon as video of the incident was posted on the internet later on election day, the racial grievance industry went into overdrive attempting to dismiss its significance. Some justified it simply by noting the precinct is largely black. This, of course, is entirely irrelevant. Thugs are no more acceptable at black precincts than they are at white ones. In fact, it is precisely in these circumstances, when the minority is particularly small, that the greatest protection is needed.

Others dismissed the incident as a clownish farce that probably did not prevent many people from voting, seeming to imply that federal voting rights laws make exceptions for stupid or ineffective attempts at intimidation—which they do not. Finally, some justified the Panthers' actions by noting that Jackson was a registered Democratic poll watcher, as if those credentials permit someone to bully and intimidate voters.

Purveyors of these excuses entirely overlooked the possible effect this abhorrent behavior may have had nationwide. Because the Drudge Report and Fox News had posted footage of the incident before noon on election day, it is not unreasonable to suspect that voters in other areas saw the video clip and were frightened by it, particularly if they had heard of the Panthers' nationwide deployment campaign.

I was in Washington on election day helping to manage the information traffic coming into the Voting Section while nearly every other lawyer and section employee was scattered across the nation doing election coverage. Joining the Voting Section staff were hundreds of federal observers and employees borrowed from other federal agencies.

I received an early report about the Panther incident in Philadelphia. Voting Section chief Chris Coates had kept me at the Washington desk for just this sort of eventuality. Normally another lawyer would manage all the traffic on election day, but Coates didn't trust him because there were already signs within the DOJ that some attorneys had used their position and power to aid the Obama campaign. Not only were key DOJ election officials large donors to Obama, but a wave of questionable inquiries and requests had come in over the previous few months from people such as Obama campaign lawyer Robert Bauer. Other Voting Section lawyers had spouses or friends deeply involved in the Obama campaign who referred matters to their DOJ contact, who then initiated a line of inquiry.

A hair trigger seemed to afflict the place throughout the fall. For example, McCain supporters had protested a government decision in Fayetteville, North Carolina, to allow voting before the election and outside of normal voting hours, conveniently timed to coincide with a nearby Obama campaign rally. When election day came early in Fayetteville, attendees of the Obama rally streamed out of the stadium and straight into the specially opened polls.[40] Add the fact that the change in poll hours had not been pre-cleared under Section 5 of the Voting Rights Act, and reasonable people can understand McCain supporters' concern. But the chief concern of DOJ lawyers was that McCain backers were engaging in voter intimidation by holding demonstrations to protest the rule change.

When the initial information reached the Voting Section about the Panther incident in Philadelphia, I related the report to Coates. He in turn contacted Deputy Chief Robert Popper, who was already managing election coverage in Philadelphia, and Popper quickly sent DOJ staff to investigate. In the meantime, in Washington we immediately encountered the first sign of resistance within the DOJ to pursuing the case.

A key component at the DOJ for monitoring federal elections is the Election Crimes Branch in the Public Integrity Section. This branch consisted almost entirely of one man, Craig Donsanto, who had been with the DOJ for years and was considered an expert in election issues. When the first reports about the Panthers filtered in, Donsanto almost smothered the investigation in the cradle. At 2:53 p.m. on election day, he emailed Coates,

> A resident of that building who's some kind of poll watcher, and another fellow who's apparently not, were at one point standing outside the poll wearing attire that could be viewed as ideated to the Black Panthers. One of these guys also was carrying a stick of some sort. The GOP poll watcher at this poll called the police who came and removed the guy who was carrying the stick. The other fellow is apparently still standing outside the poll wearing a black beret.
>
> Fox News has got hold of this incident (guess is that the GOP poll watcher who called the cops also called Fox News) and that network has been running broadcasts about this. NO VOTERS—OR POTENTIAL VOTERS—OR POLL WORKERS—HAVE COMPLAINED TO ANYONE ABOUT THIS. AUSA [redacted] advises that this seems to be entirely "media invented incident." If we

interview the GOP poll watcher (who's at the moment the only "victim" identified here), he'll go to Fox News and the entire incident will be further escalated.

Thus, AUSA [redacted] and I agreed that for the moment we (FEDS) will do NO INVESTIGATION here unless and until we receive a complaint from a voter.[41]

Donsanto's email is astonishing for several reasons. First, it contains a glaring error—neither of the Panthers was "a resident of that building." The DOJ would later rely on Donsanto's error to deflect congressional scrutiny before having to eat crow and correct the mistake. Second, Donsanto is clearly concerned with preventing Fox News from getting information about the event—this seems to outweigh his concern about discovering what actually happened. Third, Donsanto displays contempt toward Republican poll watchers, bracketing the word victim in quotes and explicitly referring to the victim's political affiliation in his direction not to investigate the case. And finally, Donsanto dismisses the entire episode as a "media invented incident." This was the same excuse used by 1960s-era southern segregationists to dismiss media reports of civil rights violations. It was most memorably claimed by Neshoba County Sheriff Lawrence Rainey in the case of the three missing civil rights workers who later turned up dead.

Furthermore, Donsanto's wording skillfully minimizes important facts—Panther uniforms become "attire that could be viewed as ideated to the Black Panthers," and a nightstick becomes a mere "stick of some sort" that the Panther is "carrying" as opposed to the more accurate term "brandishing." The email is a classic example of how Washington bureaucrats attempt to kill off inquiries they oppose.

Thankfully, Coates would have none of it. He shot back with an email exclaiming, "If standing in front of a polling place with a stick in Black Panther clothing and talking about how you are going to keep whites from voting (that is what the guy on tape complained of) does not violate the intimidation prohibition in 11(b), I don't know what does."[42]

Two hours after sending his "NO INVESTIGATION" email, as the story spread beyond Fox News, Donsanto reversed course. He wrote in an email, "The man who was carrying the stick has been identified as a suspected member of the New Black Panthers Gang. Also, in the late afternoon of Election Day at least two individuals have come forward and claimed that they were threatened by this man when coming to vote.... As this incident is currently receiving fairly wide media attention (both Fox and CNN have picked it up), it is currently thought reasonable that further victims can be expected to self identify in the future. Interviews with victims will await end of the election."[43] Suddenly, Eeyore had become Tigger.

Note that Donsanto unequivocally states that "at least two individuals" had claimed they were threatened by the Panthers. For weeks, the Voting Section sought the identities of these voters from Donsanto, but he never revealed them. His reticence was a big help to those opposed to pursuing the Panther case, who continually argued that no voters had been intimidated. A 2011 report from the DOJ Office of Professional Responsibility (OPR) on the Panther case never clarifies Donsanto's claim to know of at least two voters who were intimidated. In a footnote, the report states, "Donsanto retired from the Department in early 2010 for health reasons, and OPR was unable to interview him."[44] The note leaves several questions unanswered: Why didn't OPR ever interview Donsanto, even when the investigation was ongoing and he still worked at the DOJ? Why couldn't they interview him then, or even after he retired? Did he refuse to be interviewed?

Regardless of the answers, we would later discover that Donsanto's actions marked the beginning of a long campaign of political resistance to the Panther lawsuit that ultimately resulted in the dismissal of most of the case—after we had effectively won it.

The Voting Section offices were mostly empty on the day after the election, as the employees were still scattered around the country. Most of the people in the office were employees of the Housing Section, which shared space with the Voting Section and was managed by Steve Rosenbaum.

Throughout the day, I heard disparaging commentary in the halls from these employees about the attention the Panther incident was receiving. Some dismissed the incident as "no big deal," while others, echoing Craig Donsanto, called it a media generated event. I was stunned that the Panthers' blatant act of voter intimidation would immediately find so many apologists at the Civil Rights Division. Meanwhile, video of the incident had gone viral on the internet, eliciting shock and outrage from the American people. As Andrew Breitbart of BigGovernment.com observed, regardless of what Panther apologists might argue, "The American people are going to be the final word. They see this for what it is. This is a whitewash of an incredibly troubling trend in Obama's America."

We continually heard that we should not pursue the case because no one came forward to claim they had been victimized by the Panthers. This contention willfully ignored federal law. Section 11(b) of the Voting Rights Act outlaws coercion, threats, or intimidation directed at voters or those who are aiding voters, including relatives and poll watchers. Crucially, the law does not just outlaw coercion, threats, or intimidation, but also any *attempt* to do the same. This was important language from Congress, which understood that if voters were too frightened to show up to the polls, there might not be any actual threat or act of coercion that could be punished. So under the statute, even if no voters came forward, the mere attempt to intimidate them is a violation of law.

The proponents of the lawsuit against the New Black Panthers had a more robust, inclusive view of the law than did our opponents. It is a view that protects a wider class of voters from intimidation. One of the tragic ironies of the lawsuit's dismissal is that, by narrowing the range of protected voters, it will mostly harm black voters in the future—unless, of course, you lower or raise the bar depending on the race of the perpetrators. The weakening of Section 11(b) is a dangerous development, as these protections are arguably more important than other sections of the Voting Rights Act, such as prohibitions against race-based election discrimination by state actors, provisions for federal oversight of election changes, or guaranteed access to foreign language ballots and voting assistance. Section 11(b) is the key to the clean functioning of elections because it provides for free access to the ballot box—without that protection, all the other protections are largely irrelevant.

Thus, under Section 11(b), even if no one came forward to claim they were intimidated by the Panthers, the Panthers' actions still broke the law. At any rate, this whole question is moot because, contrary to the claims of many, Panther victims *did* come forward. One was Army veteran Christopher Hill, a GOP poll watcher who gave a sworn statement released by the Civil Rights Commission testifying that both Jackson and Shabazz attempted to block him from entering the polling place. When he tried to enter, he said, Shabazz menacingly slapped the nightstick in his hand. Hill also testified to the Civil Rights Commission about the chilling things the Panthers said to him: "I was called a cracker, white devil. Told that I was going to be ruled by a black man on the next day, and I would have to get used to being under his boot. Similar things to that."[45]

Another poll watcher that day was Bartle Bull, a veteran civil rights activist. Although he was working for the GOP on election day, Bull has a long history working for Democratic candidates, including Charles Evers in Mississippi, Robert F. Kennedy, and Jimmy Carter. He is also a former publisher of the leftwing *Village Voice*. When I visited with Bull in his New York City brownstone, he proudly showed me a medal that Senator Ted Kennedy had given him a few years earlier for his work with the leftwing Lawyers Committee for Civil Rights Under Law.

Bull was incensed about the Panthers' actions in Philadelphia, declaring, "Bobby Kennedy didn't die so jackbooted thugs could stand out in front of polls." In a sworn affidavit, Bull says he witnessed King Samir Shabazz point his nightstick at people and "slap it in his hand." He further states, "I watched the two uniformed men confront voters, and attempt to intimidate voters.... The weapon was openly displayed and brandished in plain sight of voters." Bull notes that in his forty years of involvement in politics and civil rights, he had "never encountered or heard of another instance in the United States where armed and uniformed men blocked the entrance to a polling location."[46]

I interviewed Bull and other witnesses to the Panthers' actions in Philadelphia. One notable interview was with a black husband and wife, Larry and Angela Counts, who were GOP poll watchers. On election day, the Philadelphia GOP headquarters had received reports that the Panthers had verbally abused the Counts. During our interview, they said they were afraid of the Panthers, so afraid that Angela specifically mentioned her fear of something being bombed. When the Counts were deposed by the Civil Rights Commission, however, Mr. Counts denied even meeting us. His testimony was disappointing but not surprising considering the Counts live just blocks away from the polling place where the intimidation occurred.

Over the Christmas holiday, Acting Assistant Attorney General Grace Chung Becker approved a J-memo recommending the DOJ file suit against the Panthers. Those of us involved in the case moved it forward without hesitation, feeling a sense of purpose and a sense of pride that we were fulfilling our duty to secure the integrity of America's voting system. It struck us as an open-and-shut case that was neither novel nor terribly difficult to prove.

In another voter intimidation case, the DOJ had cast a wide net. In 1991, the DOJ went after North Carolina Republicans for intimidating voters by sending them a postcard. The postcard related there was a 30-day residency requirement for voting and then described the federal penalties for giving false residency information to an election official. The description of the residency requirement was inaccurate and incomplete, and its positioning next to the accurate description of federal penalties led the DOJ to go after anyone involved with the postcard. This included the North Carolina Republican Party, the Jesse Helms campaign, and even several mailing and paper businesses that had simply helped to construct or mail the postcard.[47] There were no nightsticks or thugs patrolling a voting precinct—just an erroneous postcard. The DOJ's political leadership would adopt a far more reserved approach toward the Panther case. There was one key difference between the cases, however—in North Carolina, the defendants were Republicans.

Our complaint in the Panther case, filed on January 7, 2010, had four separate causes of action under Section 11(b): intimidation of

voters, attempted intimidation of voters, intimidation of those aiding voters, and attempted intimidation of those aiding voters. The
case was brought against four defendants—King Samir Shabazz
and Jerry Jackson (the two Panthers at the polls), as well as Panther
party chairman Malik Zulu Shabazz and the New Black Panther
Party itself.

Just four days after we filed the complaint, I got a taste of the
Panther apologetics that would feature prominently in media coverage of the case. I contacted producers of a new National Geographic
documentary on the Panthers, hoping to see if they had any important Panther footage that was left on the cutting room floor and
seeking to obtain a copy of the documentary for myself. But the
producers did not want to cooperate, confessing they were conflicted about the whole documentary project. In a blog post on the
making of the documentary, one producer wrote that Samir Shabazz
"calls for violence against whites and police officers. I wasn't certain
how I would feel about him when we finally talked."[48] As his team
researched the group, they asked themselves, "Is the New Black
Panther Party's anti-white and anti-Semitic rhetoric merely giving
voice to the righteous anger of an oppressed people upset about their
conditions or is it hate speech?"[49]

One hopes they clearly answered that question by the end of their
research; the documentary captures King Samir Shabazz, one of
the defendants in the Philadelphia case, ranting against an inter-
racial couple and then calling for the murder of white babies. "I hate
white people. All of them. Every last iota of a cracker I hate them,"
he yells. "You want freedom, you're gonna have to kill some crackers.
You gonna have to kill some of their babies."[50]

At the Voting Section, we decided the documentary could be a
valuable educational tool about the Panthers. An announcement

went out to the entire section, comprising at least seventy employees, that we would hold a viewing of the show. Exactly two people showed up—and one of them was the paralegal on the case who had to operate the VCR.

After the defendants were served a copy of the summons and complaint, the next step was for them to file an answer. Malik Zulu Shabazz declined to do so. As a licensed attorney, Shabazz undoubtedly knew that refusing to respond to the summons meant the allegations in the complaint would be deemed admitted, opening the way to a default judgment against him. The other defendants also ignored the lawsuit. As described in the pleadings filed by the DOJ, I spoke on the phone with Michael Coard, who purported to be the attorney for Jerry Jackson. Coard, a prominent Philadelphia lawyer, radio host, and self described "pan-African socialist,"[51] told me he would be representing Jackson after he got "some homicide cases out of the way." [52] Despite my warning that the DOJ could seek a default judgment, we never heard from Coard again. Neither he nor any other lawyer ever appeared in court on behalf of the defendants. The Panthers were acting as if the lawsuit would simply vanish—which, eventually, it mostly would.

With no response from the defendants, the United States filed a motion for entry of default on April 1, 2009. After the clerk of court entered default, the case seemed to be on cruise control toward resolution. The simplest, most responsible outcome could include slapping the defendants with injunctions prohibiting the Panthers from staging any more deployments at polls. But as the deadline approached to file paperwork for the final injunction, all hell broke loose.

★　★　★

Similar to the Ike Brown case, DOJ lawyers working on the Panther case ran into institutional resistance within the DOJ from the very beginning, including from the historian who had hobbled the Brown case, Peyton McCrary. In March 2009, McCrary was tasked with looking for an expert to explain the history of voter intimidation tactics and the intimidating nature of the Panther organization. After he made little or no effort even to identify an expert, we suggested one we had been working with informally on the case. McCrary tried to scuttle our recommendation, claiming the expert wasn't competent to testify about the organization. To the contrary, this expert had given testimony in numerous federal civil rights cases of the exact nature we were seeking, including testimony about the Ku Klux Klan, but somehow that wasn't good enough for McCrary. In the end, McCrary's obstructionism damaged the case because the lack of expert testimony on this point later created some points of attack for DOJ political appointees who wanted to throw out the case.

The problem extended far beyond McCrary; from the advent of the Obama administration in January 2009, it was clear resistance to the case went to the top of the Civil Rights Division and beyond. The Voting Section's political overseers, Acting Assistant Attorney General Loretta King and her deputy Steve Rosenbaum, both of whom had been promoted to their political positions by the Obama administration, had been kept apprised of the case in weekly meetings. Chris Coates had told me he briefed King on the case shortly after Obama's inauguration, but there were no inquires in the case for months, and neither King nor Rosenbaum showed any interest in pursuing it.

Late on April 29, 2009, two days before the filing for the final injunction was due, King and Rosenbaum suddenly began zealously attacking the case, making meritless arguments about the evidence that one would have expected to hear from a Panther defense lawyer. In a tense meeting with Coates, they proved to be largely unfamiliar with the facts of the case, with Rosenbaum admitting he had not even read the initial J-Memo on the matter. Coates told me when he further learned Rosenbaum and King had not read the Bartle Bull affidavit, he read every word of the document to them aloud. King leered at Coates as he read it, appearing incensed.

King argued to Coates that the complaint didn't "pass the Rule 11 test," a reference to Rule 11 of the Federal Rules of Civil Procedure. King was essentially asserting that Coates, myself, and the other two lawyers on the matter had brought a phony case. Given her history of attracting court sanctions, King should have known a thing or two about Rule 11—at least enough to know that the Panther case met the requirements of Rule 11 because there were facts to prove every single claim.

As the May 1 filing deadline approached, King and Rosenbaum continued to stridently oppose the case. On May 1, a motion for a two-week extension of the deadline was filed under orders from Rosenbaum. The motion was granted, and the case lawyers spent the next two weeks drafting reports to counter Rosenbaum and King's flimsy arguments, which included the amazing claim that some of the Panthers' actions were protected by the First Amendment.[53]

On May 15—the deadline to file the documents outlining the requested relief—the team gathered in Coates' office to await a phone call with a definitive order on how to proceed with the case. When the phone rang, Coates picked it up, quietly took some notes, and then hung up. Our orders were to dismiss the case entirely against Jerry Jackson, the New Black Panther Party, and Malik Zulu Shabazz. Only King Samir Shabazz would be subject to legal penalty, and only for a few years, and only within the city limits of Philadelphia.

We sat in stunned disbelief. This was a blatant act of voter intimidation by a race-hate group that was caught on tape and seen by
the whole nation, yet we were being ordered to do almost nothing
about it. At that moment, it became clear to me that the people running the division under the Obama administration were irredeem-
ably rotted and corrupt. Our superiors had sided with thugs, and all
we could do was silently look at each other, helpless and beaten.

I dutifully volunteered to write the motion for dismissal, noting
that we were filing a voluntary dismissal because the defendants
never answered the complaint. It read like a dispatch from legal
wonderland—essentially, we argued that we were dismissing the
case against the defendants because they had refused to defend
themselves. It was madness to anyone but a few Obama political
appointees.

Bartle Bull later testified to the Civil Rights Commission that
the only reason he signed his damning sworn declaration was
because I told him the DOJ would never drop the lawsuit. Well
aware of the Panthers' violent inclinations, he didn't want to put
himself at physical risk if the DOJ wasn't serious about ending the
Panthers' voting abuses.

Indeed, I had told him that. Even after we began butting heads
with King and Rosenbaum, never in my wildest dreams did I think
the DOJ would drop a lawsuit that had already gone to default. This
is the only regret I have in the entire Panther episode—I told a good
man who was willing to stick his neck out to protect the right to vote
that he could count on the DOJ. And I was wrong. After a lifetime
fighting for civil rights, Bull deserved better from his government—
and so did the American people.

★   ★   ★

In a congressional committee meeting on March 1, 2011, while questioning Attorney General Eric Holder about the DOJ's reported hostility to race-neutral law-enforcement, Texas Congressman John Culberson read out the following passage from Bartle Bull's sworn statement on the Panther incident in Philadelphia: "To me, the presence and behavior of the two uniformed men was an outrageous affront to American democracy and the rights of voters to participate in an election without fear. It would qualify as the most blatant form of voter intimidation I have encountered in my life in political campaigns in many states, even going back to the work I did in Mississippi in the 1960's."[54]

Visibly agitated, Holder responded, "When you compare what people endured in the South in the 60s to try to get the right to vote for African Americans, and to compare what people were subjected to there to what happened in Philadelphia … to describe it in those terms I think does a great disservice to people who put their lives on the line, who risked all, for my people."[55]

It was a telling moment. One might think the Attorney General of the United States would regard the entire American people as "his people." But no—for Holder, only one race of Americans is his people.

His exclamation gave the country a glimpse into the sort of racialist partiality that prevails inside the DOJ's Civil Rights Division. It is the same worldview that drove the opposition to bringing the Ike Brown and Panther cases. Holder, like other opponents of race-neutral enforcement of civil rights laws, cannot countenance civil rights violations by black wrongdoers because they jolt the narrative America has heard over the last half century. Bartle Bull's affidavit derails history in a deeply uncomfortable way for these people. For them, it is always 1965 in Selma, when oppressors and victims had predictable skin colors.

★ ★ ★

CHAPTER FIVE

Anatomy of a Scandal

In the two years since the Department of Justice dismissed the Black Panther case, more and more information has trickled out of the DOJ about the decision. Some of the details had to be pried out by congressional committees or by FOIA requests from groups like Judicial Watch. Ultimately, a picture emerges of a Civil Rights Division whose political leaders were absolutely consumed by the racialist worldview.

It is now clear that the DOJ's dismissal of the Panther case was part of the thorough "transformation" of the Civil Rights Division that Obama officials continually trumpeted. They did not explicitly say what this transformation really entailed—that is, abandoning race-neutral law enforcement—but that was made perfectly clear to the entire Voting Section in the summer and fall of 2009, a few months after the Panther case was abandoned.

A major sign of trouble came during a meeting between Chris Coates and his supervisors in late summer. Returning from the meeting, Coates explained to me there was open hostility toward bringing cases against minorities who violate the civil rights of white victims. "It will be up to the U.S. attorneys in the states to bring them, but we aren't going to do it anymore," Coates was informed. The ninety-three U.S. attorneys are presidential appointees who typically lack any specialization in the complicated civil rights statutes enforced by the Civil Rights Division. As a result, they are unlikely to bring a case that the DOJ's Washington leadership wouldn't bring. In other words, whites can no longer be recognized as victims of discrimination, regardless of the facts of the case.

To ensure the Voting Section rank and file got the message, a series of "brown bag" policy luncheons were scheduled with new Deputy Assistant Attorney General Julie Fernandes, wife of my old DOJ mentor Avner Shapiro. Each lunch would have a designated statute as the topic of discussion, and Fernandes used these talks to convey the Obama administration's new approach toward law enforcement. Some employees referred to Fernandes' edicts from these meetings as our "marching orders"—that's clearly what they were intended to be, and that's generally how they were received.

The first brown bag, held in September 2009, involved Section 2 of the Voting Rights Act, the law outlawing racial discrimination that was used against Ike Brown. Fernandes led a detailed discussion of "the Bartlett problem," which is how the civil rights industry refers to the outcome of the United States Supreme Court opinion in *Bartlett v. Strickland*. This case established that before a plaintiff can sue under Section 2 to establish a single member election district designated for a minority, the plaintiff had to show that a minority group could comprise at least 50 percent of a proposed election district. The decision is widely opposed by lawyers (who lose opportunities for litigation), by race-based activist groups (who lose opportunities to racially gerrymander voting districts), and by Democrats (who lose opportunities to create multiple safe Democratic voting districts).

After a discussion of outlandish proposals for working around *Bartlett* such as proportional representation theories or cumulative voting remedies, a Voting Section staffer asked what sort of Section 2 cases the Civil Rights Division was interested in pursuing. According to Coates' sworn testimony, Fernandes replied that the Obama DOJ "was only interested in bringing traditional types of Section 2 cases that would provide equality for racial and language minority voters."[1] Coates added, "Everyone in the room … understood exactly what she meant: no more cases like Ike Brown and no more cases like the New Black Panther Party case."[2]

The Holder DOJ has repeatedly denied it is hostile to race-neutral law enforcement, but it never denied that Fernandes made this statement—it can't deny it, because she said it in front of Coates, myself, and about sixty other people. What's more, she reiterated the statement at another brown bag lunch in December while discussing election coverage by federal observers.[3] During the Bush DOJ, racialists at least had to disguise their hostility to race-neutral law enforcement, similar to the specious legal arguments Loretta King and Steve Rosenbaum made against the Panther case. But now, Fernandes was openly declaring that view as DOJ policy.

Another brown bag meeting was convened in November 2009, this one to discuss the National Voter Registration Act (NVRA), widely known as Motor Voter. Section 8 of Motor Voter requires states to implement systems to purge voter lists of dead and ineligible felon voters. If states have too many ineligible voters on the voter rolls, the DOJ has the power to sue to clean up the rolls. Section 8 is crucial for ensuring the integrity of American elections, but Fernandes, along with most of the civil rights industry, is deeply hostile to enforcement of Section 8. Instead they prefer to enforce Section 7, which requires voter registration services at welfare and food stamp offices. The Bush administration enforced both Section 7 and Section 8, respecting the balance that Congress had written into the law.

At the November meeting, which I also attended, Fernandes made it clear that the days of enforcing the law as written were over. Robert Popper, the deputy chief who was overseeing Section 8 investigations, asked her point blank, "What about Section 8 cases?" The Voting Section had already recommended opening eight investigations into states with serious problems with the voter rolls. Fernandes seemed confused by the question and the statutory reference. "Um, you mean voter purging cases?" she asked. "Yes," Popper responded. Fernandes then grew agitated and dismissive. "Oh, no, no. We have no interest in enforcing that provision of the law. It has nothing to do with increasing turnout, and we are just not going to do it. That's a barrier to the ballot box, not something that increases access." That was the end of that.

Despite the fact that many states and counties had more registered voters than members of the voting age population, the Obama administration had summarily vetoed a portion of a federal statute designed to aid election integrity. Exposed, the DOJ would eventually cite "resource concerns" for not enforcing the law at the same time that numerous Voting Section lawyers would spend hours of work time watching movies, reading novels, or disappearing from the office because they had nothing else to do.[4]

Fernandes' comments reflected a seismic shift in DOJ policy, resulting in the cancellation of numerous investigations into corrupted voter rolls and racial discrimination by minorities. Chris Coates described the damage: "When the Deputy Assistant Attorney

General comes down to the Voting Section and says the kind of things that she said in terms of what you are interested in and what you are not interested in, it has tremendous impact because she is speaking for the AAG, the Assistant Attorney General, for Civil Rights and ultimately for the Attorney General."[5] Her comments were not understood as mere generalities or suggestions; they were a frontal attack on the equal enforcement policies of the Bush DOJ.

Fernandes had been a long-standing opponent of race-neutral law enforcement before arriving at the DOJ in 2009. In 2007, while working for the Leadership Conference for Civil Rights, Fernandes plainly said, "How can it be that the biggest case involving discrimination in Mississippi was brought on behalf of white voters.... The law was written to protect black people."[6] This comment, of course, referred to the Ike Brown case. Fernandes was apparently unmoved by the United States District Court's opinion that detailed Ike Brown's massive voter fraud operation and the systematic disenfranchisement of Noxubee County's white voters. It was simply unacceptable to her that "the biggest case" in Mississippi was brought to protect whites.

Fernandes' comments echoed those of her former boss at the Leadership Conference, Wade Henderson, who had argued to a congressional committee that "the [Civil Rights] Division must deal with and respond to growing distrust among minority communities who feel increasingly abandoned and marginalized by the Division's litigation choices and priorities."[7] After the Ike Brown case, the Bush DOJ commenced or brought many Section 2 cases on behalf of national racial minorities, including two I brought to protect black victims—*United States v. Georgetown County* and *United States v. Town of Lake Park*. By contrast, the Obama administration has not filed another Section 2 case on behalf of black victims or anyone else in over two years. Indeed, the DOJ's entire voting enforcement operation has flat-lined under Obama, yet after much research, I cannot find a single instance of Henderson complaining about minorities feeling "abandoned or marginalized" by the Obama DOJ.

At the same time Fernandes was reorienting the Voting Section's priorities, the DOJ's dismissal of the Panther case was attracting widespread attention in the right-leaning media. The issue was covered prominently on Fox News, with legal analysis by Megyn Kelly and Lis Wiehl, as well as in the *Washington Times* and on the websites of prominent conservative bloggers like Michelle Malkin. Jennifer Rubin at the *Weekly Standard* and Quin Hillyer at the *American Spectator* also covered the case dismissal. The DOJ showed some early signs that it would respond to the reports by blaming the Bush DOJ and particularly the case lawyers for bringing a bad case. The DOJ political leadership seemed determined to kill two birds with one stone—find a scapegoat for the outcome of the Panther case, and discredit the case lawyers, particularly Coates, who was still Voting Section chief.

The DOJ received its first letter from Congress about the Panther case dismissal in late May 2009, after Congressman Lamar Smith, the ranking member of the House Judiciary Committee and soon to be chairman, wrote to Loretta King demanding a briefing and asking why the DOJ voluntarily dismissed a case it had already won. Suspecting King would not be entirely forthcoming and driven by my fears that the administration would blame the case lawyers for the dismissal, I contacted a friend who was a congressional staffer and explained the predicament. A meeting between me and five senior members of the House Judiciary Committee was arranged for June 5, 2009, to brief them about the dismissal.

At our meeting on June 5, 2009, I explained to the congressmen that the Panther case was solid, but Rosenbaum and King had scuttled it because they opposed race-neutral law enforcement. I explained the key moments leading up to the case's dismissal, such as Rosenbaum showing his unfamiliarity with the J-Memo and with the general facts of the case. I further explained how we could have obtained a nationwide injunction against the Panthers to prevent similar outrages from happening in future elections. One congressman, perhaps only half jokingly, asked whether I owned a gun to protect myself. I replied that I had no shortcomings on that point. Another congressman asked whether I was seeking whistleblower protection, and I told him I was. Eventually, Coates would seek the same protection.

Three days after the meeting, Congressman Frank Wolf, who had received information about the Panther case, sent his first of many letters to Attorney General Eric Holder demanding answers. Wolf, then the ranking member overseeing the DOJ budget, received no response. On July 8, 2009, he sent a letter to House Judiciary Committee Chairman John Conyers and ranking member Lamar Smith asking for a hearing on the dismissal of the case. The next day, Smith, Wolf, and eight other congressmen sent a letter to DOJ Inspector General Glen Fine demanding an investigation.

Meanwhile, House members asked their Senate colleagues to hold up the confirmation of Tom Perez for Assistant Attorney General for Civil Rights until they received some answers. Perez had been voted out of the Senate Judiciary Committee with only two Republican objections—Senators Jeff Sessions and Tom Coburn. But his Senate confirmation would be delayed until October over the Panther controversy and the DOJ's intransigence.

The DOJ responded to Wolf on July 13. The letter, most likely written by Rosenbaum, maintained that the facts and law did not support going forward with the case. This implied the case attorneys were at fault for bringing forward a weak case—the same argument I had sensed the DOJ brass was preparing. After his confirmation, Tom Perez would make the argument explicitly, testifying to the Civil Rights Commission that Rule 11 and similar local court rules mandated the case be dismissed.[8] This was a direct attack on the four lawyers on the case, for Rule 11 is an ethical obligation that attorneys don't bring frivolous claims.

The letter offered a slew of irrelevant or inapplicable justifications for dismissing the case, including the Panthers' First Amendment rights, Jerry Jackson's status as a certified poll watcher, and the fact that the Panthers did not specifically call for *armed* Panther members to patrol voting precincts. The letter also contained a naked factual error: "The Department decided not to proceed with its claims against Jackson, who was a resident of the apartment building where the polling place was located and was certified by city officials as a poll watcher."[9] In fact, Jackson lived a few blocks away, but incorrectly presenting him as a resident of the building, just as Craig Donsanto had done in his initial "do not investigate" email, implied he had a reason to be at that location other than intimidating voters.

The letter further claims that the DOJ "is committed to comprehensive and vigorous enforcement of both the civil and criminal provisions of federal law that prohibit voter intimidation."[10] In reality, however, the dismissal of the Panther case would inevitably constrain the DOJ's actions against voter intimidation; by raising the factual floor on voter intimidation to justify dismissing the Panther case, the DOJ raised the bar on voter intimidation cases.

Most astonishingly, to justify dismissing the case, the letter claims the New Black Panther Party had disclaimed its members' actions in Philadelphia—despite the fact that Panther Party chief

Malik Zulu Shabazz went on Fox News after the election and defended King Samir Shabazz's brandishing of a nightstick. The DOJ letter ignored that statement by Malik Zulu, instead pointing to a disclaimer the Panthers later posted on their website that disavowed their members' actions in Philadelphia and claimed they had suspended the Philadelphia Panther chapter. This self-serving notice, an obvious attempt to limit the Panthers' legal liability, was also invoked by Loretta King and Steve Rosenbaum when they were attacking the case in front of the case lawyers.

For perhaps the first time, the DOJ was arguing that wrongdoers' disavowal of their own actions—a disavowal not even provided in a pleading, but rather on a website—would serve as absolution. This position directly contradicted a brief that Steve Rosenbaum had worked on in spring 2009 while he was overseeing the Panther case. In *United States v. Sturdevant*, a real estate company whose employee had used racial slurs asked to be dismissed from the lawsuit because the firm disavowed her actions and claimed her comments were not company actions—in other words, they made the same argument the Panthers made. Yet Rosenbaum was adamant in legal pleadings that the company's disavowal in *Sturdevant* was irrelevant.[11] Of course, in *Sturdevant* the victims were black, so apparently Rosenbaum held the defendants to a different standard than the Panthers. In a telling sign of the quality of Rosenbaum's work, he would eventually be slapped with sanctions in the *Sturdevant* case for not complying with discovery rules and providing inadequate answers to interrogatories.

Congressmen Wolf and Smith signed a five-page letter flaying the DOJ's response. Referring to the DOJ's note that the Panthers did not call for their precinct patrollers to be armed, they asked, "Is the Justice Department's position now that a paramilitary organization is free to send its members en masse to polling places—in uniform no less—without fear of legal repercussions, as long as there is no explicit mention of weaponry?" They continued, "Had the Ku Klux Klan or Aryan Brotherhood made a similar announcement prior to November 4, 2008, would the Civil Rights Division have viewed the group's failure to mention weapons as an exculpatory omission?"[12]

The letter also makes note of the curious lack of discovery in the case. This is an essential point. If Rosenbaum and King had doubts about the case, it would have been a simple matter to conduct some discovery via leave of court. But by ordering the case dismissed, the DOJ removed investigators' ability to dig deeper into the nationwide Panther deployment on election day. As the letter by Wolf and Smith notes, the DOJ "should have responded by at least conducting a deposition of the Defendants and engaging in some minimal discovery to determine the full composition and character of the Defendant's intimidating activities."[13]

Like Rosenbaum and King, Panther Party chief Malik Zulu Shabazz was also averse to discovery. When the United States Commission on Civil Rights subpoenaed him for a deposition on February 2, 2010, Shabazz simply failed to appear. Although the law dictates that the DOJ should have enforced the subpoena against him, it mysteriously declined to do so. And we saw the same pattern with King Samir Shabazz and Jerry Jackson; the Civil Rights Commission deposed both men on January 11, 2010, and both refused to testify, invoking the Fifth Amendment. Refusing to enforce the subpoena against either man, the DOJ didn't seem to want a lot of facts about the Panther deployments to reach the public.

★ ★ ★

Throughout the summer, conservative media outlets continued to draw attention to the inexplicable decision to dismiss the Panther case. The cascade of stories included a *Washington Times* report that Associate Attorney General Tom Perrelli played a role in spiking the case.[14] This contradicted assertions made in the DOJ's July 13 letter to Congressman Wolf that only career employees had made the call. At the end of July, Wolf demanded that the DOJ refile the case against the Panthers, a move available to the DOJ because the dismissal was without prejudice.

Media coverage of the story led to another major development— on September 11, 2009, the United States Commission on Civil Rights voted to make the Panther case dismissal the subject of its annual statutory report. Had the DOJ been more forthcoming with its reasons for dismissing the case, the Panther case probably would not have become such a major focus for the commission. But that kind of transparency wasn't an option, since those who dismissed the case had no reasonable explanation for their actions that could withstand public or congressional scrutiny.

Established by President Eisenhower, the Civil Rights Commission is a fact-finding body meant to aid Congress and policy makers. Thanks to its broad mandate, the commission has stood at the forefront of race policy for more than half a century. On June 6, 2009, just weeks after the Panther case was dismissed, the commission had sent the DOJ a letter seeking answers. In response, the DOJ trotted out its arguments about the Panthers' First Amendment rights and the party's supposed renunciation of its members' actions. Unsatisfied by these weak excuses, a few months later, on August 10 and September 30, the commission sent more letters demanding answers, but received no reply.

On November 10, I was served with a subpoena to testify before the commission. I immediately informed Voting Section chief Chris Coates, who was served with a subpoena later that day. After a few days, I received an email from an official in the DOJ's Federal Programs Branch ordering me not to comply with the subpoena. It stated, "You are not authorized to disclose any information or produce any material acquired as part of the performance of your official duties without prior approval of the proper Department official."[15] Members of Congress and Civil Rights Commissioners were shocked at the brazen command to disregard a subpoena.

I was in a bind. On the one hand, the DOJ was refusing to allow me to testify. On the other hand, federal law requires all federal agencies to comply with a commission subpoena; ironically, the DOJ itself is vested with the power to enforce those subpoenas.[16] I hired several lawyers to help me navigate the legal thicket. One of them, Jim Miles, the former South Carolina Secretary of State, wrote to the DOJ on November 25 begging them to reach a resolution with the commission:

> I respectfully suggest that a command to ignore this subpoena appears, at a minimum, to disregard entirely the interests of my client and appears designed solely to assert a prerogative of the Department. Of course the Department is wholly within its power to assert this prerogative. But this assertion forces my client to choose between his obligations under 42 U.S.C. 1975(e) and 42 U.S.C. 1975b(e), and his lesser obligation under a federal regulation. The potential sanctions for failing to comply with the statutory obligations are plainly more serious than violating the federal regulation you cite.[17]

Miles also reminded the DOJ about 8 U.S.C. §1505, which states that anyone who corruptly or threateningly "influences, obstructs, or impedes" the due and proper exercise of the commission's subpoena process is subject to fine and five-year imprisonment. Miles noted, "Given that the actions of the Department appear to be one subject of the investigation, the order places my client in a particularly difficult position." The DOJ's response to my attorney was something akin to a pact among thieves—don't worry, they assured him, we don't have any intention of prosecuting your client.

Around this time, a leftwing blog published a false story claiming I was "fighting to testify." To the contrary, I was afraid of the legal bind in which the subpoena had put me. The story was the fruit of an unsavory alliance between the DOJ and various leftwing blogs that became the DOJ's mouthpiece as the Panther scandal unfolded. The "fighting to testify" story appeared on a little-read blog called Main Justice whose writers, Ryan Reilly and Mary Jacoby, obviously kept in close contact with my critics at the DOJ. Department officials would use the website to relay smears against me, Coates, and other supporters of the Panther case.

After Coates was subpoenaed, he began having talks with Assistant Attorney General Tom Perez regarding his transfer out of Washington to South Carolina. Coates had told former DOJ attorney and leftwing activist Gerry Hebert two reasons why he was considering a transfer—because Obama's political appointees were stripping him of his authority, and because he wanted to be closer to his family. Yet, Hebert was quoted in the press only relating the second reason; the fact that Obama's officials were systematically disempowering Coates somehow disappeared from the story.

Indeed, Coates had been gradually relieved of all authority over case assignments, litigation, and Voting Section policies. He was even excluded from meetings to decide how the Voting Section would react if the Supreme Court were to strike down Section 5 of the Voting Rights Act as unconstitutional. Given that half the Voting Section employees administer Section 5, it would have seemed prudent for their manager to participate in these contingency plans. Meanwhile, a DOJ source told me others in the Voting Section were secretly reporting directly to Rosenbaum and King about Coates. (These informants have since been promoted.) In light of all this as well as his family obligations, in late 2009, Coates opted for a detail in South Carolina. Given the reach of the Civil Rights Commission subpoena was limited to 100 miles, Tom Perez quickly approved moving Coates 450 miles away from Washington.

Coates used the occasion of his farewell party at the Voting Section to deliver one last message to his colleagues. In front of a large audience including Julie Fernandes and Coates' wife, daughter, and granddaughter, he unleashed his own closing argument defending the rule of law and race-neutral enforcement of civil rights laws. Coates declared,

> Before I became a DOJ attorney, I read the Voting Rights Act to protect all voters; but especially as a government lawyer, I have *never* assumed that I was entitled to *ignore* that clear language in federal law and therefore ignore incidents where evidence showed white voters were discriminated against or where the wrongdoers were themselves members of a minority group.... Since many minority officials are now involved in the administration of elections in many jurisdictions, it is imperative that they believe that the anti-discrimination and anti-intimidation provisions of the Voting Rights Act will be enforced against them by the Justice Department, just as

it is imperative that white election officials believe that Justice will enforce the provisions of the Voting Rights Act against them.[18]

The audience was frozen in shocked silence. Those of us who knew the slow roast was coming had the luxury of watching the reactions of Coates' most vociferous critics. They mostly stared at some fixed object, whether a picture on the wall, a notepad in their lap, or the top of Coates' head. Coates continued,

> I fear that actions that indicate that the Justice Department is not in the business of suing minority election officials, or not in the business of filing suits to protect white voters from discrimination or intimidation, will only encourage election officials, who are so inclined, to violate the Voting Rights Act.... I cannot imagine that any lawyers who believe in the rule of law would want to encourage violations of the Voting Rights Act by anyone, whether the wrongdoers are members of a minority group or white people.[19]

I looked at Fernandes. She squirmed, seemingly about to blast steam from her ears and nose. Coates kept up his momentum:

> One of these most basic standards is equal protection under the law. When that is violated, America does not live up to the true meaning of its creed. When it is followed, the country functions the way it was intended to. For the Department of Justice to enforce the Voting Rights Act only to protect members of certain minority groups breaches the fundamental guarantee of equal

protection, and could substantially erode public support for the Voting Rights Act itself. My fourth reason for this kind of law enforcement is very simple: Selective enforcement of the law, including the Voting Rights Act, on the basis of race is *just not fair and does not achieve justice.*[20]

After about fifteen minutes, the speech was over. Skipping the punch and cookies, some employees fled the room the moment the speech ended. A number of Coates' long-time friends stuck around, though even they were too stunned to say anything to him. And with that, Coates was gone.

A few days later, on January 18, 2010, my attorney Jim Miles again pleaded with the DOJ to find a way to get me out of the subpoena. He asked if the president had asserted Executive Privilege, which would trump any of my other obligations and settle the issue. (We soon learned Obama had not made the assertion.) Miles also corrected numerous errors that had been reported by the Main Justice blog. He wrote, "For example, contrary to the inaccurate and false reporting on number of blogs, my client does not 'seek to testify' and is not 'fighting to testify.' Retractions of these false statements have been sought without success, and I suspect will not be forthcoming even now. To the contrary, my client simply seeks to do what the law requires."[21]

Miles further suggested that the "Department initiate a judicial proceeding to quash the subpoena served upon him."[22] This move, too, would have settled the issue, but the DOJ declined to take it. Instead, the DOJ announced that AAG Perez would testify in our stead. The department's hand had been forced by devastating testi-

mony provided to the commission on April 23, 2010, by three eye-
witnesses to the Panthers' actions in Philadelphia—Bartle Bull,
Chris Hill, and Michael Mauro. They left no doubt that Jerry Jackson, whose case had been dismissed in its entirety, had violated
federal law, that Panthers had called black poll watchers "race traitors," and that voters were, in fact, intimidated from voting. The
DOJ suddenly needed a reliable appartchik to rebut this testimony,
so it decided to replace me and Coates with Perez.

In response, Coates and I wrote separate emails to the DOJ
director of federal programs warning that Perez had no firsthand
knowledge about the case, so he could conceivably testify falsely if
he based his information on statements by Loretta King and Steve
Rosenbaum. My warning went even further: "Over the last several
months, unattributed statements about the case by Department
officials have been cited in media reports that are demonstrably
false. Because the statements are never attributed, it is impossible
to know whether these are people entirely unfamiliar with the
matter, or, are individuals upon whom the scheduled witness will
rely."[23] Essentially, I was saying that someone at the DOJ was lying
to the press.

My email also cited personal reasons why the DOJ should recon-
sider sending Perez as a witness: "I have been assured that the
Department has no designs on compelling me to honor the subpoena. As someone who has taken an oath to obey the law, this
provides little comfort. Informing a potential criminal that he may
commit a crime because the police will not prosecute him does not
excuse the crime. Administrations change."[24] This referred to Eric
Holder's reopening of the investigation into CIA interrogations of
terrorism suspects.

Another concern I had was that the DOJ's false spin on the case
was emboldening the Panthers. In my email, I explained how

Panther members were becoming more aggressive toward me and the other case attorneys:

> Finally, the New Black Panther Party has personally targeted me and the trial team in their rhetoric and publications … and the statements made about this case are not mere rhetoric to me…. One of the defendants has explicitly called for the murder of white babies "in their cribs" in a National Geographic documentary. Further, in the official New Black Panther Party newsletter, my photograph has appeared along with former AAG Grace Chung Becker and two Congressmen over the caption: "The Lynch Mob, Wolf, Smith, Adams, Becker out to get the Panthers." The defendants have become increasingly belligerent in their rhetoric toward the attorneys who brought the case.[25]

Nobody at Justice expressed a whiff of concern or any trace of reassurance to anyone involved. Why would they? The DOJ's spin that the facts and law didn't support the case echoed the Panthers' own arguments, leaving the case attorneys looking like we had concocted a groundless lawsuit against the group. The Left was even comparing the case to COINTELPRO, a decades-old FBI operation meant to discredit the original Black Panthers, the NAACP, and other groups.

Our emails clearly hit their mark, because the DOJ hastily arranged a meeting for May 13 between the Panther case attorneys and Tom Perez, with some other officials sitting in as well. The purpose, obviously, was to defuse our argument that Perez was unfamiliar with our experiences working on the Panther case. At the meeting, Coates explained via speakerphone from South Carolina the long and detailed history of hostility toward race-neutral law enforcement inside the Civil Rights Division. Popper explained the merits of the case and the legal and factual basis for proceeding against all the defendants. I explained the history of the law and why enforcing the Voting Rights Act in a race-neutral manner was consistent with the Constitution and the history of the civil rights movement. We thought there was a chance our arguments would affect Perez's upcoming testimony to the Civil Rights Commission, but only a small chance.

When Perez testified the next day, he justified our pessimism. He regurgitated the DOJ's standard argument that the facts and the law did not support going forward in the case. While he conceded the case was not frivolous, he still maintained that Rule 11, the ethical obligation not to bring a case without factual and legal support, demanded dismissal. He also compared the case to a case against the Minutemen in Arizona that the Bush DOJ had decided not to pursue. Unsurprisingly, his recounting of the Minutemen case—that "three well-known anti-immigrant activists," one of whom was "brandishing a weapon," were "approaching" several voters[26]—was so distorted and so at odds with the findings of the Voting Section investigators that he must have been either willfully lying or depending on fantastical accounts prepared by his underlings. In fact, the Voting Section investigation revealed that no one brandished a weapon and that the Minutemen did not even approach any voters.

But no underling could be blamed for Perez's answers when Commissioner Todd Gaziano asked him whether he was aware of anyone in the DOJ who was hostile toward race-neutral law enforcement. "We don't have people of that ilk, sir," Perez replied.[27]

Gaziano pushed harder. "If someone in your Division … came to you and said 'a supervising attorney' or 'a political appointee' made the statement that the voting rights laws should never be

enforced against blacks or other racial minorities, you would investigate the report wouldn't you?"

Perez grew flummoxed. "I thought the subject matter of this
hearing was what we did in the New Black Panther Party case," he
said. "I'm having difficulty understanding the nexus."[28] Obviously.

Gaziano persisted, asking Perez if he would ever investigate
statements of the sort Julie Fernandes had made at the brown bag
meetings. Perez testified, "If you have such a statement, bring such
a statement to our attention."[29] Essentially, Perez was arguing that
he had never heard anyone at the Civil Rights Division ever mention
hostility toward race-neutral law enforcement, something Coates
had warned him about just before his testimony.

Perez's obfuscations met with some deep skepticism. Commissioner and law professor Gail Heriot, for example, ridiculed the
DOJ's core argument that injunctions could not be obtained against
the three dismissed Panther defendants. She lectured Perez, "I am
a remedies teacher. This is what I do for a living. I teach remedies.
If a student came to me and wrote on an exam that, because there
was a default here, that there was some problem or some difficulty
in getting the judgment, I would flunk them. This is not a tough
case here."[30]

For me, Perez's testimony was the last straw. He completely
ignored everything we had told him the day before, instead defending Rosenbaum and King to the hilt. In light of the corrupt nature
of the Panther case dismissal, DOJ statements falsely characterizing
the case, and the indefensible orders for the career attorneys not to
comply with lawful subpoenas investigating the dismissal, I felt I
could no longer continue in my position. So a few hours after Perez
concluded his testimony, I gave a letter of resignation to Voting Section chief Chris Herren.[31]

The following week, I received an unexpected phone call from Roger Simon asking me to become a contributor to his media site Pajamas Media, one of the leading conservative news websites. I accepted his offer, and soon began writing about issues such as civil rights and the ongoing activities of the Obama DOJ. I also did a round of media interviews on the Panther case including a widely seen interview with Megyn Kelly on Fox News.

The Kelly interview catapulted me into the media spotlight. On my flight from Washington to New York City to film the segment, I stared out the window, contemplating how everything was about to change. It was like dropping down a chute with no way back out the top. I hadn't prepared for the interview except by chatting with Megyn Kelly the night before on the phone. As the plane approached LaGuardia, I said a prayer asking for help to choose my words wisely and judiciously. Given the circumstances, I also prayed for courage and discernment. The Gospel the previous Sunday was Saint Luke's story of the seventy-two being sent like "lambs among wolves" to spread the good news, being ready to shake the dust off when they encounter hostility to their message and simply move to the next town undiscouraged. I knew no matter what venomous attacks might follow, truth was the more powerful force.

After the interview aired, DOJ officials began spreading information, usually anonymously, designed to undermine my arguments and smear my reputation. The whole operation ran like clockwork. Even before I sat for the interview, Kelly's show received an email from a person, almost certainly a DOJ political appointee, claiming I was a disgruntled employee who was angry because I had been "moved out of my position." In reality, two weeks before my resignation I had been promoted to a GS-15-9 position. The allegation in the email was a desperate, bald-faced lie that, incidentally, conveyed private employment information protected by law.

As the fallout of the Panther case continued to reverberate, the racialists found a useful tool in Abigail Thernstrom, a Republican Civil Rights Commissioner who criticized my testimony and dismissed the Panther case as "small potatoes." But Holder's supporters didn't ever mention that Thernstrom was previously a strong supporter of the commission's investigation of the Panther case. On June 22, 2009, she sent a letter, along with Commissioner Ashley Taylor, to Loretta King stating, "We are gravely concerned about the Civil Rights Division's actions in this case and feel strongly that the dismissal of this case weakens the agency's moral obligation to prevent voting rights violations, including acts of voter intimidation or vote suppression. We cannot understand the rationale for this case's dismissal and fear that it will confuse the public on how the Department of Justice will respond to claims of voter intimidation or voter suppression in the future."[32]

By the end of the year, her dramatic about-face on the case would, as Jennifer Rubin would write, mark "a sad coda on Thernstrom's impressive career."[33] Indeed, Thernstrom had spent years cataloging similar racially charged and lawless decisions by the DOJ Voting Section, even titling a chapter in her latest book, "The Lawless Civil Rights Division." On an episode of CBS *Face the Nation*—in which none of the case lawyers or any Civil Rights Commissioners who disagreed with Thernstrom appeared—Thernstrom argued, "We certainly have no direct evidence" of a racial double standard in the DOJ's handling of the Panther case. She added, "I'm an evidence girl, really. I want evidence." Thernstrom already had plenty of evidence, and she was about to get more.

The final act of the Thernstrom saga played out in September 2010 in a restaurant in Washington, D.C. It occurred shortly before the *Washington Post* ran a front-page story citing multiple current DOJ officials who confirmed that a culture of hostility exists toward using civil rights laws to protect whites.[34]

Abigail Thernstrom was at lunch with former Voting Section chief John Tanner. According to a source familiar with the lunch, Thernstrom wanted to ask Tanner a question about Chris Coates. Although Coates was widely expected to avoid testifying to the Civil Rights Commission after he moved to South Carolina, Thernstrom seemed worried that he might surprise everyone and defy the DOJ's orders not to testify. So she asked Tanner, "If Chris Coates were to testify, what would he say?" Tanner, who had worked closely with both me and Coates, replied, "He would corroborate Christian Adams."

According to my source, Thernstrom went speechless and buried her face in her hands. She had repeatedly stuck her neck out on national TV belittling my testimony. The militant left was wielding her like a club, and now she faced the specter of another DOJ attorney affirming my testimony.

Thernstrom's motives are still mysterious to me. My best guess is that she was being brutally consistent with her long-standing hostility to certain portions of the Voting Rights Act. Thernstrom opposes Section 5, which requires pre-clearance of many election changes, and she is also against Section 2, as amended, particularly when it results in litigation to establish single member districts for racial minorities. Simply, she has long opposed key portions of the Voting Rights Act and the enforcement of those parts of the law. In the Panther case, perhaps she was being slavishly consistent to her broad opposition to the exercise of federal power under the Voting Rights Act, this time to Section 11.

With Thernstrom's criticisms front and center, the controversy about the Panther case dismissal raged through the summer of 2010. Stoking public anger was the video aired in the National Geographic documentary showing King Samir Shabazz calling for the murder of white babies.

The Left seemed determined to defend the DOJ's dismissal of the case simply as a function of defending President Obama regardless of the case's merits. Consider an email sent to me by Tommy Christopher at the blog site Mediaite. After I testified to the Civil Rights Commission, Christopher wrote me, "Mr. Adams—Did you ever have conversations with any member of the Commission, or their staff, regarding the political implications of your complaint? If so, with whom, and what was the substance of those conversations?" Of course I had no such conversations—I was concerned about stopping voter intimidation, not the "political implications" of my complaint. I asked Christopher whether it would make any difference to him if Coates confirmed my allegations under oath. He replied, "As for Coates, without a stronger case up front, no, I don't think his testimony is necessary." To Tommy Christopher and his ilk, the facts of the case were irrelevant—what mattered was circling the political wagons.

By September 2010, Chris Coates had concluded the DOJ was falsely describing the dismissal of the Panther case. Still subject to the Civil Rights Commission subpoena, he decided to act. He called me from Charleston and informed me bluntly, "I'm going to come to Washington to testify." Otherwise, he said, the DOJ was "likely to be successful in providing a false and incorrect description of the dismissal of the Panther case."

Taking a week's leave, he boarded a train for Washington to testify at the commission hearing scheduled for September 24. He worked secretly on his testimony in Washington and prepared a letter for Civil Rights Commission Chairman Gerald Reynolds announcing his intent to testify. This was delivered late on September 22 and posted immediately at Pajamas Media.[35] Coates' appearance in Washington was such a surprise that a CNN reporter called me on September 23 to ask whether the letter was a hoax. At the same time, Coates provided Congressman Frank Wolf a full copy of his written testimony and invoked the full slate of applicable whistleblower protections.

On September 23, Wolf fired off a letter to Attorney General Eric Holder warning that Coates was not to be interfered with before his testimony the next day.[36] "I write to strongly support Mr. Chris Coates' decision to comply with a federal subpoena to appear before the U.S. Commission on Civil Rights. I also want to make you aware that prior to appearing before the Commission, Mr. Coates contacted me to share similar information relating to the equal enforcement of federal voting laws." Wolf further warned, "[I] will do everything in my power to enforce [whistleblower laws] should any negative actions be taken against Mr. Coates."[37]

Pajamas Media quickly posted Wolf's letter to the internet. To forestall any attempts to block Coates' entry to the building, Pajamas Television posted cameramen with live internet uplinks around the office of the Civil Rights Commission. Pajamas TV later streamed the entire hearing live over the internet.

Coates' testimony was filled with firsthand details about the Civil Rights Division's hostility to race-neutral law enforcement. He began by challenging the accuracy and veracity of prior DOJ testimony and statements about the dismissal: "Based upon my own personal knowledge of the events surrounding the [Civil Rights] Division's actions in the Panther case, and the atmosphere that has existed and continues to exist in the Division and in the Voting Section against fair enforcement of certain federal voting laws, I do not believe these representations to this Commission accurately reflect what occurred in the Panther case and do not reflect the hostile atmosphere that has existed within the Division for a long time against race-neutral enforcement of the Voting Rights Act."[38]

Coates described "widespread" opposition within the Voting Section to the Ike Brown case, explaining how the section historian "flatly refused to participate in the investigation" and would later impede the Panther investigation as well.[39] He related how Mark Kappelhoff, then-chief of the Criminal Section of the Civil Rights Division, worried that the Brown case was causing the DOJ problems with "its relations with civil rights groups."[40] Perhaps most damning, Coates testified how Loretta King had banned him from asking attorney job applicants whether they were willing to equally enforce the law regardless of the race of the victim.

He also testified how Kristen Clarke of the NAACP Legal Defense Fund attended a meeting in the fall of 2008 with Bush-era AAG Grace Chung Becker and spent a "considerable amount of time criticizing" the decision to bring the case against Ike Brown.[41] At that time, mind you, the district court had already found Brown liable for discrimination, yet an NAACP representative was still arguing the case should not have been brought.

Coates' testimony was a tour-de-force from the DOJ's former Voting Section chief, laying bare the systematic racial biases infecting the Civil Rights Division. Commissioner Thernstrom did not ask Coates a single question during the hearing, but various racialists quickly struck back afterward. Ignoring entirely the substance of Coates' remarks, DOJ spokeswoman Tracy Schmaler issued a written statement launching more barbs against Bush. "Let's not forget the context in which these allegations are being made," she intoned. "The politicization that occurred in the Civil Rights Division in the previous administration has been well documented by the Inspector General, and it was a disgrace to the great history of the division."[42]

Notably, instead of denying Coates' claims, some of his critics implicitly conceded his argument and denounced the very notion of race-neutral law enforcement. American University law professor Allan Lichtman, who has been paid thousands of taxpayer dollars to act as a DOJ voting expert, told the *Christian Science Monitor*, "You can try to force [the Voting Rights Act] to be equal, but it's not.... If these are the worst examples you can find, then, by God, white people in America are pretty safe."[43] Mary Jacoby of the Main Justice blog wrote, "Let's not forget that the Civil Rights Division exists because of racial discrimination against blacks."[44]

Bowing to public outrage and congressional demands, the DOJ assigned the Office of Professional Responsibility to conduct an internal investigation of the Panther dismissal. The entire investigation was a farce. The first "career civil servant" lawyer picked to investigate the dismissal, Mary Aubry, had donated $3,850 to Obama's presidential campaign, $2,500 to the Democratic National Committee, and $1,000 to Hillary Clinton.[45] (Aubry was eventually yanked from the investigation, but not before the investigation was well along.) What's more, a week after appointing Robin Ashton to head the OPR, Eric Holder told the *New York Times* the Panther affair was a "made up controversy." He added, "All I have on my side with regard to that is the facts and the law."[46] With Holder publicly pronouncing his expectation of what the investigation would find, it was unsurprising that the OPR, led by Holder's own appointee, would produce results to Holder's liking.

Democrats on the House Judiciary Committee leaked a heavily redacted version of the OPR report to the press. The report repeatedly accepts versions of facts that defend Obama administration positions while dismissing facts to the contrary. For example, according to the report, some witnesses "explained that hostility [within the DOJ] to the *Brown* case stemmed from anger that after five years in which no section 2 cases were brought to remedy discrimination against racial minority voters, the first one approved by the Bush administration was one to protect white voters." Yet the report "makes no finding regarding the accuracy of these claims."[47] Why not? The investigators only needed to check the DOJ website, where they would have found that the Bush administration filed Section 2 cases in Crockett County, Tennessee, in 2001 to protect black voters; in Berks County, Pennsylvania, in 2003 to protect Hispanics; in Osceola County, Florida, in 2005 to protect Hispanics; and then a flurry of cases from 2006 through 2008. The OPR should never have published this claim, and if they did, simple honesty demands that they reveal it as a falsehood.

These arguments—that the Brown case was the first Section 2 case brought by the Bush DOJ, and that for five years no case was brought to protect minority voters—are common untruths told by critics of the Bush administration. Stanford Law professor Pam Karlan peddled this nonsense in a published law review article that falsely states "for five of the eight years of the Bush Administration, [they] brought no Voting Rights Act cases of its own except for one case protecting white voters."[48] In a footnote, Karlan says she relied on Obama Voting Section chief Chris Herren for information for her article.

The OPR report also runs interference for Julie Fernandes, disguising her hostility toward enforcement of Section 8 of Motor Voter, which requires states to remove dead and ineligible felons from the voter rolls. While Fernandes definitely declared in my presence that the law would not be enforced by the Obama administration, she only admitted to the OPR that Section 8 wasn't her "top priority."[49] She told other tall tales to OPR about Section 8—namely, that she would "consider authorizing a suit in a meritorious Section 8 case if one were presented to her."[50] Coates could not even get Section 8 *investigations* authorized much less actual litigation commenced, yet OPR casually accepts Fernandes' excuse even though it had direct evidence to the contrary from Coates.

Despite the report's overall whitewash of the malfeasance at the Civil Rights Division, at key points it actually corroborates what Coates and I had been saying all along. Multiple named DOJ lawyers interviewed under oath testified that some Civil Rights Division employees don't believe civil rights laws should be used to protect white victims. Even Loretta King acknowledged this belief was evident in the division, despite Perez's sworn testimony denying it.[51] Likewise, the report found that Voting Section lawyers widely understood that Julie Fernandes had informed them that the Obama DOJ would only bring cases to protect national racial minorities: "The attendees recalled Fernandes making remarks to the effect that the Division was interested in pursuing 'traditional civil rights' enforcement cases ... which many understood meant cases in which racial minorities were the victims."[52]

Needless to say, the media entirely ignored these aspects of the report. The *New York Times'* Charlie Savage set the tone by reporting that the OPR had "cleared all department lawyers of wrongdoing" without ever mentioning that confirmation of my allegations and those of Coates was buried in the report.[53]

The report contained another startling revelation overlooked by the media: Steve Rosenbaum and Loretta King wanted to dismiss the entire Panther case, including the portion against the weapon-wielding King Samir Shabazz. After reviewing the evidence, the report found, the pair "did not believe the case should have been brought."[54] But this was too much even for Associate Attorney General Tom Perrelli, who had prohibited Rosenbaum and King from dismissing the case against Shabazz. In other words, Perrelli believed that a thug brandishing a nightstick should not be allowed to intimidate voters, even if the voters are white—and Rosenbaum and King disagreed. Americans might rightfully ask whether Rosenbaum and King are fit to continue in their positions as top enforcers of our nation's civil rights laws.

In the end, the OPR report revealed few details about the real reason the DOJ dismissed the Panther case. I believe, as do Chris Coates and many others within the DOJ, that the decision resulted from the Civil Rights Division's institutional hostility to protecting white victims of voting discrimination from minority wrongdoers. The fact that the Panther case had already effectively been won before it was dismissed indicates a slavish subservience to ideology by key decision-makers such as Rosenbaum and King.

But the OPR report shows that discussions about the Panther case went above Rosenbaum and King, ultimately to Attorney General Eric Holder himself, who warned King that bad press might follow a dismissal of the case.[55] Holder's failure to discuss the other ramifications seems a dereliction of his responsibilities, considering he had the power to order King to pursue a strong remedy against all the defendants. Did he ever consider how a dismissal would constrain future DOJ actions when the intimidation victims are black? Or did he simply presume it was okay to enforce the law unequally?

There are other indicators that the Panther case was closely followed at the top levels of the Obama administration. For example, the *Washington Times* reported that DOJ officials involved in the Panther dismissal visited the White House on key dates related to the case.[56] Furthermore, the White House visitor logs note an unnamed official participated in these West Wing meetings.[57] Who was it? Notwithstanding Obama's vaunted commitment to transparency, we'll probably never know.

In a clear effort to insulate top Obama administration officials, the OPR report strives to attribute the decision to dismiss the Panther case solely to Rosenbaum and King. For the sake of argument, let's assume that was true. In that case, has the Obama administration punished the pair in any way for refusing to protect white voters from weapon-wielding members of a race-hate group? Of course not. In fact, the administration has praised them, rewarded them, and kept them in positions of enormous importance and power. Why would it do otherwise? After all, Rosenbaum and King are faithfully implementing the vision of their superiors.

The unanswered questions about the Panthers' connection to the Obama administration reach back past election day to the afternoon in 2007 in Selma, Alabama when Obama, desperately seeking racial authenticity, accepted greetings from the Panthers, shared a podium with them, and marched with them through the streets, Panther fists raised high above his head in a black power salute. Did the Obama campaign know the Panthers would be there? Was their appearance coordinated with his campaign? What did Obama say to Malik Zulu Shabazz that day? Who was responsible for later posting the Panthers' endorsement on Obama's official campaign website? These questions were unasked for over four years.

Ultimately, the biggest casualty of the Panther case was the rule of law. The DOJ set a dangerous precedent by giving its seal of approval to voter intimidation, so long as the victims are a certain race. Thus, it did not shock me to see that during the November

2010 elections, an emboldened New Black Panther Party staged another election day deployment at the polls not only in Philadelphia,[58] but also in Houston, Texas. Led by chapter President Quanell X, Panthers in Houston sought to bully white poll watchers, just as they had done in Philadelphia. They even successfully persuaded minority polling officials to have white poll observers ejected from the polling places.[59] The Panthers had no right under Texas law to enter the polling place much less order the expulsion of white poll watchers, but what does the law matter when you have the federal government on your side?

Predictably, the DOJ has taken no action to determine if the Houston New Black Panthers violated the Voting Rights Act.

CHAPTER SIX

* * *

Payback Time Nationwide

Incidents of racially charged vote fraud and voter intimidation are by no means limited to Noxubee County and Philadelphia. While hardly ever attracting media attention—the Panther case was an exception in that regard—these cases for years have sparked pitched battles inside the Department of Justice between those who believe in equal enforcement of the law and those who do not. Unfortunately, despite the best efforts of many DOJ attorneys, DOJ officials have repeatedly chosen not to enforce the law faithfully—and often deliberately take the side of wrongdoers—in corrupt displays of racial and political favoritism.

Many of these battles involve implementation of the Voting Rights Act. Along with the Civil Rights Act of 1964, the Voting Rights Act was a landmark law providing the federal government with powerful tools to ensure legal equality after a century of failed attempts to do so. However, DOJ radicals have so thoroughly manipulated this law—refusing to enforce some sections while exploiting others to broaden federal power far beyond what Congress intended—that they have transformed the act into an all-purpose cudgel for bludgeoning those they perceive as their political and ideological enemies.

As argued earlier, and as this chapter will further demonstrate, the racialist camp was wreaking havoc inside the Civil Rights Division long before the Obama administration came along. But under Obama's presidency, these radicals now populate the division top to bottom. Both the entirety of the senior management and the vast majority of the rank and file are in this camp. This is what Eric Holder really meant with his promises to "reinvigorate and restore" the division. The media unquestionably applauds Holder's efforts, unwilling to report that the division's vaunted transformation has entailed blatant racial favoritism, legally unsupportable interpretations of civil rights laws, and selective enforcement of the law for political ends.

This has ominous implications concerning the conduct of the 2012 presidential elections, for the Civil Rights Division is now being utilized to energize the president's political base and alter the electoral ground rules to benefit Obama's campaign. There are glaring flaws in our electoral system, from corrupted voter rolls to the lack of voting rights protections for military personnel stationed abroad, that the Civil Rights Division is clearly intent on perpetuating. If this situation continues, the division's bias could well influence outcomes in close swing states in 2012. Since the division vehemently denies these biases exist, it is unlikely to take any remedial action until public pressure forces its hand.

Hale and Perry Counties, Alabama: "I'm Not Interested in Helping the Minority *Here*."

Hale County and Perry County, Alabama lie about sixty miles to the southeast of Noxubee County, Mississippi. All three counties are in the "Black Belt," a 25-mile-wide crescent-shaped swath of land stretching from McNary County, Tennessee, south into Mississippi, then turning east into Alabama. Its name originally stemmed from the region's rich, deep black soil, but later came to refer to the area's black-majority population as well.

Hale County (60 percent black) and Perry County (70 percent black) have similar demographics to Noxubee. And like Ike Brown's stomping ground, they also have a history of voter fraud designed to disenfranchise the white minority. DOJ officials ignored this malfeasance for years, when they weren't outright supporting the wrongdoers.

During the 1990s, Hale and Perry Counties witnessed a series of racially charged elections dominated by two competing camps—an all-black faction and a biracial one. Both counties are certified for federal observer coverage, and the DOJ sent federal election observers there more than twenty times from 1965 to 2000. Despite this large DOJ presence, or perhaps because of it, a disturbing pattern of voting abuse emerged: loads of black voters were brought to the polls by bus or van, led by a wrangler who ostensibly "helped" them to vote.

It was a similar situation to the abuse of "voting assistors" under Ike Brown. In Hale and Perry, the voters weren't asking for assistance; the wranglers simply announced they were assisting the voters, who submissively complied and then watched silently as the wranglers marked their ballots, one after another, all day long.

Having monitored numerous elections in the counties, the DOJ was well aware of the wranglers' activities. The department issued a press release on June 5, 2000, announcing that eleven federal officials would be sent to Hale "to ensure that African American voters are not subject to discriminatory treatment at voting sites and are not prevented from receiving assistance from the person of their choice."[1] In other words, the DOJ would watch the wranglers, but do nothing to stop their lawless activities.

In another echo of Noxubee, before election day, unusual numbers of absentee ballots were sent by mail in both counties from the circuit court clerk. They ended up at addresses where people had never requested them to be sent, and like magic, notary publics appeared on doorsteps holding absentee ballots they had snatched out of mailboxes, offering to help people vote and even voting the ballots while the voters stood by, passive and disinterested.

The burgeoning lawlessness sparked a backlash among law-abiding citizens. One prominent critic was Faye Cochran, a member of the board of registrars in Hale County, the body responsible for voter registration. Fighting to ensure that the voter rolls were clean and any ineligible voters were removed, Cochran identified circuit court clerk Gay Nell Tinker and Greensboro City Councilman Aaron Evan as the primary culprits behind much of the voter fraud.

These activities earned Cochran a visit from a DOJ Voting Section attorney, my old mentor Avner Shapiro. In an interview, Cochran described for me how she provided Shapiro voluminous details about the racially motivated election fraud corrupting Hale County, including the forced imposition of assistance on black voters and the illegal absentee ballot scheme.[2] Her information was dynamite evidence of possible violations of Section 2 of the Voting Rights Act—the precise kind of behavior that the district court would later find had violated Section 2 in Noxubee.

Although Shapiro was sworn to enforce Section 2, he grew agitated while listening to Cochran's story. "I am not here to help you," he dismissively told her during one interview in 2000. "I'm here to help the minorities only." Stunned, Cochran interjected that whites constituted a 39 percent minority. Shapiro was unmoved. "I'm not interested in helping the minority *here*," he declared contemptuously. "I'm here to help the national racial minority—blacks."[3]

Through the 1990s and as the century turned, absentee ballots began to swing election results, as more and more were cast in each successive election to the benefit of the all-black faction. The multiracial faction faced increasing odds against a well-tuned political machine employing voter fraud.

By 2004 and 2005, elections in Hale and Perry Counties featured open lawlessness both in the polls and in the collection of absentee ballots. Cochran and others discovered false voting registration addresses, including abandoned houses with trees growing through them and vacant lots sporting only a fire hydrant. Meanwhile, teams of notaries swarmed the counties collecting absentee ballots from black voters. After questionable absentee ballots were seized and placed in a bank vault to await further scrutiny, the bank was burned to the ground overnight, destroying the evidence.[4]

In 2005, frustrated with the explosion of voter fraud in western Alabama, Cochran helped to organize the Democracy Defense League (DDL). The group, along with similar organizations like True the Vote in Harris County, Texas, is part of a wave of grassroots organizations that have sprung up across America to combat voter fraud. These efforts are made necessary by a combination of inept enforcement of voting laws, the minimization or outright denial of the problem in academia and in the national media, and political opposition to stamping out voter fraud because the wrongdoers are political allies of the Democratic Party.

In 2005, the DDL's complaints finally reached Chris Coates. Then a DOJ special litigation counsel, he contacted Faye Cochran to investigate further and decided to visit Hale County to monitor an upcoming election. Cochran was thrilled; the DOJ was coming to Hale to do something other than interrogate *her*.

Avner Shapiro, however, was upset by Coates' interest in the case. He furiously confronted Coates, shouting, "This is my case!" Coates later told me that "Avner was like a rocket about to go off, he was so angry." Shapiro may have been outraged by Coates' attention to complaints from white victims—after all, Shapiro himself had told Coates he "didn't join the Justice Department to sue black people." Then again, his outburst may have merely been part of a petty turf war. Regardless, he thundered at Coates, "What gives you the right to work on a case I had been working for years?"

"Because Assistant Attorney General Brad Schlozman assigned me to go there," retorted Coates. A Bush appointee, Schlozman was dedicated to race-neutral law enforcement, an outlook that made him the target of a legion of leftwing critics. When he approved Coates' investigation of Hale County, the civil rights industry issued an all-hands-on-deck, sink-the-Bismarck battle cry against Schlozman. The industry had a vested interest in defending a well-running political machine in Hale that manufactured an illegal gusher of racially polarized votes. Avner Shapiro's wife, Julie Fernandes, initially helped lead the charge against Schlozman from her perch as a senior counsel at the Leadership Conference on Civil Rights.

After observing the elections in Hale County, Coates drew "the clear impression that some African Americans there in those counties were involved in acts of racial discrimination against whites."[5] Unable to follow up on his investigation due to his subsequent promotion to principal deputy chief of the Voting Section, Coates had Joshua Rogers, a fantastic attorney who had distinguished himself on the Ike Brown case, assigned to Hale. But Rogers quickly ran into difficulty when the Voting Section chief allowed Avner Shapiro to return to the case team. Rogers and Shapiro were an incendiary mix on this case—Rogers believed in race-neutral law enforcement while Shapiro did not. Nevertheless, both were sent to Hale and Perry Counties to monitor the June 2006 elections.

The contrasting approaches of the two attorneys were evident in their initial task of training election observers from the Office of Personnel Management (OPM) in Tuscaloosa. Focusing exclusively on white-on-black discrimination, Shapiro encouraged the OPM observers to "play detective" and "play investigator" to uncover white wrongdoing. Rogers, recognizing that Shapiro had entirely omitted the most serious problems afflicting the area, described all the wrongdoing and racially motivated illegal assistance the DDL had uncovered. He explained the importance of memorializing instances when "assistors" cast a ballot without the input of the voter, whether black or white.

The presentations starkly illustrated the competing philosophies of civil rights enforcement. Shapiro's approach chooses sides and turns the DOJ's guns into covering fire for racially motivated wrongdoing. Rogers' approach, meanwhile, assumes that all voters possess the right to vote free from interference or coercion. All voters, to Rogers, are blessed with an individualized dignity to voice their own opinion about who should govern them, and no one has the right to hold their pen and vote in their name.

On election day, June 6, the situation between Shapiro and Rogers deteriorated further. According to a DOJ source, when Shapiro learned that Rogers had witnessed black political operatives forcing "assistance" on black voters inside the polls in Sawyerville, Shapiro quickly ordered Rogers to leave Sawyerville for Newburn, on the opposite side of the county. Rogers, smelling a rat, called Coates in

Washington. Coates countermanded Shapiro's instructions and told Rogers to stay in Sawyerville to ensure that OPM observers memorialized all instances of forced assistance.

Rogers later received a call from Harvey Kanutzen, captain of the OPM teams. He blasted Rogers' activities in Sawyerville, insisting, "You are not to enter one more polling site." This was a remarkable command, considering Rogers was in control on the scene and did not answer to Kanutzen. But Kanutzen continued issuing orders anyway. "You are to go to the courthouse to watch absentee ballot counting, and I'm sending two observers to the courthouse also— and they are going to be observing *you*," he barked. In other words, Kanutzen was ordering Rogers to a place where he could not observe or record any instances of forced assistance or other kinds of voting fraud. No one was voting at the courthouse, of course, and instances of absentee ballot fraud, having occurred beforehand in the field, could not be uncovered simply by observing the ballots being counted.

When Rogers called his superior—Shapiro—to protest Kanutzen's behavior, Rogers quickly discovered Shapiro was part of the fix. Shapiro backed Kanutzen fully and made clear he wanted nothing to do with Rogers' evenhanded approach. Not wanting to blow up the entire monitoring effort by defying Shapiro again, Rogers obliged and headed off to the courthouse, where two OPM observers appeared as promised to monitor Rogers. Thus, an experienced DOJ lawyer was bottled up in a meaningless courthouse room while pervasive voter fraud was perpetrated across the county.

According to my source, the day after this incident, Shapiro berated Rogers in personal terms, mentioning his Christian faith and blasting him for communicating with the Alabama Secretary of State and for initially following Coates' instructions to continue monitoring wrongdoing in Sawyersville. Referring to how Shapiro had effectively neutered his monitoring activities, Rogers responded, "I think you got exactly what you wanted out of yesterday's election coverage." Shapiro yelled back, "Delusional! You think I want to mess with some Federalist Society attorney under a Republican administration?!" At last, the truth was revealed. Rogers, who had simply been trying to fulfill his duty to record wrongdoing, was seen by Shapiro as a species of enemy political operative. Projection can be a funny thing when it explodes openly in anger.

Alabama Attorney General Troy King eventually opened a vote fraud investigation in Hale and Perry Counties, sparking outrage from the civil rights industry. State Senator Bobby Singleton—husband of one of the investigation's key targets, circuit court clerk Gay Nell Tinker—accused the investigators of harassment. Singleton, the dignitary who had welcomed candidate Barack Obama to Selma on behalf of the "Alabama black legislature," also professed shock that an investigator for the attorney general wore a weapon during the investigation—a routine practice.[6] Remarkably, according to an October 2, 2007, affidavit submitted to the Alabama Court of Criminal Appeals by investigator George Barrows, Singleton himself was under investigation for voter fraud as well.[7]

Faye Cochran told me the backlash to the investigation was so frantic that local police officers arrested one of Attorney General King's investigators based on complaints of harassment.[8] This sounds eerily familiar to what happened to the police officers who cooperated with the investigation into Ike Brown.

Naturally, the perpetrators of the vote fraud scheme denounced the entire investigation as a racist act of voter suppression. This false allegation, which DOJ investigators have encountered whenever they have looked into voter fraud by black wrongdoers, is meant to discourage law enforcement through personal attacks while creating solidarity among potential witnesses against the investigation.

As the investigation wrapped up, Attorney General King described "a systemic problem of corruption" in Hale. "It is a culture problem, an elite believing they have the right to decide who holds office," he declared.[9] Eventually three women active in the all-black political faction would face justice. Two of them, Valada Paige Banks (who had previously been convicted of welfare fraud)[10] and Rosie Lyles, were indicted on multiple felony voter fraud counts in August 2007. In a stunning display of racial solidarity, more than 200 people, almost all black, packed their arraignment hearing and loudly applauded when not guilty pleas were entered. In a corrupt appropriation of the moral authority of the civil rights movement, they wore t-shirts that said, "Greensboro 2: Injustice Anywhere is a Threat to Justice Everywhere."[11] Outside the courthouse, supporters held hands in a huge circle, sang songs from the civil rights movement, and prayed for the defendants' legal deliverance.

Hale County circuit court clerk Gay Nell Tinker was also indicted for felony absentee ballot fraud. Her charges included possession of a forged instrument (a phony absentee ballot), promoting and soliciting illegal absentee votes, and perjury relating to who actually signed absentee ballots.

The voter fraud indictments of Lyles, Banks, and Tinker were assigned to Hale County Circuit Court Judge Marvin Wiggins. Attorney General King asked Wiggins to recuse himself because Gay Nell Tinker was the judge's sister. Wiggins refused. That's justice, Hale County style.

Even before the indictments, Wiggins had tampered with the investigation of his sister—which also touched upon his brother-in-law Bobby Singleton as well as his cousin Carrie Reaves—by quashing a search warrant and grand jury subpoena without even being assigned to the case or giving the attorney general a chance to respond. The Alabama Court of Criminal Appeals ultimately reversed Judge Wiggins and ordered him off the voter fraud cases. Wiggins, however, ignored the order for almost a month and refused to step aside.[12]

Eventually, a judicial complaint was filed against Judge Wiggins. He was later rebuked by the Alabama Court of the Judiciary, suspended without pay for ninety days, and given a public reprimand.[13] Alas, the incident ultimately had little effect on his career. In November 2010, the voters in Alabama's Fourth Judicial Circuit reelected Judge Marvin Wiggins to a six-year term with 100 percent of the vote. Wiggins ran for the position unopposed.

Two months before Wiggins' reelection, his sister Gay Nell Tinker entered guilty pleas to five felony counts of illegal absentee ballot fraud.[14] These convictions did little to impede her career advancement either. Despite five felony convictions, Tinker now serves as the judicial magistrate for the city of Greensboro, Alabama.

In August 2009, Rosie Lyles reversed herself and entered a guilty plea to possessing forged absentee ballots. The following month, Valada Paige Banks did a similar about-face and entered a guilty plea to possession of forged absentee ballot applications.[15] The convictions of Tinker, Lyles, and Banks all involved actions identical to the ones Faye Cochran had complained about to DOJ lawyer Avner Shapiro a decade earlier.

By this point, it may come as little surprise that Rosie Lyles, the convicted vote fraudster, was one of the people in Hale County upon whom Avner Shapiro most relied in deciding whether to recommend that elections be monitored. In fact, when Shapiro interrogated Faye Cochran, he cited Lyles' complaints about her. The iron restraints of hindsight prove that the DOJ had been on the side of the racially motivated lawbreakers while it abandoned law abiding citizens. And all because, as Shapiro told Cochran point-blank, the victims were white.

After the farce of the 2005 elections in Hale County, election monitoring by the Bush administration and an aggressive state investigation kept the worst electoral abuses in check. However, there has been a resurgence of voter fraud under the Obama administration. Prior to the June 2010 election, Alabama Secretary of State Beth Chapman begged the DOJ to send "the maximum number of federal agents and poll observers" to monitor Hale County elections.[16] Instances of suspected fraud included ballots cast from false addresses and more than a dozen voter identification cards being mailed out and returned as undeliverable after those same voters had cast absentee ballots.[17] Meanwhile, former Greensboro police officer Aaron Evans, who had been convicted on fifteen counts of voter fraud back in 1998, was busy in the field collecting and assisting the casting of absentee ballots. Gay Nell Tinker, even while under indictment for absentee ballot fraud, was also assisting voters with absentee ballots.

Eric Holder responded to Chapman's desperate plea by sending precisely zero monitors. A month later, however, he sent election observers to Barbour, Lee, and Russell Counties in Alabama. In November, he also sent a cadre of observers to Autauga County, Alabama. Care to guess what the common characteristic of these counties is? They are all majority white. Eric Holder has clearly chosen his priority minority.

Wilkinson County, Mississippi: The Flames of Fraud

The empowerment of formerly oppressed people often creates a volatile situation where much can go wrong and much can go right. In those situations, there is a natural human instinct toward vengeance and retribution that must be controlled by the law. In the transition from white rule to black rule in Zimbabwe, we find a stark example of what happens when the law fails to control these instincts—legally sanctioned terror against the white minority, gangsterism, and economic collapse. We find a counter-example in South Africa, where Nelson Mandela presided over a peaceful transition from apartheid that, though imperfect, was marked by adherence to the law and full legal protections for all races.

In some American counties, as the black majority became empowered after passage of the Voting Rights Act, new political leaders emerged who sought racial payback. While they did not unleash wanton violence on the scale of Zimbabwe, the same sense of racial animus animated their cause.

This was the case in Wilkinson County. Located at the southwestern tip of Mississippi along the Mississippi River, the 70 percent black county has a white minority that maintained political power for years through racial discrimination, threats, and the wholesale disenfranchisement of black residents. Black empowerment in Wilkinson created a political dynamic similar to that of Hale and Perry Counties—an all-black political faction became locked in a running battle with a racially-integrated faction. And as in Noxubee, the Democratic Party's domination of Wilkinson County meant that the Democratic primaries effectively determined who would be elected.

On November 7, 2006, a special election was held for Seat Two on the Wilkinson County Board of Supervisors. In that contest, Kirk Smith, a white candidate, defeated black candidate Richard Hollins by forty votes. But absentee ballots threw the results to Hollins in an election that featured the familiar slew of voting fraud machinations. Reports reached Smith throughout election day that two of Hollins' sisters were stalking voters at the polls and forcibly "assisting" them to vote for Hollins. Similar to Noxubee elections, no preventive action was taken by the poll workers, who had been chosen by the local Democratic Executive Committee. There was also no help forthcoming from the uniformed sheriff deputy who was standing vigil at the polls and openly supporting Hollins. Naturally, Hollins was declared the victor and then served as county supervisor.

The Bush DOJ began investigating Wilkinson County for potential violations of the Voting Rights Act. Thus, federal election observers, along with monitors from Mississippi Secretary of State Delbert Hosemann's office, were in place when Hollins faced Kirk Smith again in the Democratic primary held the following year. On election day, August 7, 2007, Smith led the contest when all the machine votes were tabulated but, once again, was overtaken by Hollins after absentee ballots were counted. In light of widespread irregularities in the absentee ballots, however, this time the Democratic Executive Committee tossed out all the absentee ballots, swinging the election back to Smith.

Smith's wife was present at the review of the absentee ballots and spoke out against committee members who wanted to approve questionable ballots. For her efforts, she was arrested by a sheriff's deputy who was a political ally of Hollins. Tensions rose further a few days later following a heated skirmish between Smith's wife and a law enforcement member of Hollins' faction. Then, during the early morning hours of August 10, the Smith family awoke to find their house engulfed in flames. Escaping from the house, the family later found an empty gasoline can on the premises.

Wilkinson County Sheriff Reginald Jackson, part of the all-black political faction, declined to send investigators to the charred remains of the Smith home to collect evidence in the days following the fire. According to Chris Coates, Sheriff Jackson said Smith and his wife "probably set [the fire] themselves."[18] To this day, no one has been arrested in connection with the fire.

In order to win, Smith had to overcome an astonishing amount of illegality. According to a report by the Mississippi Secretary of State, election monitors recorded improper voter assistance being imposed on black voters "by pollworkers, other election officials, representatives of candidates, and members of the public."[19] In one precinct, a single person "consistently and repetitively provided assistance to individuals who did not appear to be qualified to receive assistance, did not request assistance, and did not communicate their wishes in any perceptible manner to that pollworker providing assistance."[20] Astoundingly, in one precinct "approximately half to 75% of all voters received assistance."[21] Voters who were shown to have cast absentee ballots were contacted by the Secretary of State and reported that they had never requested the ballots.

The report further describes interference in the election by advocacy groups, which "attempted to block access to law enforcement personnel. They also expressed a perception that the Secretary of State employees' uniform (slacks and a polo shirt with the Secretary of State's seal) was inappropriate and intimidated voters."[22] The laughable charge that voters were intimidated by the sight of slacks and polos comes straight from the NAACP playbook. And sure enough, it was the local chapter of the NAACP and the national NAACP Legal Defense Fund that were facilitating the illegal conduct in Wilkinson County election by aggressively interfering with the Secretary of State's law enforcement activities.

Ultimately, Richard Hollins filed a court challenge to Smith's victory, challenging the wholesale rejection of the absentee ballots by the Democratic Executive Committee. The court fight between Hollins and Smith dragged on until 2008 when a special master was appointed to oversee a do-over. Just like in Noxubee, the Democratic Executive Committee proved so untrustworthy in staging elections that a court gave someone else the power to run them. The do-over primary on June 26, 2008 saw Richard Hollins defeat Kirk Smith 552 to 523.

In August 2011, the DOJ announced it would send observers to monitor elections in both Wilkinson and Noxubee Counties. The fact that it took the Obama administration nearly three years to make this move shows that protecting white voters remains a low priority. The Civil Rights Division was clearly reluctant to take this decision, which undoubtedly stemmed from the rising tide of criticism its racialist policies have attracted in the right-leaning media. Moreover, DOJ sources told me the only Voting Section attorneys willing to accept the assignment were Bush hires—Obama's recruits, of course, didn't sign up to protect white voters. But because there are so few Bush hires left in the Voting Section, the division had to pluck another Bush hire out of the Housing Section to complete the monitoring team.

As the racialist camp solidifies its grasp on the Civil Rights Division, the end result is eminently predictable: just as the New Black Panther polling patrols resurfaced in 2010 after the DOJ dismissed its case against them, in the near future we can expect counties like Wilkinson, Hale, Noxubee, Perry, and others to bubble over with fraud, forced assistance, and lawlessness. These outrages, which somehow never attract the attention of our apathetic media corps, are a direct result of the DOJ's ideological allergy to protecting voters of all races. The department's "restoration and reinvigoration" carries a price Americans should not have to pay.

In light of the rampant fraud that marred elections in Wilkinson, Hale, Perry, and Noxubee, it is important to note that there is an enormous and well-funded industry of voter fraud deniers that provides an intellectual smokescreen for this lawlessness. Justin Levitt, then of the Brennan Center for Justice, summed up the industry's outlook when he claimed voter fraud was as pervasive as "Sasquatch."[23] Closely linked with fellow travelers in academia, this movement comprises leftwing activist groups and think tanks such as Project Vote, the Brennan Center for Justice, and Demos. The NAACP is also a voter fraud denier, and there are no signs it will change its view even though a local NAACP executive committee member, Lessadolla Sowers of Tunica, Mississippi, was found guilty in April 2011 of ten counts of absentee ballot fraud.[24] In her photograph at the NAACP website, Sowers is sporting an "Obama for President" button on her blouse.[25]

Another voter fraud denier, Tova Wang at Demos, rushed to the internet with a six-page report just two days after the 2010 congressional election claiming there had been no vote fraud.[26] Wang could not possibly have known this so soon after the election. In Wang's world of partisan advocacy, voter fraud in any election can immediately be discovered or ruled out, depending on which finding is politically useful. But in the real world, voter fraud usually reveals itself over time. Rumors start, perpetrators gossip, questionable patterns emerge, and victims eventually come forward. But Tova Wang, sitting in her Manhattan office, was somehow able to rule out voter fraud with confidence in a nationwide election that had concluded less than forty hours earlier.

A primary goal of vote fraud deniers is to abolish voter identification requirements, which are the target of some of their most overwrought rhetoric. For example, NAACP president Benjamin Jealous extravagantly described voter ID laws as an attempt to disenfranchise minorities through some "of the last existing legal pillars of Jim Crow," adding that those laws originate with "the worst and most racist elements" of the tea party movement.[27]

The Democratic Party has heeded this call-to-arms. The party's national chairwoman, Congresswoman Debbie Wasserman Schultz, dismissed the need for voter ID laws by claiming that "you're more likely to be hit by lightning than be a victim" of vote fraud.[28] In a separate interview, she made it clear that she is encouraging her ideological comrades at the DOJ to act on the issue. "The assistant attorney general for civil rights, Tom Perez, has assured Americans and members of Congress that the Voting Section is looking very closely at the laws that have recently passed," she said. "They've acknowledged the concern that both I and others have expressed about the potential for these laws to have an undue and dispropor-tionate impact on racial minorities and the poor. I trust that Tom Perez and Attorney General Eric Holder are reviewing these laws very seriously."[29]

Vote fraud deniers claim photo ID laws are racially discrimina-tory because minorities disproportionately lack driver's licenses. What the deniers don't mention is that most states allow numerous forms of photo identification to satisfy the law, and some even pro-vide state photo identification for free. Far from being a nefarious attempt at voter suppression, voter ID laws are crucial, common-sense tools for preventing the sort of in-person voter fraud I have witnessed with my own eyes. They are also perfectly consistent with the Constitution; in fact, the mere potential of fraud was enough for the United States Supreme Court to find Indiana's voter identifica-tion law to be constitutional.

Millions of dollars go to funding voter fraud denial organizations that provide cover for criminal wrongdoing in American elections. Instead of truthfully reporting on voter fraud crimes, they produce distorted and outright false analyses that are published unquestion-ingly in the *Washington Post* and other newspapers. Attorneys in the DOJ Voting Section actually believe these fables, sometimes posting the articles on office doors.

Who pays for all this? Unsurprisingly the George Soros-funded Open Society Institute is a major contributor. But so too are many corporate foundations—the Ford Foundation, Carnegie Corporation, Rockefeller Foundation, and PEW Charitable Trusts have provided millions of dollars to support voter fraud deniers.

It is a bad omen that the Civil Rights Division listens to these groups and seems more concerned by voter ID laws than by racially motivated voter fraud in Mississippi, Alabama, and elsewhere. H. L. Mencken once wrote that "conscience is the inner voice that warns us somebody may be looking." If the ones who are scrutinizing our conduct are themselves purveyors of lawlessness, however, it is nearly impossible for America to move in the right direction. Thus, as the 2012 election draws near, we can expect to see spreading electoral lawlessness.

An Ironclad Commitment to Voting Rights—For Felons

In order to better impose its fiats on the American people, the DOJ constantly struggles to seize more and more power from the states. This is evident in the Voting Section's long-standing campaign to protect the right to vote for convicted felons. Although the Fourteenth Amendment to the Constitution specifically contemplates states' revocation of felon voting rights, the Civil Rights Division tries to use the Voting Rights Act to strip states of this authority. Courts have repeatedly rejected this power grab, which is strongly supported by the civil rights industry and its backers in the Democratic Party who believe Democrats will win the mass of felon votes.

DOJ radicals pressed this agenda in an ugly incident less than eight months after the Bush administration took power. In September 2001, then-Voting Section chief Joe Rich sent a letter to Alabama

Attorney General Bill Pryor warning that Alabama could not enforce a 1994 law because it had not been submitted to the DOJ for preclearance under Section 5. The statute in question required felons to submit to a DNA test as a mandatory precondition to applying to the state's Board of Pardons and Paroles for a restoration of civil rights, including the right to vote. Part of a nationwide effort to build up DNA databases, the program was facilitated by Congress through federal legislation and through DOJ-administered federal grants to states.

Rich's letter was based on a legal memorandum he received from his deputy Gilda Daniels (now a law professor teaching critical race studies) and from Kristen Clarke (who eventually left the DOJ to work for the NAACP Legal Defense and Education Fund). The memorandum cited a *New York Times* article on voting rights that quoted Pryor's views of the Alabama statute as well as a critical report by the Sentencing Project, a group that lobbies against felon disenfranchisement laws.

Rich sent his warning letter to Pryor without the approval of the Civil Rights Division's new political leadership, thereby violating internal procedures. While Rich no doubt knew he was contravening DOJ protocols, he may or may not have known that his letter also conflicted with a major DNA testing initiative launched by another DOJ division that had granted Alabama more than half a million dollars for its DNA testing program.

Unlike many state attorneys general who surrender even to the most outrageous demands of the Civil Rights Division, Bill Pryor decided to fight back. Pryor, who is now a federal appellate judge on the 11th Circuit Court of Appeals, returned a defiant letter to Rich noting that Supreme Court precedent specified that this kind of law, which outlines pardon procedures, does not directly affect voting and therefore is not covered under the Voting Rights Act. In fact, that Supreme Court case, *Presley v. Etowah County Commission*, was an Alabama case.[30]

Pryor's defiance put Joe Rich in a bind—the only thing he could do about it was to file a lawsuit against Alabama. But that would require the approval of the assistant attorney general for civil rights, meaning Bush political appointees would discover what Rich had concocted. Stymied, Rich left the case file to sit in the bowels of the Voting Section without offering any response to Pryor. Then, in the late summer of 2002, Voting Section lawyer Hans von Spakovsky discovered Rich's actions. He informed the front office about the matter and wrote a detailed memorandum for the new administration's leadership explaining why Pryor's legal analysis was correct and why that of Rich, Daniels, and Clarke was wrong.

Three months later, von Spakovsky was promoted out of the Voting Section and into the front office to become the division's main voting counsel. After getting the approval of his new supervisors, von Spakovsky forced Rich to send a letter to Pryor on March 10, 2003, acknowledging the veracity of Pryor's legal analysis. Withdrawing the division's demand that Pryor submit the DNA testing law for review, Rich informed Pryor that the DOJ was closing its file on the matter.

The case serves as a lesson to state officials who receive questionable demands from the Civil Rights Division—it pays to push back. State officials are tragically naïve if they assume the division's activities are reasonable or even valid. Bill Pryor recognized that fact back in 2001, and his principled stand forced the division to follow the law. One can only hope other state and municipal leaders will follow in his footsteps.

Selective Law Enforcement

Most Americans probably associate the National Voter Registration Act, known as the "Motor Voter law," with their option to register to vote at the local DMV. The law, however, goes far beyond that, mandating many significant voting registration procedures. And in a recurring theme, the Obama DOJ only enforces those provisions of the law that jibe with the new administration's ideology or help its political cause.

Section 7 of Motor Voter requires all state "public assistance" agencies and any state office offering "disability services" to serve as a proxy voter registration office. With the beneficiaries of these services voting overwhelmingly Democratic, the Obama DOJ has shown continual zeal in enforcing this rule. A recent consent decree in a case brought by the Voting Section against the state of Rhode Island shows the vast obligations the DOJ believes Section 7 imposes. In addition to welfare and motor vehicle offices, Rhode Island was forced to convert food stamp offices, cash assistance offices, behavioral treatment centers, utility payment grant offices, and even drug treatment centers into voter registration offices. At every site, the consent decree requires the taxpayers of Rhode Island to fund a Motor Voter "site coordinator" to guarantee that the recipients of government services are receiving their voter registration materials. [31]

Furthermore, Rhode Island will have to generate mountains of paperwork detailing every instance in which voter registration materials are rejected at any of the state's offices. In other words, officials must create a record *every time* someone doesn't want to register to vote, and these records must be turned over to the bureaucrats in the Civil Rights Division's Voting Section on demand. All welfare agency site coordinators must attend training sessions, presumably on the taxpayers' dime. And if social services are provided through private entities like a church charity, they must "amend" their terms of the contracts.

Tellingly, the consent decree admits that its terms go far beyond what Section 7 actually requires. Nevertheless, Rhode Island rolled over and agreed to these extra-legal burdens, thereby tipping further the balance between state and federal power beyond what Congress envisioned when it passed Section 7.

Now, compare the DOJ's enthusiastic enforcement of Section 7 with its approach to Section 8, which requires voter rolls to be kept free of dead and ineligible voters. Keep in mind that the Motor Voter law stemmed from a careful, bipartisan compromise. Congress knew that turning welfare offices and drug addict treatment agencies into voter registration offices would create more potential problems for maintaining accurate voting rolls. That's why it insisted in the same law that voter rolls be kept up-to-date. In other words, without Section 8, Section 7 would never have become law. Failing to enforce one of these provisions would directly defy the will of our lawmakers.

Yet I was present at a brown bag luncheon for the Voting Section in November 2009 when Deputy Assistant Attorney General Julie Fernandes glibly proclaimed that the DOJ would no longer enforce Section 8. The meeting, focusing on Motor Voter enforcement decisions, occurred at a time when the DOJ political leadership was considering a formal recommendation by Chris Coates to investigate eight states for having too many dead and ineligible voters on the rolls. Coates had found indications of serious problems in the voter rolls in these states. For example, shortly after taking office, Colorado Secretary of State Scott Gessler discovered the voter rolls were so polluted that thousands of non-citizens may have illegally voted in the 2010 general election.[32]

At the meeting with Fernandes, Deputy Chief Robert Popper asked her point-blank whether a decision had been made to move forward with any of the Section 8 investigations recommended by Coates. As recounted in chapter five, Fernandes replied that the Obama DOJ had "no interest" in enforcing Section 8, ostensibly because such actions create a "barrier to the ballot box." That settled the issue almost a year before the 2010 midterm elections.

Some lawyers in the room were stunned at Fernandes' arrogant lack of judgment, while others wearily accepted that we'd just been ordered not to do our job. A Voting Section manager later described to me how another supervisor reacted to Fernandes' comments: "The look on her face when Julie said that was as uncomfortable as if someone had disrobed entirely."

Although investigating any of the states identified by Coates would have been easy, initially entailing a few calls to state officials to verify the public data and to ask why they had not removed any dead voters in years, no green light ever came. The excuse the higher-ups gave was a common one: limited resources. This was hard to accept, considering the attorneys who recommended the investigation watched months go by with little work to do. In reality, the investigations were rejected purely out of raw politics.

The DOJ never denied that Fernandes had rejected Section 8 enforcement at the brown bag meeting. In fact, her remarks were all but confirmed in the Office of Professional Responsibility Report on the Panther case dismissal, though the OPR couches the discussion in the phony terms of resource concern.[33] Ironically, her instructions to enforce some laws but not others were precisely what Obama, his current Assistant Attorney General Tom Perez, and the entire racial grievance industry had accused the Bush DOJ of doing—they called it "cherry picking at the buffet line." In reality, as is easily proved by statistics at the DOJ's own website, the Bush

Civil Rights Division enforced every voting statute on the books, even those likely to harm Republicans at the ballot box.

While the Obama DOJ was rejecting cases that could help prevent voter fraud, it was also busy spiking similar cases begun under the Bush administration. For example, in the early days of the Obama administration, it dismissed a Bush-era case against Missouri, where some counties had more registered voters on the rolls than voting age citizens. Nothing was too surprising about the dismissal, except perhaps the willingness of some media outlets at the time to publish stories, without a whiff of skepticism, claiming the new president had purged politics from DOJ decision making.

The Obama administration's selective approach to law enforcement has another wrinkle: while the administration goes above and beyond the law to make voting more convenient for welfare recipients, it shows much less resolve in ensuring the vote for U.S. military personnel stationed overseas—a group that, by a stunning coincidence, tends to vote Republican.

To better protect military voting rights, Congress passed the MOVE act in 2009 mandating, among other things, that absentee ballots be sent to military personnel at least forty-five days before an election, and that a voter registration office be opened on every military installation before the 2010 mid-terms. Yet the Obama administration has made it clear that protecting military voting rights is not an urgent matter—in February 2010, a DOJ official openly informed a convention of state officials that litigation to enforce MOVE wasn't a DOJ priority, a convention attendee told me. In fact, after MOVE passed, it took the DOJ nine months just to update its website with the new standards. Then, as the 2010 election approached, the DOJ allowed states to widely ignore the MOVE act, absentee ballots were not mailed out forty-five days before the election, and military installations were not informed until after the election of the mandate to create voting offices. As a result, according to a 2011 report by the Military Voter Protection Project, participation rates by uniformed service members actually declined in the 2010 election despite the MOVE Act.[34]

At Eric Holder's confirmation hearing, he testified, "I think in some ways you can measure the success of an attorney general's tenure by how the Civil Rights Division has done."[35] On that score, the division's selective law enforcement doesn't speak well of Holder's own tenure. By refusing to enforce laws designed to ensure election integrity, the DOJ will inevitably erode the public's confidence in the sanctity of the electoral process. And in the end, this malfeasance—instead of the will of eligible voters—may determine who wins and loses. Indeed, in the 2010 general election in Colorado—one of the elections Coates had sought to investigate—the U.S. Senate seat was decided by a mere 1.5 percent of the vote.

Holder himself, of course, is fully aware of the problem, and has been asked about it repeatedly at congressional oversight hearings. He could have simply overruled Julie Fernandes and insisted that the DOJ enforce all the laws, as it had done under Bush. But Obama promised to bring change, and Holder has certainly delivered it. With so much at stake in 2012, we can expect more of the same.

Kinston, North Carolina: Protecting the People by Defying Their Will

Kinston, North Carolina is a town of 23,000 in Lenoir County, in the eastern part of the state. Visitors will find a classic tobacco town with a turn-of-the-last-century business section with department stores named Duprees and H. Stadiem Inc. Kinston also hosts what's left of the hull of the CSS *Neuse*, one of only three remaining Confederate ironclads. Locals enjoy summer baseball with the Kinston Indians, a Carolina League affiliate for Cleveland, as well as races at the Kinston dragstrip. Kinston is, in short, a classic small-to-midsize southern town.

Because Kinston, which has a 67 percent black majority, is in a county covered by Section 5 of the Voting Rights Act, any voting-related change in the town, no matter how minor, must be pre-cleared by the federal government, either by bureaucrats at the DOJ Voting Section or by a three-judge federal court in Washington, D.C. The enormous power of Section 5 is supposed to be used to protect racial minorities. But in Kinston, it has been used as a bludgeon to protect the political power of Democrats. And the individual primarily responsible for this misuse of federal authority is none other than our old friend Loretta King.

The problem began in November 2008, when a local ballot referendum asked voters if they wanted to make Kinston city elections non-partisan. In practice, this would mean ceasing to identify candidates' party affiliations on the ballot. By an overwhelming margin of about two to one, voters approved the change. Their vote tracked the trend within the rest of North Carolina, where only eight of 551 localities held partisan elections.

Under Section 5, the DOJ had to approve the change before it could take effect. Approval should have been routine, considering a majority of blacks in a majority-black town had approved the referendum. But that wasn't good enough for Loretta King, who opted to block Kinston's switch to non-partisan elections.

Her October 2009 objection letter was an absurd case study in twisted logic. She began by arguing that blacks weren't *really* a majority in Kinston. The town's demographic data proved otherwise, but her assertion was necessary in order to apply Section 5 to the situation; if King conceded the town had a black majority, then Section 5 protections should also apply to the white minority. So King argued that even though blacks comprise an overwhelming majority in the town, *sometimes* they don't in *some* elections: "Although black persons comprise a majority of the city's registered voters, in three of the past four general municipal elections, African Americans comprised a minority of the electorate on election day; in the fourth, they may have been a slight majority. For that reason, they are viewed as a minority for analytical purposes."[36]

This ridiculous sophistry essentially holds that Kinston blacks are entitled to Section 5 protections because many of them voluntarily choose not to vote in certain elections. What King disingenuously fails to mention is that blacks actually did comprise a majority of voters in the election where the referendum was approved.

King's bizarre arguments turn offensive when she concludes that Kinston blacks aren't capable of knowing whom to vote for without the partisan "Democrat" label next to a candidate's name. In her words, "Removing the partisan cue in municipal elections will, in all likelihood, eliminate the single factor that allows black candidates to be elected to office."[37] She takes her plantation-era analysis even further by claiming that Democratic Party-sponsored campaign events "provide forums for black candidates to meet with voters who may otherwise be unreachable without the party's assistance." That's right, without partisan beer and barbeque, black candidates would apparently be unable to venture into the white neighborhoods to seek support. The letter then plunges headfirst into vintage leftwing class analysis: "The party provides campaign funds to candidates, without which minority candidates may lag behind their white counterparts in campaign spending."[38]

Of course, non-partisan elections would not prevent the Kinston Democratic Party from sponsoring events with candidates or raising political contributions for them—candidates would only lose their partisan affiliation on the ballots on election day. But King enjoys peddling the well-worn fable of black candidates who, fearing to campaign in white neighborhoods, rely on their kindly political benefactors in the Democratic Party to provide safe forums to meet with whites. King also ignores campaign finance reality by describing downtrodden blacks unable to raise enough money from the 67 percent black majority in Kinston to defeat candidates supported by the white minority. Without a "D" appearing next to those black candidates' names on election day, King assumes that somehow the entire engine of Democratic Party fundraising is prevented from supporting them. In the end, King's objection letter combines statistical dishonesty, obsolete racial stereotypes, and factual clumsiness, but it achieved the Obama DOJ's goal of protecting Democrats via the expansive use of the civil rights laws.

The DOJ's formal objection to the Kinston referendum sparked considerable anger in the town. But the Kinston City Council—comprising incumbents who owed their offices to the partisan election scheme—refused to challenge the ruling in federal court, where the non-partisan election plan surely would have been approved. In fact, if Kinston had added a constitutional challenge to Section 5 of the Voting Rights Act, the DOJ would probably have capitulated in short order since DOJ leaders would be mortified at having the constitutionality of Section 5 tethered to such a legally flimsy case. Thus, Holder and his minions owe a debt of gratitude to the fierce partisans on the Kinston City Council who brazenly ignored their constituents.

These days, Voting Section bureaucrats have begun openly urging black lawmakers to oppose—or at least not to support—certain election changes. DOJ sources tell me Voting Section management is emphasizing to front line staff the importance of engaging with black and Hispanic officials and plainly explaining that it is unhelp-ful for them to support certain electoral changes. In effect, the bureaucrats are telling minority elected officials, "If you support the plan, it will be harder for us to object when it reaches us." Obama puts forth a vision of a post-racial society with biracial coalitions, but if that vision is sincere, it's strange that he allows his own DOJ to sabotage it so thoroughly.

Harlingen, Texas: Ensuring the Right Race Wins

In May 2009, a few months before the Kinston objection letter was issued, Loretta King and the DOJ engaged in an even more abusive act of Section 5 enforcement, or in this instance, non-enforcement. Less than two months before a scheduled May elec-tion, Harlingen, Texas, adopted changes to its method of electing city commissioners. The new, single-member district lines needed to be pre-cleared under Section 5 before the election could take place. But on the eve of the election, the new lines had not been approved.

Normally, when a change has not received Section 5 approval shortly before an election, the DOJ sues to block it. Federal law is unambiguous on this point—if an election change has not been pre-cleared, it cannot be implemented. This was routine practice under the Bush DOJ, which sued in October 2008 to stop a change in Waller County, Texas, that had not been pre-cleared,[39] and sued again later that month over a similar situation in Calera, Alabama.[40] And even if an election goes forward without DOJ action, the depart-ment can still sue afterward, essentially to overturn the illegal out-come. This means that in Harlingen, the election itself would be a nullity because the new district lines had not been pre-cleared. But in no circumstance, at least no circumstance governed by the rule of law, should the winners of an unapproved election be sworn in—unless of course the rule of law was less important than racial politics.

Like so much in the Obama DOJ, however, in Harlingen these clear and obvious legal steps were jettisoned so as to engineer a corrupt, racially driven outcome. According to multiple DOJ sources with direct knowledge of the matter, when Voting Section lawyers assigned to Harlingen gathered to discuss the matter with King the week before the May election, they recommended filing an action in federal court to enjoin the election. King reportedly made this stunning reply: "I want to wait to see the race of whoever wins the election instead." She was predicating the application of federal law on whether or not a Hispanic won the election. And when the candidate of the right race won, no further action was taken.

King resorted to utter lawlessness in her selective and politicized enforcement of Section 5, which obviously is not structured to sanctify illegal election results whenever the candidate of the favorite race wins. She was using the law as a political cudgel, precisely the sort of thing that could jeopardize the constitutionality of Section 5 if it reaches the United States Supreme Court. This incident should illustrate to the justices that Section 5 is prone to abuse, as if the history of court sanctions against the DOJ wasn't enough.

Resource concerns cannot justify King's command. If they could, then enforcement of Section 5 would degenerate into a simple exercise in watching to see if favored political candidates win elections. Had the Bush administration waited in Waller County until the victors were known before pursuing an enforcement action, it would have been rightfully denounced for corruption. If it had allowed the elections to go forward in Calera and sued only after taking into account the race of the winners, the media would have correctly decried the injustice. Yet this is the precise kind of corruption that has infected the entire Civil Rights Division since Loretta King assumed control of it—and the media could not care less.

Back in Washington: Beware the Red Files

As we have seen, Obama and his backers have engaged in a strange form of political projection, baselessly accusing the Bush Civil Rights Division of the exact kind of malfeasance and bias that have become hallmarks of the division under Obama's presidency. This is evident time and again in the administration of Section 5, which during the Bush years was one of the chief areas critics claimed had become politicized.

For example, in 2003, Voting Section bureaucrats recommended an objection to a mid-decade Texas congressional redistricting, arguing it would dilute the electoral power of blacks and Hispanics. But DOJ political appointees ultimately pre-cleared the plan, sending the *Washington Post* into a front-page frenzy about "allegations from Democratic lawmakers and lawyers that the Texas case provides additional evidence that the [DOJ's] work has been politicized during the Bush administration."[41]

Democrats delved deep into their lexicon of abuse to blast the DOJ decision. Then-House Minority Leader Nancy Pelosi denounced the DOJ's "contemptible politicization,"[42] while House Democratic whip Steny Hoyer conjured vaguely sinister possibilities, declaring that "Americans have every reason to believe there is something darker going on in the Civil Rights Section."[43] Piling on, ranking member of the House Judiciary Committee John Conyers proclaimed, "As I had always feared, the Section 5 process had been compromised at the highest levels of Congress and the Department of Justice.... I will ask Chairman Sensenbrenner to schedule hearings next month to get to the bottom of what is going on within the

Department."[44] Congressman Henry Waxman was predictably incensed. "The reports of political interference in the Civil Rights Division are extraordinarily serious," he intoned. "The right to vote is fundamental to our democracy, yet two reports in recent weeks indicate that political considerations may be overriding the obligation of the Justice Department to protect the voting rights of all Americans."[45]

Eventually the U.S. Supreme Court almost entirely agreed with the Bush political appointees, rejecting wholesale the notion that political gerrymandering in Texas might justify an objection under the Voting Rights Act.[46] Of course, none of the Democratic Cassandras withdrew their accusations, and they have been remarkably quiet as the Obama DOJ has adopted the very tactics they had falsely accused the Bush administration of using in Section 5 enforcement.

To understand the Obama administration's duplicity, it's important to understand how Section 5 enforcement works. DOJ Section 5 regulations give the Assistant Attorney General for Civil Rights the authority to *interpose an objection* to a state law. The regulations, however, do not allow the AAG to *approve* state election changes. As a matter of longstanding practice, the career bureaucrats inside the Voting Section review state submissions. They gather facts, conduct interviews and, if they are satisfied the proposal does not discriminate, approve the plan. Approval comes by a pre-clearance letter purportedly signed by the chief of the Voting Section, but more often than not, by an underling. Submissions that are pre-cleared don't reach up into the political ranks of the department. If the technicians down below, armed with the relevant data, think a proposed voting change is not discriminatory, then the internal presumption is that they are best suited to stamp a submission approved. Only if the technicians, lawyers, and statisticians detect problems justifying an objection do the political appointees get involved.

The exercise of an objection to a submission is a profound power. Such federal oversight is at the farthest frontier of federal power under the Constitution. Thus, it is understandable that the AAG alone, and not the bureaucrats in the Voting Section, has the authority to object to a submission. Voting Section bureaucrats will recommend an objection by producing an objection recommendation memorandum. The AAG remains free, despite the howls of Conyers, Hoyer, Pelosi, and Waxman, to reject or accept the recommendation. But the important point is that internally, the Voting Section is responsible for pre-clearances, while the political appointees are responsible for accepting or rejecting a Voting Section recommendation for an objection.

The Obama DOJ has turned this process upside down. According to sources inside the Voting Section, Deputy Assistant Attorney General Julie Fernandes has implemented a new Section 5 process that shifts massive power to approve state laws into the DOJ's political ranks. It works like this: when a politically important submission comes in, Fernandes or some other Obama appointee now tags it as a "red file"—it is literally placed into a red file so everyone knows this is a state law that keenly interests the Obama political appointees. Red files are treated much differently from other submissions because the staff members know their work is being watched at the highest levels of the department. It also sends a signal to the career technicians that they should be extra aggressive in collecting evidence of discrimination.

Longstanding DOJ practices have been jettisoned when it comes to red files. Instead of the Voting Section technicians deciding to pre-clear the submissions, only the political appointees inside the Civil Rights Division are allowed to pre-clear them. Under every prior administration, complex objection memos were required to support any objection. With red files, up has become down and complex pre-clearance memos are now required to *justify* a pre-clearance. Sources inside the DOJ tell me they have to work as hard for a pre-clearance now as they used to for an objection. This review process is a corrupt, politicized deviation from standard procedures. Politics enter the process the moment the Obama political appointees scan the submission horizon for state laws they want to subject to hyper-scrutiny.

Obviously, states long targeted by the Obama DOJ such as Arizona are justified in fearing the red file process. Sources also tell me every statewide redistricting submission for Congress, state house, and state senate will be stuck in a red file automatically by order of the Obama political appointees. That means redistricting plans in states like Florida, South Carolina, New York, California, Arizona, Georgia, South Dakota, and others will all suffer politicized scrutiny. If this isn't enough reason for states to bypass the DOJ entirely and submit plans directly to the federal court for approval, then nothing is.

The new procedures for red files inject political manipulation into the review of election laws in nearly a third of all the states in the run-up to the 2012 presidential election. It means Obama political appointees will be deciding whether or not certain election laws are effective in states that are home to more than half of the American population. This is exactly the sort of alleged politicization that was vehemently condemned by Democratic politicians, leftwing academics, and the media during the Bush years. But not one peep will be heard from them about red files—unless, of course, a Republican defeats President Obama in 2012 and keeps the red file policy in place. Only then will we hear the familiar cries of protest.

CHAPTER SEVEN

Through the Looking Glass

Absurdity at the Obama Department of Justice

T he Mellon Auditorium sits on Constitution Avenue in Washington, D.C. When it was built, it was the largest government-owned assembly space in the city. President Roosevelt initiated the selective service lottery here in 1940, and the North Atlantic Treaty was signed in the auditorium on April 4, 1949, giving birth to the most powerful military alliance in world history. The structure is described as "among the very finest classical buildings in America," with a "gilded auditorium and lobbies [that] are among the nation's most magnificent interiors."[1] It has served as a spectacular setting for balls, diplomatic events, and lavish formal functions. But on April 27, 2010, the Mellon Auditorium hosted nearly one thousand Justice Department employees for a farce from the other side of the looking glass.

On that day, the Civil Rights Division hosted a "retreat" that included free lunch for every employee and a speech by Eric Holder. The attorney general trumpeted his work transforming the division, even though his Voting Section had hardly filed any litigation in the entire fifteen months of the Obama administration. But nobody really cared—it was time to celebrate. Among the fantastical offerings were "inspirational presentations" and a "review of Division-wide survey and listening tour results." Listening tours were very popular after Obama's inauguration.

The keynote address was delivered by Dr. Freeman A. Hrabowski III, the president of the University of Maryland (Baltimore County), who is known for mixing science with his passion to see people of particular races study science in college. Adopting a speaking style more of a preacher than a professor, he intoned, "Some of us remember when we couldn't have imagined an attorney general that would look like Eric Holder. Would you give him a hand please?" The DOJ audience dutifully cheered. Hrabowski later warned of the rise of Nazism, clumsily using the famous Martin Niemöller quote, "First they came for the communists, then they came for the Jews," to describe the importance of the modern civil rights industry. One employee described the remarks to me as a "WTF moment." But the day would be filled with WTF moments from this taxpayer-funded legal Wonderland.

There were breakout sessions discussing topics such as "emerging areas" in civil rights practice, "outreach to Muslims," and "environmental justice," as well as a session of the "LGBT [lesbian-gay-bisexual-transgender] Working Group." A session on "collaboration opportunities" included speeches on "collaboration with sister agencies," "anti-immigration discrimination," and something called "place based initiatives." These are hardly pressing civil rights issues for most Americans, but like Lewis Carroll's March Hare, many in the Civil Rights Division have "murdered time." To them, it's always 1964, with Jim Crow devising new schemes; and to the green-tinged radicals, it's always 1982, when Shocco Township, North Carolina, was selected as a landfill site, giving birth to the "environmental justice" movement.

No bother that few federal statutes even remotely within the Civil Rights Division's jurisdiction have any connection to these "emerging" areas; such inconveniences matter not to the political leadership. It's all about the crusade, not the laws on the books.

None of this could have surprised anyone familiar with the DOJ's new political leadership. Proudly calling himself a progressive, Assistant Attorney General Tom Perez was characterized by the *Washington Post* as "about as liberal as Democrats get."[2] Perez's top deputy, Samuel Bagenstos, earned his keep by vehemently attacking the Bush Civil Rights Division. Ironically, the Supreme Court later validated the Bush politicos' legal position (and rejected the contrary argument advanced by Bagenstos) on a major voting rights case from 2004, but no apology, needless to say, was forthcoming. When he moved to the Obama DOJ, Bagenstos argued a pleading for the DOJ in federal court in New York that was so poorly written the judge compared it to the work of a *pro se* litigant.

Matt Nosanchuck, a counsel to Perez, took the lead for candidate Obama's outreach to the transgender and homosexual community before arriving in the friendly confines of the Civil Rights Division. He also served as co-counsel in NAACP lawsuits against firearms manufacturers. Another counsel, Jocelyn Samuels, was previously an officer with the National Women's Law Center, one of the most radical "progressive" feminist groups in the country.

Between the breakout sessions at the retreat, outlandish comedy took center stage. Like a campfire program at Cub Scout camp, all the Civil Rights Division's sections participated in a skit contest. For weeks leading up to the retreat, DOJ employees spent work time writing scripts, singing songs, and rehearsing. Despite the festive nature of the skits, all scripts had to be submitted well ahead of time to a designee of the assistant attorney general for approval. The Civil Rights Division leaders couldn't help themselves—their instinct to control extends even to bad community theater.

In all there were twelve skits to fill the day. The Voting Section sang songs about elections. Another section presented a faux TV newscast featuring clips from the TV show *Glee*. Lawyers took the stage to sing, dance, and act out. Even the staff of the assistant attorney general frolicked and sang along with their own production. Only the Criminal Section seemed to push back against the childish absurdity, presenting two opposing lawyers engaged in a closing trial argument. One DOJ employee told me that earning a six-figure salary while watching the skits made him feel such shame, embarrassment, and disgust that he felt physically ill.

Before the night ended, it was announced that no prize would be given for best skit. As part of a trend often seen in elementary schools, all were pronounced winners this day, and all skits received an award. Only the taxpayers, who paid for this absurd waste of time, ended up as losers.

The retreat demonstrates the ideological extremism and jarring unprofessionalism that characterize the nation's top law enforcement agency. Instead of dutifully defending the law, the Obama administration has used the DOJ to impose a fringe political agenda on the American people.

Some Civil Rights Division employees recognize the off-kilter priorities of the place. They roll their eyes at the worst of it and simply carry on, considering themselves trapped in a well-paying Wonderland. I am reminded of the scene when Alice protests to the Cheshire Cat that she doesn't want to associate with mad people. The cat replies, "You can't help that. We're all mad here. I'm mad. You're mad." Alice wonders how the cat could know she was mad. Easy, he says, "You must be, or you wouldn't have come here."

Before the Obama administration, the most fringe elements of the civil rights industry never had complete hold over the levers of power at the Civil Rights Division, not even during the Clinton presidency. Sure, there were plenty of abuses, but the place was never run with the messianic zeal it has now. These kinds of radicals long ago seized control of the academy, where universities have welcomed former DOJ lawyers like Gilda Daniels to teach "critical race studies" and other nonsensical dribble. But for the first time, the cultural, racial, and legal extreme now firmly controls a powerful government agency that maintains massive influence over the economy and many other aspects of American life.

The most effective check against these abuses is an informed citizenry. Americans want civil rights protected, but they don't want militant ideologues trampling upon common sense. In that spirit, this chapter will inform readers about what is really going on far away from the media spotlight at the Civil Rights Division.

Pink Wigs and Stiletto Heels

Americans might be shocked to learn that the Obama DOJ thinks it is a federal civil right for boys to wear stiletto high heels and pink wigs to a public high school. In the Mohawk Central School District near Utica, New York, a 15-year-old male student wanted to come to class dressed as a flamboyant transvestite. Unsurprisingly, other students teased the boy, and the school attempted to enforce a reasonable dress code to maintain classroom order. But in the age of Eric Holder, this became a federal civil rights issue.

The Civil Rights Division intervened in the affair to force the school to allow for child-transvestites. Where in the Constitution might this power be found? What could the legal theory possibly be? What federal right was at stake that could overcome the well established power of schools to enforce order to facilitate learning? The answer, incredibly, is sex discrimination. "Gender non-conforming" behavior has been elevated to a federal civil right under the Obama DOJ's bizarre legal application of Title IX.[3] This is not even within paddling distance of the mainstream. The law was intended to prevent discrimination against women, not against those who fantasize about having a different gender.

The school district was forced to pay the transvestite-child $50,000, pay for counseling services with a psychiatrist specializing in "gay, bisexual and transgender youth issues," hire an expert to review the school's "gender expression" programs, and hire a second expert to conduct annual training on "gender identity and gender expression" discrimination. In short, the DOJ rolled the school district. Obviously, the school district's lawyer, unlearned in the lawless proclivities of the Civil Rights Division, recommended this complete capitulation and settlement terms far beyond what the law required.

How the Amazon Kindle Violates Your Civil Rights

In 2009, Amazon planned a product launch in conjunction with numerous universities that would use the second-generation Kindle as a textbook platform. The launch for the new Kindle, which promised to significantly cut student spending on textbooks, was developing swimmingly until the participating schools received a letter from the Obama Civil Rights Division. The letter explained that the Kindle's talking book function failed to comply with the Americans with Disabilities Act (ADA). Never mind that the closest competit̶o̶r̶ ̶a̶ ̶b̶o̶u̶n̶d̶ ̶f̶ ̶ ̶rmer tree with ink used to make words, had ̶ ̶nctionality, meaning the Kindle was a vast ̶ ̶lternative. The government decided to stick ̶ ̶way, claiming the new Kindle violated the ̶ ̶n buttons to launch the talking capabilities

̶ ̶gone mad could make this argument. If ̶ ̶Bush had known that the ADA would be ̶ ̶oubt he would have signed it into law. But ̶ ̶e these kinds of unintended consequences. ̶ ̶nded me of the fateful compromise secured ̶ ̶ in 1982 to pass amendments to the Voting ̶ ̶e realize that his efforts would usher in an ̶ ̶ndering. The "Dole Amendment" explicitly disavowed any goal of proportional representation—that is, drawing legislative districts to achieve racial outcomes in proportion to the racial percentages in the general population. Dole assumed his amendment would be adequate to prevent this outcome. But proportional representation is precisely what the DOJ considers every time it decides whether or not to bring a lawsuit under the statute. Indeed, every Section 2 case commenced by the Civil Rights Division is preceded by a consideration as to whether the proportion of minority elected officials is the same as the proportion of minorities in the population. The Dole Amendment has become a meaningless scrap of paper. Yet without it, the extraordinary changes to the Voting Rights Act—which allowed for lawsuits to replace electoral systems if, among other reasons, they were not producing enough victories for minority candidates—would have never passed. The civil rights industry got what it wanted. And Bob Dole got tricked.

Fast forward thirty years. After sending the letter announcing the Kindle investigation, the DOJ demanded that the universities stop distributing the new devices as a textbook platform.[4] If the Kindle doesn't have Braille functionality, then nobody should be allowed to use it, Holder's DOJ argued. The universities capitulated, forcing Amazon to halt its product launch and redesign the Kindle to satisfy the whims of a few crusading bureaucrats. The saga could have been lifted straight from the pages of *Atlas Shrugged*—though I doubt any DOJ employees involved in the Kindle action are familiar with the book's plot.

Business groups should carefully note these thuggish DOJ tactics. Yesterday's threat to the Kindle could be tomorrow's threat to any corner of the American economy. Merely listen to Attorney General Eric Holder's own words. On April 25, 2011, he gave a speech to the entire DOJ proclaiming, "The agenda of the Department of Justice is … always boundless."[5] To the contrary, *law* binds bureaucrats. But Holder encouraged them to change the world in their own image: "This is our time. This is our moment … to create a world that reflects our aspirations for future generations."[6] Needless to say, history has demonstrated time and again the extreme danger posed by government employees with utopian visions.

The attack against the Kindle might have been moderated if the process involved attorneys who had experience representing businesses that actually produce goods. Only a group of bureaucrats who have spent their entire careers inside the government or inside the professional civil rights industry could so thoroughly misunderstand economic reality. But the Obama Civil Rights Division is stuffed with lawyers who view American business as a strange, foreign enterprise at best, or more often, as an enemy to be restrained and controlled. Until business groups start to fight back and challenge the misapplications of the law, the bureaucracy will keep finding new ways to expand its power while sucking the life from American ingenuity.

Arizona: The New Alabama

Nowhere is the disconnect between the American people and the Obama DOJ more apparent than in the DOJ's attack on Arizona's law aimed at reducing illegal immigration. On April 23, 2010, Arizona Governor Jan Brewer signed into law the Support Our Law Enforcement and Safe Neighborhoods Act, commonly referred to as S.B. 1070. The law requires Arizona police to attempt to determine a person's immigration status incident to an arrest for a separate crime. Individuals cannot be released from jail until their legal immigration status is confirmed. Risk of flight is an ancient legal basis to deny bail, and S.B. 1070 codified this long tradition through the common-sense recognition that an illegal alien is more likely to flee when facing criminal charges.

Arizona enacted the bill because of the federal government's failure to secure the southern border. In southern portions of Arizona, ranchers live in continuous fear for their lives and property. Arizona rancher Roger Barnett has apprehended on his land more than 12,000 illegal aliens, who leave behind trash and wreck his property. Rob Krentz, another Arizona rancher, lost over $8 million from illegal aliens destroying water pipelines, harming cattle, and breaking down his fences. Then he lost something even more valuable—his life. On March 27, 2010, Krentz was found shot to death along with his dog. In the last radio transmission he made to his brother, Krentz said he was aiding an illegal alien he had found in the desert.[7]

Despite the dire need for the new law, it offended the deepest sensibilities of the civil rights industry and the Civil Rights Division.

The law drew immediate condemnation from Attorney General Holder, who declared on NBC's *Meet The Press*, "I think it has the possibility of leading to racial profiling and putting a wedge between law enforcement and a community that would, in fact, be profiled." Four days later, Holder confessed to the House Judiciary Committee he had never actually read the law he was denouncing.

Notwithstanding the embarrassment, every component of the Civil Rights Division was placed on high alert in an effort to leverage federal power against Arizona. The Special Litigation Section intensified its investigation of Maricopa County Sheriff Joe Arpaio, delivering various ultimatums seeking access to Maricopa jail records. Just forty-nine days after Obama's inauguration, Loretta King had announced that Arpaio was being investigated for adopting English-only policies inside the jails.[8]

The DOJ broadened its assault on Maricopa on August 30, 2010, when it filed a lawsuit against the Maricopa County Community College. The lawsuit alleged that the college required noncitizen job applicants to present documentation to establish their eligibility to work in the United States. Three days after the lawsuit was filed, the Civil Rights Division filed a lawsuit against Sheriff Arpaio seeking to tour his facilities and obtain documents.

The Voting Section also ramped up its monitoring of Arizona elections, particularly in Maricopa County. On August 23, 2010, the DOJ also sent election observers to Apache and Navajo Counties. At the direction of the Voting Section, dozens of federal observers fanned across Arizona to monitor the November 2, 2010 election as well. A pro-amnesty group described the DOJ decision as a success. "We asked our supporters to send a message to the DOJ to send monitors down to Maricopa County, Arizona. Guess what? The Department of Justice responded swiftly, thanks in part to your concern."[9] On March 8, 2011, the DOJ was back again, flooding

Maricopa County with teams of federal election observers to cover municipal elections.

Once again, I am reminded of Alice in Wonderland. The Red Queen demanded of Alice, "What's one and one and one and one and one and one and one and one and one and one?" Alice couldn't answer. She had lost count. Likewise, the DOJ's rapid fire attack on Arizona is meant to wear Arizona and its people down and force them to submit. It's also designed to send a message to other states and counties that might pass laws against illegal immigration.

Before DOJ political appointees decided to monitor Arizona elections, they would have read and approved "election coverage memoranda." Submitted by DOJ attorneys, these election coverage memoranda undoubtedly referred to S.B. 1070. Of course, that law has nothing to do with elections. But when a DOJ attorney seeks approval from the political appointees to do election coverage, it never hurts to repeat the party line. Researchers or groups opposing illegal immigration would no doubt find a treasure trove of golden nuggets if they request these memos through a Freedom of Information Act submission—that is, assuming the DOJ complied.

One related memorandum has already surfaced. In 2002, the DOJ's Office of Legal Counsel (OLC) concluded that police officers plainly have the "inherent power" to detain illegal aliens.[10] This is significant because the OLC acts as the DOJ's internal lawyer, and its views are binding as internal legal policy. Cecillia Wang of the ACLU Immigrants' Rights Project has called for the policy to be withdrawn, which would be an extraordinary step that the DOJ may be contemplating. Wang told the *Washington Post*, "The fact that this memo is lurking out there gives cover and comfort to people in Arizona and other states who want to pass these overbroad and extraordinary anti-immigration measures."[11]

Holder and his minions show no signs of relenting. Indeed, on April 26, 2011, the DOJ hosted training sessions on battling "anti-immigrant" laws through the auspices of the "National Origin Working Group," an ad hoc group of attorneys from different DOJ agencies, including the Civil Rights Division. At the sessions, Monica Ramirez described how the Civil Rights Division is actively "monitoring anti-immigrant" laws. This is a common and deliberate distortion of language within the DOJ, since there are no "anti-immigrant laws," just anti-*illegal* immigrant laws. The civil rights industry conveniently jettisons the concept of legality or illegality from its language. Unsurprisingly, before she joined the DOJ, Ramirez worked at the ACLU Immigrants' Rights Project, the same outfit that sued Arizona.

In case there was any doubt over the Civil Rights Division's commitment to this issue, around a year after filing suit against Arizona, the division sued the state of Alabama over a law aimed at stemming illegal immigration. The message is clear: it is futile to resist illegal immigration into your state, so don't even try.

As Arizona Goes, So Goes the Nation

The DOJ's efforts to protect illegal aliens extend far beyond Arizona and Alabama. Time after time, I saw the department target localities with election law investigations merely because they had adopted policies to try to address illegal immigration.

Consider, for example, Kane County, Illinois, which had the audacity to pass a non-binding ordinance declaring English as the official language and to consider an ordinance to ban employers from hiring illegal aliens. In response, teams of DOJ lawyers descended on the county to monitor elections, interview witnesses, threaten litigation, and ultimately file suit against the county.[12] Of course, Kane capitulated in the mistaken belief that the DOJ can't be beaten. The memorandum of agreement requires the county to maintain a Hispanic "advisory group," implement publicity programs invariably purchased in Spanish media, and to concede the feds' power to place observers in Kane to monitor future elections.

It was only later that the DOJ's creepy motives in attacking Kane were exposed. In an email, the Voting Section manager who pushed the case wrote, "Please join me in congratulating the Kane County team.... One of the towns in Kane County, Carpentersville, was at the heart of our lawsuit and during our investigation was spotlighted in the *New York Times Magazine* regarding its anti-immigrant ordinance and *attitudes*" (emphasis added). Apparently, the county's residents had to be punished for their thought crime of harboring the wrong attitudes about illegal immigration.

Farmers Branch, Texas, was next in line. This Dallas suburb adopted an ordinance to reduce illegal immigration, and as day follows night, so too appeared DOJ investigators. Of course, they weren't investigating immigration matters, for they do not have authority to enforce immigration-related laws. But their ideological quiver was not empty—voting laws would do.

It is important to note these corrupt investigations were not launched because of complaints from voters or from anyone involved in the election process. They were purely efforts to please Hispanic activist groups like MALDEF and LULAC. Regarding Farmers Branch, a Voting Section official wrote that he simply "considered anti-immigrant statutes and their impact on Hispanic voters" as the basis for his investigation. Teams of lawyers were sent to monitor elections in Farmers Branch, over and over again.

After passing an ordinance against illegal immigration, Prince William County, Virginia, became the next target of the DOJ witch hunt. This time, however, there was absolutely no nexus to any voting law enforced by the Voting Section. Not to worry—after some employees pressed for the legal basis for DOJ scrutiny, a manager replied in an email I obtained that there "has been considerable public protest over their anti-immigration ordinance, and feelings are running high there, a la Farmers Branch. The sentiment may spill over into the election process." Not one bit of evidence actually indicated anything was about to "spill over into the election process," but offended "feelings" and "sentiments" were enough for the DOJ to concoct a legal predicate to investigate a county that had not broken a single law enforced by the investigators. Noting the sticky problem, one DOJ staffer suggested the campaign against immigration ordinances be limited to those places actually covered by Section 203 of the Voting Rights Act. But the lawless quest against Prince William County continued unabated.

The absorption of the Civil Rights Division into the open borders movement is perhaps unsurprising in light of the division's current leadership. For example, Assistant Attorney General Tom Perez is a long-time advocate for illegal aliens who served as president of *Casa de Maryland*, a radical open borders advocacy organization that encourages illegal aliens not to speak with the police and urges local governments not to enforce federal fugitive warrants against them. He also fought to mandate that Mexican identification be recognized as valid photo ID in the United States, even though the documents are so rife with fraud that twenty-two of Mexico's thirty-two states and districts refuse to recognize the documents.

Likewise, two Voting Section managers have given multiple presentations to *Consejo de Federaciones Mexicanas en Norteamérica* (COFEM), a group dedicated to helping illegal aliens thwart U.S. immigration laws. Funded by the Mexican government, the organization promotes cultural loyalty to Mexico among Mexicans living inside the United States and provides Mexican social studies textbooks to U.S. schools with large illegal alien populations. Voting Section staffers were even allowed to take the day off work to attend a COFEM rally in Washington, D.C.

These open borders radicals interpret immigration policy purely through the lens of race. In their minds, racial animus is the only explanation why towns such as Farmers Branch and Carpentersville enacted their ordinances. It never occurs to the crusaders that in a nation built on the rule of law, many people may oppose rampant law-breaking regardless of any racial factors.

Police Officers in the Crosshairs

Shortly after Eric Holder became attorney general, the Civil Rights Division hired Jonathan Smith to head its Special Litigation Section, the unit that generally investigates police departments and other law enforcement agencies accused of violating individuals' constitutional rights. Smith is ideally suited for such an assignment in the Obama administration, having previously served as executive director of three leftwing advocacy organizations—the Legal Aid Society of the District of Columbia, the Public Justice Center, and the District of Columbia Prisoners' Legal Services Project. Smith has spent his entire career badgering prison guards and the police, so who better to put in charge of the DOJ's work in this area?

The DOJ has a long history of suing police departments. A flag-ship case was brought in the 1990s against the Los Angeles Police Department when Eric Holder was the deputy attorney general. The 93-page consent decree, so lengthy and onerous that it has a table of contents, requires federal micromanagement of nearly every aspect of LAPD operations.[13] The most dangerous part of the decree requires police officers assigned to the gang and narcotics unit to disclose their personal finances and submit to random audits, a stipulation that has discouraged many officers from serving on these units. As a result, gang units vanished in places like Watts and the 77th Street Division of the LAPD.

The paperwork requirements form a less dramatic but equally burdensome part of the decree. The LAPD has spent $100 million complying with these provisions. Racial data have to be collected every time a police officer stops someone for any reason. Over 300 police officers were pulled off the street to work on compliance issues. They faced dozens of reporting deadlines from a federal monitor who was appointed to oversee LAPD operations.

The investigation and lawsuit against the LAPD was managed and approved by Steve Rosenbaum, the same attorney who helped to get the New Black Panther case dismissed. He is so proud of the draconian remedy in the case that he has a large, framed newspaper article about it hanging on his office wall.

The decree was set to expire in 2011. But in November 2010, the Civil Rights Division sent a letter warning that the LAPD had done an insufficient job eradicating racial profiling. According to the letter, the DOJ had uncovered a "perception and attitude of some LAPD officers on the street" that suggested "a culture that is inimical to race-neutral policing."[14] Showing some amusing hypocrisy in light of its racially motivated dismissal of the Panther case, the DOJ's threatening missive claimed the LAPD had failed to comply with the requirements of the ten-year-old consent decree and could now be subject to years of additional oversight.

What was the basis for this allegation of systemic racism inside the LAPD? A single conversation in which two police officers were unknowingly recorded speaking with a supervisor. When told they had been accused of stopping a motorist because of his race—a common allegation throughout the country—one police officer replied, "So what?" The second officer said he "couldn't do his job without racially profiling."

These comments may not have put the LAPD in the best light. But as Heather MacDonald has noted, the department can hardly be accused of ignoring accusations of racial profiling. She reported,

> A complainant can outright admit making up the profiling charge in retaliation for being arrested, and the LAPD's special profiling investigation body, the Constitutional Policing Unit, will continue diligently poring over his complaint as if it had been made in good faith. After the department logs a whopping average of 100 hours on each complaint, devoting more resources to these knee-jerk accusations than to any other kind of alleged officer misbehavior, the LAPD's civilian inspector general will audit the department's work with a two-part, 60-question matrix, subjecting claims made by arresting officers to a reflexive skepticism unmoored from reality.[15]

Yet based on a single conversation between a few officers, the Civil Rights Division claimed that one of the nation's largest police departments had a systemic problem on an issue that it had already spent one hundred million dollars to address. Complaints like that should not get out of the section, much less be approved by political leadership—unless, of course, the political leadership has priorities other than ensuring the nation's law enforcement capabilities.

And there's the rub. Assistant Attorney General Tom Perez has described civil rights industry advocacy groups such as the ACLU and NAACP as the "eyes and ears" of the division.[16] (Helpfully for Perez, these groups are also the near-exclusive source for the division's hiring pool.) But while these outside groups might be the eyes and ears, when it comes to shaking down institutions such as the LAPD, the DOJ is the muscle.

To the LAPD, the DOJ's trap must have sounded like the Red Queen: "The rule is, jam tomorrow and jam yesterday—but never jam today." When Alice objects that "it must sometimes come to jam today," the Queen retorts, "No, it can't. It's jam every other day: today isn't any other day, you know." After a decade of federal oversight, with millions of dollars spent to comply with the consent decree, the LAPD learned that a single tape recorded conversation, to the bureaucrats at DOJ, means today isn't any other day, and may well never be.

A stable of academics serving as paid consultants help to fuel the DOJ's fixation on racial profiling by the police. One such consultant, Dr. Jack McDevitt of Northeastern University, heads the Institute on Race and Justice (IRJ). Past collaborators with the IRJ include Angela Davis, a former member of both the Communist Party USA and the original Black Panther Party. The IRJ receives at least $440,448 in DOJ funds to teach department lawyers about racial profiling by police departments. But the IRJ's reports on this issue have another deep pocketed benefactor—George Soros and his Open Society Institute.[17] Soros sponsored the IRJ's project "Confronting Racial Profiling in the 21st Century: Implications for Racial Justice," the very same work that IRJ is doing for the DOJ. Thus, police departments are subjected not only to DOJ muscle, but DOJ muscle with the financial backing of George Soros.

School Discipline Is Racially Discriminatory

In every American community, students are expected to behave in school. If a student breaks the rules—such as disrupting a classroom, insulting a teacher, or fighting—who would question that school officials should punish the student? Such simple truths are part of the American experience. But to Eric Holder's Civil Rights Division, these bedrock principles are evidence of racial discrimination.

The DOJ's reasoning goes like this: if minorities face school discipline at rates greater than their overall percentage in the population, then the school is engaging in racial discrimination. As Civil Rights chief Tom Perez explained, "Black boys account for 9 percent of the nation's student population, but comprise 24 percent of students suspended out of school and 30 percent of students expelled."[18] This preposterous racial bean-counting is an affront to the very concept of individual responsibility.

In January 2011, Perez announced that the DOJ would use a "disparate impact" analysis on school discipline cases to determine whether discipline policies were racially discriminatory. Thus, if blacks were disciplined in higher percentages than their share of the population, the DOJ would bring a lawsuit to stop the discipline policy. The new policy was on display at a DOJ conference on September 27 and 28, 2010, entitled "Civil Rights and School Discipline: Addressing Disparities to Ensure Educational Opportunity." Attorney General Holder addressed the gathering and sought to "better understand the causes, and most effectively remedy the consequences, of disparities in student discipline."[19] Perez then complained that minority "students are being handed Draconian punishments for things like school uniform violations, schoolyard fights and subjective violations, such as disrespect and insubordination."[20]

Some might argue American schools have already allowed far too much disrespect and insubordination among students. That Tom Perez gives quarter for these acts illustrates the cultural demographic he and his fellow Obama political appointees seek to protect—the disrespectful and insubordinate. Once political leaders are excusing bad behavior on racial grounds, it isn't much of a leap to take a blasé attitude toward uniformed New Black Panthers stalking the polls. Increasingly, revered institutions are no longer upholding American values—they're actively destroying them.

In Defense of Failure

Defenders of race-based employment preferences typically claim they "don't support quotas." This is a rhetorical trick employed by the civil rights industry and their political backers, who understand that racial preferences are wildly unpopular in the nation at large. But don't let the rhetoric fool you—the racialist camp remains committed to hiring employees based on the color of their skin.

This abiding commitment to race preferences was brazenly displayed in the DOJ's attack on police and fire departments that use entrance exams in hiring decisions. The department sued numerous police or fire departments where black applicants failed the entrance exams at higher rates than white or Hispanic applicants. The remedy sought by the DOJ requires the police and fire departments to hire black employees who had lower test scores than their white counterparts.

Consider the New York City Fire Department. In 2007, the DOJ joined a decade-old case filed by three failed fire department applicants. After Obama's inauguration, the case took a radical turn when the DOJ demanded that full-time jobs be doled out to black firefighters who outright failed the entrance exam and had displayed a shocking lack of knowledge of basic fire safety. Unsurprisingly, this remedy was pursued by Loretta King, who penned a memorandum to the federal court on September 30, 2010, mandating that NYFD hiring policy introduce "proportional" quotas—that is, hiring that is "representative" of the overall racial population.

Few Americans understand the technical components of employment discrimination law, such as disparate impact theory and regression analysis. As a result, with little public or media scrutiny, Loretta King and other DOJ radicals have used these extremist decrees to create a litigation-based system of racial spoils. To the extent that they're publicly defended at all, these policies are touted as part of the noble, on-going effort to escape America's unjust past. People who notice and understand these cases often remain silent out of fear of being called racist.

Thankfully, that situation is slowly changing. Before the internet and the rise of citizen journalism, the executive branch could hide waste, fraud, and abuse from public scrutiny. The millions of dollars in fines and sanctions imposed against DOJ lawyers like Nancy Sardeson and Loretta King would never see the light of day. But things are different now. Although the mainstream media is still loath to report on the malfeasance of a Democratic administration, Americans can increasingly turn to citizen journalists, internet news sites, and Fox News to learn what's really happening. With these outlets drawing attention to the DOJ's outrageously unfair and unjust policies and the toll they take on public safety, public tolerance for these decrees is beginning to wear thin.

Public opinion may well be the only check against the racialist abuses of the Civil Rights Division. After all, the opinions of the United States Supreme Court don't seem to matter. Consider the recent landmark civil rights ruling in *Ricci v. DeStefano*. In this case, White and Hispanic firefighters who had passed a promotional exam in New Haven, Connecticut, sued the city after it denied them promotions due to its system of race-based hiring preferences. In repudiating the city's actions and ordering that the firefighters be promoted, the Supreme Court emphatically underscored that Title VII of the Civil Rights Act demands evenhanded law enforcement. Unsurprisingly, the Obama administration took a contrary position and submitted a brief defending the city's actions. The brief was authored by some of our familiar friends, including Loretta King and Steven Rosenbaum.[21]

After being thrashed by the Supreme Court in *Ricci*, Assistant Attorney General Tom Perez reacted by defiantly announcing that the division will continue bringing aggressive disparate impact cases. The law is little more than a distraction for the Civil Rights Division bureaucrats who feel they have a higher moral calling. In fact, just months after *Ricci* was decided, the Civil Rights Division sued the state of New Jersey. The offense? Administering police officer applicant tests that blacks pass 73 percent of the time and whites pass 89 percent of the time. [22]

In Dayton, Ohio, the DOJ took an even more radical position, demanding the city hire black police officer applicants who, as was the case with the New York firefighters, actually failed the test. Prior to the DOJ's intervention, Dayton had been hiring applicants who received a "D" score on the entrance test, namely 66 percent correct. But because not enough blacks were being offered jobs even with this barely passing grade, the Civil Rights Division demanded that the city hire black applicants who failed. This was too much even for the local NAACP, whose president, Derrick Foward, declared, "The NAACP does not support individuals failing a test and then having the opportunity to be gainfully employed."[23]

But no criticism seems to faze the DOJ. Unbowed, it still insists that police and fire departments cannot use competency exams that might result in a "disparate impact" against black applicants. These departments are forced to choose between hiring unqualified candidates and risking a DOJ lawsuit. This is just the sort of justice dispensed by the Red Queen: "Either you or your head must be off! Take your choice!"

The Unshakeable Right to a Paid Vacation in Mecca

Safoorah Khan was a math lab instructor in the Berkeley School District just outside Chicago. She had been on the job just nine months when she asked the school district superintendent for three weeks off in December 2008 to go on a Muslim pilgrimage to Mecca, Saudi Arabia.

Her timing was terrible. Khan's trip was planned for the final days of the semester when teachers are expected to administer tests and compile grades. She was the only teacher who taught her subject in the school, which understandably denied her request to vanish from her job for three weeks. But this was a mere inconvenience for Khan, who resigned her job and went to Saudi Arabia anyway. One would think that would have ended the matter. But to the Civil Rights Division, it was just the beginning.

Sensing anti-Muslim discrimination, the Employment Litigation Section compiled a line-up of attorneys on the case that reads like a Who's Who of the radical Left. Leading the team is Aaron Schuham, a prominent gay activist and the former legislative director for Americans United for Separation of Church and State, a militant atheist group. One of the line attorneys working with Schuham on the case is Varda Hussain who, before coming to the DOJ, spent hundreds of hours working pro bono to help Egyptian terrorists held at Gitmo. Now, there is nothing inherently unethical about taking on such representation, but it can give a good indication of a lawyer's worldview. As former DOJ lawyer Andy McCarthy has written, representing terrorists "doesn't make any lawyer unfit to serve. It does, however, show us the fault line in the defining debate of our lifetime, the debate about what type of society we shall have. And that political context makes everyone's record fair game. If lawyers choose to volunteer their services to the enemy in wartime, they are on the wrong side of that fault line, and no one should feel reluctant to say so."[24]

The other line attorney on the case is Raheemah Abdulaleem. She too is active in Islamic causes outside of her DOJ duties, including involvement with the Women's Islamic Initiative in Spirituality and Equality, a quasi-feminist Islamic group.[25] And finally, no controversial Civil Rights Division case would be complete without the obligatory appearance of Loretta King, the Queen of Justice Wonderland.

Former Attorney General Michael Mukasey, a former federal judge and one of the most distinguished attorneys in the country, told the *Washington Post* that the lawsuit exhibited "very dubious judgment" and was "a real legal reach." He added that "the upper reaches of the Justice Department should be calling people to account for this."[26] Mukasey is right. Courts have never interpreted the law to require an accommodation anywhere near nineteen days. Three days of leave to accommodate a religious event is at the outer limits of the jurisprudence.

Nevertheless, Assistant Attorney General Tom Perez was out in front defending the decision to sue, demonstrating again that from root to branch, the Obama DOJ is filled with crusaders who care less about what the law says and more about advancing a political cause. Without specifying whether he thought the request was reasonable, Perez described Khan's plea for three weeks' leave as "a profoundly personal request by a person of faith." He then likened the lawsuit, which is still being litigated, to defending "the religious liberty that our forefathers came to this country for."

Actually, it's not even close. The religious liberty of our forefathers was the liberty to worship freely without being executed, jailed, or excessively taxed. They sought freedom from government intervention in matters of conscience. They did not seek something for nothing. They did not flee the bloodshed of Europe's religious wars to seek the right to disappear for weeks at a time while still enjoying full pay and benefits. They sought freedom—period. With his comments, Perez insulted the brave history of our forefathers and the experience of legions of immigrants who set off for America to escape religious persecution.

I met several devout Catholics during my time at the DOJ. In the wake of this latest embarrassment, I would now encourage them, before Lent in 2012, to request a three-week leave of absence that doesn't burn up a minute of annual leave. Send your request to Eric Holder. Tell the attorney general you wish first to visit Krakow's Divine Mercy Shrine, then the Shrine of the Black Madonna of Czestochowa, and then go off to Rome for Good Friday Stations of the Cross followed by a visit to St. Peter's Square for Easter services with the pope. Explain to General Holder that it is "a profoundly personal request by a person of faith." You might even enclose a copy of the complaint in *United States v. Berkeley School District* in your request.

But don't book your plane tickets just yet. You see, in this DOJ, some religions are more equal than others.

CHAPTER EIGHT

★ ★ ★

Ending Injustice

By now, it should be clear that what happens inside parts of the Department of Justice is not what lawyers, judges, and the public presume. The department is predominantly populated by worthy professionals, but politics, deceit, misconduct, and bias infest some of its activities, particularly in the Civil Rights Division. This is a long-standing problem that has grown exponentially under the Obama administration.

Because of the division's hostility to race-neutral enforcement of the Voting Rights Act, widespread electoral lawlessness was allowed to fester for years in Noxubee County, Mississippi, while the New Black Panther Party got away with blatant voter intimidation in Philadelphia. Meanwhile, institutional ambivalence toward military voters led to tens of thousands of U.S. service members being disenfranchised in 2010. A recurrence of these types of incidents in the 2012 elections would be an outrage, but an entirely unsurprising one.

In light of the Obama DOJ's unshakable commitment to a racialist agenda, there is little we can do now to stem its abuses aside from closely monitoring its activities and spreading the word about every new instance of misconduct. But it is not too early to prepare a plan for overhauling the department if a new administration were to gain power after the next election.

The next Republican administration cannot repeat its predecessors' mistakes in its management of the Civil Rights Division. During most of the Bush I and Bush II presidencies, the division's political leadership either deployed a defensive strategy or outright surrendered to bad policies. The guiding philosophy was "stay out of the news." Instead of countering the civil rights industry by articulating a competing vision of civil rights enforcement, GOP administrations tended to adopt little bits of bad ideas. Timidly, they abandoned political battles at the earliest signs of controversy and allowed the radicals to set the agenda, to the detriment of the American people.

Consider the role of federal election observers during presidential elections. Going back to the Clinton years, federal criminal prosecutors were routinely chosen among hundreds of other DOJ volunteers to man the polls as election observers. When nearly a thousand federal employees are needed, it makes perfect sense to tap experienced criminal prosecutors from across the DOJ. But people like Kristen Clarke at the NAACP opposed the presence of criminal prosecutors inside the polls. Why? Because in her mind, minority voters would somehow sense they were criminal prosecutors and would fear going to the polls.

Rejecting this nonsense, the Clinton and Bush DOJs continued to deploy these experienced lawyers to the polls. But in 2008, with

Barack Obama on the ballot, Clarke and her allies in the civil rights industry undertook a major campaign to get these lawyers removed from voting precincts—and the Bush administration complied. You can be sure the Obama administration won't be changing the policy. Indeed, the activists who agitated over the issue are now running the Civil Rights Division.

This capitulation, along with many others, stemmed from a management philosophy that sought first and foremost to avoid controversy. Had the Bush administration publicly rejected the preposterous demands of Clarke and her small band of professional activists, it would have earned strong support from the American people, including from independents and moderate Democrats who tend to have little patience for race-baiting schemes. Americans overwhelmingly support equal enforcement of civil rights laws and fair play. They want employment discrimination laws that don't require police departments to hire applicants who failed the entrance exam. They don't want the launch of an Amazon Kindle to be blocked simply because it does not employ Braille buttons. They don't want to see a heckler's veto triumph because of the cowardice of our political leaders.

The next Republican administration must understand that although the civil rights industry is loud, and although its accusations receive a lot of attention in the media, the modern movement itself is thinly populated and totally isolated from mainstream America. Its absurd demands should be openly repudiated, not indulged out of a misguided fear of garnering bad publicity.

A future Republican administration must unreservedly proclaim its commitment to race-neutral law enforcement. Because the vast majority of Americans support this approach, the only cost will be listening to the reflexive clang and gong of racialist groups. As long as the new vision is clearly articulated and firmly rooted in the core principles of equality and the rule of law, defying the civil rights industry will be a net positive, not a political liability.

Of course, the Obama administration also pays fealty to race-neutral law enforcement, but its proclamations are thoroughly insincere. That's why public declarations are not enough—the next administration must implement its vision through concrete policies. Some of the most useful actions it can take to advance race-neutral law enforcement are described below.

Stop Enforcing the Law Unequally

The most obvious beneficial reform is for the DOJ to stop enforcing the law unequally. The department must be willing to investigate and initiate lawsuits against people who break civil rights laws whether they are black, white, Asian, Hispanic, Christian, Muslim, or Jewish. This is particularly true in the Civil Rights Division. Including *all* Americans in the protections of civil rights statutes is essential to restoring the rule of law and guaranteeing equal protection to everyone.

This will not be easy. Every tendency of the career bureaucrats inside the Civil Rights Division will work against this change. When complaints of wrongdoing by a racial minority come into the various sections, there is a strong chance, particularly in a Republican administration, that DOJ lawyers will keep them from reaching DOJ officials who might be sympathetic. After all, hiding the ball is a classic bureaucratic tactic. That is why the next administration must have absolute confidence that the division's section chiefs can be trusted to adequately investigate complaints and keep the political leadership apprised of the progress. Regrettably, most of the current chiefs do not satisfy this requirement. Indeed, some of them are the most vociferous opponents of enforcing the law equally. The section chiefs must be made to understand that they do not set policy.

Instituting race-neutral law enforcement will entail numerous significant changes. For example, a new administration can begin to review submissions made under Section 5 of the Voting Rights Act in such a way as to protect all minorities regardless of race—an interpretation rejected by the Obama administration. Such a change would require political courage, for it will draw howls of outrage from the civil rights industry. However, the American people will roundly support the move if it is explained in straight-forward terms of using Section 5 to protect all Americans.

Find Political Appointees Who Understand the Civil Rights Industry

It would be a grave mistake for the next administration simply to choose DOJ political appointees based on prior experience at the department or on Capitol Hill. The chief qualification to become a political appointee to the Civil Rights Division should not be a Washington insider's resume. Instead, there should be two essential qualifications.

First and foremost, a political appointee should know how to play offense on civil rights issues and not merely adhere to the tried and failed defensive civil rights playbook. Republican administrations have generally tried to keep these issues under wraps and adopt a Democrat-lite civil rights program. Political appointees must discard this approach and seize the many existing opportunities to advance a new, robust, and creative civil rights agenda. They must know how to articulate and communicate a vision that rejects utterly the racialist underpinnings of the civil rights industry. Crucially, when their actions draw the inevitable opprobrium of the civil rights industry, political appointees must never hesitate to take their vision or their policies directly to the American people.

Developing and advancing this vision requires expertise in civil rights issues. To find DOJ political appointees with the right experience and the right abilities, the GOP leadership must end its historical detachment from the brightest, most forward thinking conservative civil rights experts. People who have served on the U.S. Commission on Civil Rights, for example, will have a smaller learning curve at the DOJ than someone, say, whose main experience is serving on a Capitol Hill committee or in a big law firm.

Second, any new political appointees must recognize that the bureaucracy will try to impede any policies that contradict existing civil rights orthodoxy. Political appointees will have to work overtime to ensure that every case cited by a lawyer-bureaucrat really says what is purported, every fact claimed by a bureaucrat really is true, and every hurdle a bureaucrat claims is hindering the new administration's agenda really exists. When I worked at the Voting Section, on numerous occasions I was asked to double check case law descriptions of long-time DOJ lawyers and found they had played fast and loose with the actual language of the case. Past appointees have been burned repeatedly by placing undue faith in the career managers.

This isn't to say civil servants in the Civil Rights Division are all dishonest. But many, blinded by their ideological fervor, regrettably are. Political appointees must understand they will face near-universal hostility from almost every corner of the career ranks, even if some employees can disguise it well. Skepticism will be the only way to advance the administration's agenda.

As for the hiring of attorneys, one simple change would vastly improve the division's work. Recall that former Voting Section chief

Chris Coates was told by then-Acting Assistant Attorney General Loretta King to stop asking attorney applicants if they could enforce the law equally, regardless of the race of the victim. This opened the gates to the flood of radical attorneys who have joined the Civil Rights Division under Holder's leadership. Reversing King's order should be a top priority of a future Republican attorney general. Every new attorney at the division should be required to unequivocally support equal enforcement of the law, regardless of the victim's race. The attorneys hired by King and her successor should, as a condition of their continued employment, be required to undergo extensive professional training about this issue.

Clamp Down on Politics

Assistant Attorney General for Administration Lee Lofthus issued a memo in 2007 prohibiting certain DOJ employees—including the career members of the Senior Executive Service, FBI, National Security Division, Administrative Law judges, and certain employees in the Criminal Division—from engaging in political activities. A common-sense measure to prevent the appearance of bias in the conduct of employees' duties, this restriction should be expanded by the next administration to apply to attorneys in the Office of Professional Responsibility, Office of the Inspector General, and the Voting and Criminal Sections of the Civil Rights Division.

The *Wall Street Journal* has reported that numerous DOJ lawyers responsible for managing the 2008 election were Obama financial donors. "According to Federal Election Commission data, James Walsh, an attorney in the Civil Rights Division, has donated at least $300 to Mr. Obama. His boss, Mark Kappelhoff, has given $2,250— nearly the maximum. John Russ, also in Civil Rights, gave at least $600 to Mr. Obama," the paper noted.[1] What the *Journal* did not report is how central these individuals were to the DOJ's oversight of the 2008 election.

Consider John Russ, who coordinated all the election observer coverage across the United States from within the Voting Section. He was intimately involved with decisions as to where federal observers would be deployed and for what reasons. He saw every election coverage memo and could suggest changes—suggestions that carry enormous weight with newer, less experienced attorneys. None of this implies Russ did anything improper, but campaign contributions by Voting Section employees can easily create an *appearance* of impropriety to the American public. Russ has since been promoted and will be closely involved in the DOJ's 2012 election activities.

Here's a similar example: Mark Kappelhoff, who nearly maxed out his contributions to Obama, was the head of the Criminal Section inside the Civil Rights Division during the 2008 election. One could easily forgive a person for lacking confidence in his neutrality. Kappelhoff, who according to Chris Coates was worried that the Ike Brown case would upset civil rights groups, had been a strong proponent of stretching the meaning of 18 U.S.C. § 241 to include a criminal prosecution against James Tobin and other Republican phone bankers in New Hampshire. The statute involves conspiracies to deprive citizens of civil rights, and to Kappelhoff, that included making phone calls to help Republican candidates. Kappelhoff was a zealous salesman of this flimsy legal theory before several courts and a jury embarrassingly quashed it.

Eventually the First Circuit Court of Appeals found that the statute the DOJ used to prosecute Tobin was not even "a close fit" to his behavior. After tossing out the conviction, DOJ lawyers re-indicted Tobin, this time for lying to federal prosecutors, but the federal court dismissed the charges as a vindictive prosecution.[2]

The New Hampshire Republican Party, however, was nearly bank-rupted by the case.[3] It was left with only $736 in the bank after the DOJ carnage, a mere third of Kappelhoff's generous contributions to the Obama campaign.

The Criminal Section managed by Kappelhoff has powerful jurisdiction over American elections. After the 2008 election, Kap-pelhoff was immediately rewarded with a temporary political post inside the Civil Rights Division—the number two official in the entire Division—before returning to the "career" ranks. During his brief period of political elevation, he played a role in the dismissal of the New Black Panther case.

The ban on political involvement should also apply to the DOJ's internal ethical watchdogs—that is, employees of the Inspector General's Office and the Office of Professional Responsibility (OPR). In recent years these two units have increasingly become involved in politically sensitive investigations, including a probe of the dis-missal of the Panther case and an inquiry into reported opposition to race-neutral law enforcement in the Civil Rights Division.

The facial defects in the OPR report on the Panther case show that the office must be dramatically reformed, if not abolished alto-gether. One only needs to look at the OPR's initial appointment of Mary Aubry to investigate the case. As detailed in chapter five, Aubry was a significant Democratic donor and had given money to Obama's campaign and victory fund. It was impossible to believe she would conduct an unbiased investigation of a case that was potentially explosive to the recipients of her political largess.

That was far from the only sign of bias among the OPR and Inspector General staff, as described below. Reports from these units have continually echoed campaign themes from Democratic presi-dential candidates and, in fact, became central themes of Obama's candidacy.[4] The work of these units, along with the activities of the

Civil Rights Division's Voting and Criminal Sections, arguably have the most political significance of all the DOJ's agencies. How their employees have escaped the DOJ's prohibition on political involvement is a mystery. That regulation should be applied to them on the first day a new, Republican attorney general is sworn in.

Reward Performance, Not Ideology

Few citizens are aware that cash awards from $1,500 to $3,500 are distributed to DOJ employees every year. Performance payments for government employees are generally a good thing, but at the DOJ, they are sometimes used to reward ideological reliability, not accomplishment. The next administration could improve the award process by making a simple change: don't give cash awards to attorneys when they lose a case, except in truly exceptional circumstances.

Consider the case of Lisa Stark, an attorney in the Appellate Section of the Civil Rights Division. In 2009, Stark received a cash "special commendation award" for her work in the human trafficking case *United States v. Cha*. The government's appeal argued that the trial court had improperly suppressed evidence that supported the United States—the police had conducted a twenty-six-hour warrantless search of the Chas' residence, and Stark was defending the use of evidence obtained in the search. The federal court of appeals ultimately rejected Stark's appeal, but not before the DOJ gave her a cash award for her work on the case. The awards ceremony booklet, which I still possess, commended Stark's "tireless efforts" to convince the Solicitor General's office to file the appeal, describing the solicitor general as a "skeptic" of Stark's argument. The DOJ apparently never considered the possibility that the solicitor general was right to be skeptical of Stark's argument, or that his skepticism would be shared by the federal court of appeals.[5]

The real reason Stark was rewarded even before the court ruled on her case was because of her politics. She had been a vocal critic of the Bush-era DOJ leadership and had made sizable contributions to the Obama campaign. She was recommended for the reward by appellate Section chief Diana Flynn (formerly known as David Flynn until he began the process of becoming a transsexual and started dressing as a woman), who was also an Obama contributor. Since the DOJ gives out its awards every October, the 2009 awards ceremony that recognized Stark was the first opportunity for the incoming Holder DOJ to reward its friends, even if the courts had yet to decide the merits of their work. If the next administration makes the one, simple change of no longer giving awards to attorneys who lose their cases, it will significantly boost the DOJ's credibility.

Disband the Civil Rights Division's Policy Section

Soon after taking office, the Obama DOJ concocted a scheme designed to burden any future Republican attorney general—it created a Civil Rights Division office called the Policy and Strategy Section whose role is to develop division policy. This mirrors precisely the role of the staff to the assistant attorney general; even the new office's name indicates its duplication of AAG responsibilities ("policy") and betrays an activist agenda ("strategy"). During Democratic administrations, the Policy Section is meant to hover in the background, supporting the ideas of the political appointees. But during any future Republican administration, the Policy Section is designed to energetically push for a left-leaning agenda.

On its first day in office, a Republican administration should break up the Policy Section. Career bureaucrats are not supposed to set policy and develop strategy—that is the role of political appointees who are accountable to the American people through the political process. Of course, that is precisely why the Obama administration established the Policy Section: to create a bureaucracy that advances a leftwing agenda and is *not* accountable to the voters.

Karen Stevens, a former political appointee at the Clinton DOJ, was the first appointee to run the new Policy Section. During the Bush administration, she burrowed in as a career employee. People familiar with her work tell me she worked a part-time schedule and did the absolute minimum to pass her yearly performance evaluations. When the Bush DOJ moved her to free up a slot for someone who would outperform her, she wailed that she was a humble civil servant victimized by discrimination. Before President Obama's hand barely lifted off the Bible on January 20, 2009, Stevens was elevated back into the political leadership in the Civil Rights Division.

Incoming GOP officials, perhaps in 2013, must go into the DOJ with their eyes open. The Policy Section will function like an inverse Damocles sword—instead of hanging over them, the ideological bureaucrats will lurk below them, waiting to plunge an attack upward to counteract any meaningful steps toward race-neutral and objective law enforcement.

Protect Military Voting

As discussed in chapter seven, tens of thousands of military voters were disenfranchised in the 2010 elections. For nearly a year after Congress passed a new law to improve military voting procedures, the DOJ proved incapable of the mundane task of updating its website—a task many bloggers, journalists, and website managers perform every day. Numerous DOJ sources attributed the delay to Voting Section deputy chief Rebecca Wertz, who reportedly dithered for months over a single memorandum detailing changes to the webpage.

Because the Civil Rights Division has proved unwilling or unable to protect military voters, enforcement of military voting laws should be moved out of the Civil Rights Division into the Civil or National Security Division. Furthermore, the people who have bungled military voting enforcement cannot be allowed to continue enforcing the law. Instead, the attorney general, after removing military voting enforcement from the Civil Rights Division, should appoint a section manager over military voting who has actually worn the uniform and served overseas. The job could easily be filled by numerous Voting Section alumni who served as Navy officers. One such officer is a veteran of the Iraq War as well as a highly experienced litigator in the private sector. Instead of deploying him to protect the voting rights of his brothers in arms, Rebecca Wertz stripped him of any case protecting military voters under the Obama administration.

Wertz's action was a disgrace that casts serious doubt on the Civil Right Division's commitment to protecting military voters. In the next administration, attorneys like this Navy officer should be brought back to DOJ and given a single charge—do whatever is necessary to ensure that U.S. service members have their votes counted.

Shutter the Office of Professional Responsibility

The DOJ's two ethical watchdogs, the Office of Professional Responsibility (OPR) and the Inspector General (IG), are now at the forefront of the DOJ's crusade against conservatives and Republicans in its midst. The campaign has been steadily advanced by OPR attorney Tamar Kessler, who was involved with two OPR reports slamming Bush political appointees inside the Civil Rights Division. Multiple sources close to the investigation tell me Kessler disregarded mountains of exculpatory evidence, and the final reports she authored somehow failed to mention the dozens of liberals hired into the Bush Civil Rights Division's Voting, Criminal, Appellate, Employment Litigation, and Special Litigation Sections.

Kessler also aimed her guns at the Bush administration's war on terror. Concluding that Bush-era lawyers John Yoo and Jay Bybee committed professional misconduct in giving advice about interrogation tactics for suspected terrorists, Kessler recommended disciplinary proceedings be opened against the pair. Kessler's attack mirrored a major theme of the Obama campaign—the Bush administration's allegedly lawless interrogation tactics—but it was fundamentally bad lawyering. Dana Perino and Bill Burck wrote of Kessler's work, "In college, OPR couldn't pull a 'gentleman's B' for this report, even in the era of grade inflation. Since nobody fails any more, let's call it D-minus work."[6]

Moreover, then-Attorney General Michael Mukasey and Deputy Attorney General Mark Filip recognized the shoddy nature of Kessler's analysis. They wrote a letter to the OPR arguing Kessler's work was "based on factual errors, legal analysis by commentators and scholars with unstated potential biases, unsupported speculation about the motives of Messrs. Bybee and Yoo, and a misunderstanding of certain significant ... interagency practices."[7] In an interview with Jennifer Rubin in the *Weekly Standard*, Mukasey went further: "My take was that it was a hatchet job. They quoted one guy who wasn't even a lawyer and someone who [had] represented John Walker Lindh [the American captured as an enemy combatant in Afghanistan]. They cited an unpublished opinion." He characterized Kessler's OPR report as "sloppiness combined with ill will."[8]

In the end, Associate Deputy Attorney General David Margolis—the DOJ's senior career official—threw out Kessler's report and excoriated her findings. Margolis determined Kessler had created new standards out of whole cloth and predicated her findings on the most flimsy and unpersuasive evidence.

Kessler's nakedly political attacks are the kind of thing that demands the OPR be eliminated or, at the very least, thoroughly reformed. Unfortunately, if past is prologue, ideological bureaucrats like her will not only keep their jobs, but will be esteemed by colleagues and given regular promotions and cash performance awards. More than likely, Kessler and her fellow OPR partisans view the discrediting of their work by Mukasey and Margolis as a badge of honor. It is already clear that OPR lawyers will find little offensive conduct by any political appointee or ideological companion for the duration of the Obama administration. But like the cicada that sleep dormant for years underground, the attorneys will emerge eventually and find endless wrongdoing to investigate as soon as the next Republican administration takes charge.

There is little hope the OPR will lose its partisan bent until its Holder-appointed leadership is replaced. For example, Kevin Ohlson is now in charge of reviewing recommendations before they leave the OPR. He served as Eric Holder's chief of staff and was a large contributor to the Obama campaign. Similarly, Robin Ashton, the chief of the OPR, served on the staff of Vermont Senator Patrick Leahy while Leahy was furiously attacking the Bush DOJ in 2006 and 2007. The OPR's whitewash of the Panther dismissal alone should justify a future Republican administration transferring Ohlson and Ashton out of the OPR.

The best overall solution is to shut down the OPR and fold its functions into the Office of the Inspector General. At the same time, the Inspector General should be selected for a single three-year term, like an ombudsman at a major newspaper. That way, the IG will be genuinely independent and less likely to play partisan games to obtain reappointment.

Manage the Unmanageable

The *Washington Examiner* recently reported that employees in the Civil Rights Division often pass time by playing videogames and watching movies.[9] That's got to stop. Games and other forms of entertainment need to be blocked from the division's computers.

The methodology of how cases are investigated and filed also needs to change. Separate lawyers or teams of lawyers should recommend pursuing a case by preparing a J-memo, but different lawyers should then litigate the case. The current methodology ensures that the lawyers who recommended the case will never admit its weaknesses. After all, the attorney who prepared the J-memo has already essentially argued that the case is solid. Criminal prosecutors, on the whole, are much better trained to realize it is not their job to get a conviction in every case, and that their real client is the cause of justice. By contrast, as one DOJ lawyer told me, Civil Rights Division lawyers "seem to think it's a failure if they conclude that a case is not worth bringing, and therefore try to extract a pound of flesh from every file, whether warranted or not."

Another problem with the current case methodology is that Civil Rights Division lawyers have unconstrained authority. Most cases brought by the DOJ are not heard in court until a "mutually agreed" upon consent order is filed. Criminal lawyers, in contrast, must use the grand jury process or risk getting dressed down by a judge or jury if they overreach. This most recently happened to DOJ criminal section lawyer Susan French, who was forced to dismiss a Hawaii human trafficking case in the middle of a trial because she misled the grand jury that indicted the defendants.[10] Most other parts of the DOJ have government agency "clients" that, like real-world clients, can understand litigation is not always the best option, that it might be a waste of time, or that it might distract from more important issues. In the Civil Rights Division, however, no one other than the lawyers themselves (and sometimes not even a political appointee accountable to the electorate) has any involvement with the case until it "settles," usually under extraordinary pressure. Thus, you get a spate of cases in which the Civil Rights Division spends two years and makes trips to some far-off city to get a $20,000 settlement that they can trumpet in a press release.

Consider Breaking Up the Civil Rights Division

Some long-time Civil Rights Division employees have suggested to me that the division is so dysfunctional that it should be broken up, with its functions scattered across the DOJ. In this scenario, the Civil Division would assume most of its key responsibilities like enforcing the Voting Rights Act and housing discrimination laws, and the assistant attorney general for the Civil Division would be put in charge of enforcing most civil rights laws. Although politically difficult, pursuing this option would promise numerous benefits; most notably, the division's biases and personal agendas would be diluted into the highly professional Civil Division without losing one bit of effectiveness. Eliminating the Civil Rights Division would also save millions of dollars in redundant administrative and political functions, and it would break up the DOJ's version of the thin blue line—the code of silence that reigns when attorneys like Steve Rosenbaum, Nancy Sardeson, and Loretta King engage in legal overreach or professional misconduct.

The division's problems may indeed be so ingrained as to warrant this solution. Virtually the entire division now marches in ideological lockstep. Employees consider themselves to be part of a nearly sanctified mission with roots planted in the hallowed ground of the civil rights movement of the 1950s and 1960s. They are animated by a crusading zeal to push the law further and further toward legal frontiers that Congress never authorized. I recall attending events in the Great Hall at DOJ headquarters where employees sang spirituals and spoke about how their mission was intertwined with great historic events. To them, the Civil Rights Division is more than a law enforcement agency. It is a torchbearer for future generations, a holy quest that continually renews itself and finds new reasons for its existence by reminding everyone of its glorious past.

Division employees and their backers in the civil rights industry, of course, will be outraged by the prospect of dissolving the Civil Rights Division, blind to the fact that the laws enforced by the division would remain on the books, and that the division's important functions would continue elsewhere. For them, preserving a government sanctuary for the most extreme racialists is more important than preserving the division's rightful functions.

Breaking up the division would require an act of Congress, so it is unlikely for the time being. Still, it is time to begin interjecting this idea into the public debate.

An August 2011 Rasmussen survey found that only 17 percent of Americans believe the federal government has the consent of the governed, the lowest level the survey has ever measured. A startling 69 percent of Americans say the government does not have that consent. In marked contrast, 55 percent of the political class believes the government does have the consent of the governed.[11] President Carter's former pollster, Pat Caddell, calls the result "unprecedented" and even "pre-revolutionary."[12]

Regardless of whether America is indeed in a "pre-revolutionary" state of mind, one thing is for sure when only 17 percent of Americans believes the government has the consent of the governed: it doubles the need to have elections that are free, fair, and trusted. It means election laws must ensure that people believe the outcome of elections represent the will of the majority of voters. It means systems to ensure election integrity don't face reactionary opposition. It means people need to believe their vote counts, no matter who ends up winning. Seventeen percent is a staggeringly low number. More people probably believe Elvis is still alive.

Even if Americans don't trust politicians or bureaucrats, they need to be able to trust in their ability to make their collective voice heard through fair elections. They also must have confidence that the law applies equally to everyone regardless of race. Without faith in these fundamental principles of republican government, Americans will naturally lose any sense of a shared national destiny. Once this occurs in a country, political extremism and social strife typically follow.

Ominously, the very government department responsible for protecting voting rights and enforcing equal protection has been overrun by radicals bent on furthering a fringe political agenda in which race determines everything, including your access to the political process and your entitlement to legal protection. Using all the powerful tools available to the Department of Justice, they have achieved major success in advancing this worldview largely outside the public's gaze.

This book has sought to begin the process of rectifying this problem by shining a light on the corruption, political extremism, and sheer unprofessionalism that I witnessed firsthand at the DOJ. But ultimately, exposing the problems in these pages is merely a first step. It must be followed by the empowerment of committed officials who have the courage to restore decency, balance, and fairness to the vital institutions that sustain our unique and brilliant constitutional system.

Acknowledgments

Nobody can complete a book like this alone. Many thanks are due to many people.

For their support and vision, Richard Pollock, Roger Simon, and everyone at Pajamas Media who are reconstructing the news model deserve thanks. So does Andrew Breitbart, soul brother and pied piper. I am thankful for the kindness and support of David Horowitz, Peter Collier, Jamie Glazov, David Swindle, and Karen Lugo. Thanks to David Matsio, Mark Tapscott, and J. P. Freire for providing a venue.

The country owes a debt of thanks, as I do, to Michelle Malkin, who was exposing the evil of the New Black Panther Party when few others were. Soon to follow Malkin in recognizing and revealing injustice were Jennifer Rubin, Quin Hillyer, Jed Babbin, John Fund, and Tom Fitton. Thanks to everyone at Blackrock Group including

Danielle Howe, Tom Kise, Mike Dubke, and Carl Forti for their effective air bombardment.

Many members of Congress deserve credit, including Congressman Frank Wolf and Senator Jeff Sessions for serving as the watchdogs the Constitution envisioned on issues related to the Justice Department. Those of us close to the New Black Panther saga greatly appreciate General Michael Mukasey for his dignity and supportive comments. Thanks to Gail Heriot, Todd Gaziano, Ashley Taylor, and Peter Kirsanow who have gazed into the smoking maw of the beast with me.

My humblest appreciation to DOJ alumni Asheesh Agarwal, Butch Bowers, Robert Driscoll, Greg Katsas, and Mark Corallo, who provided covering fire when I went over the top. I will never forget it.

For inspiration and opportunities, thanks along the way to Clint Bolick, Secretary of State Jim Miles, Cleta Mitchell, Garry Malphrus, and Michael Graham.

Bishop E. W. Jackson deserves special thanks for his keen understanding of these issues and the power of language as a weapon of righteousness. To Rich Bolen, who sharpened me as iron sharpens iron. To Andy McCarthy, another DOJ alumnus holding Eric Holder accountable. And to Hans von Spakovsky, for his courage and dedication to exposing injustice and abuses of power. His reporting blazed the trail that made it easy for me to follow.

Thanks to all the radio and television hosts who have allowed me to appear or mentioned this story, including Sean Hannity, Megyn Kelly, Mark Levin, Laura Ingraham, Jon-David Wells, Dana Loesch, Tara Servatius, Martha Zoller, Rush Limbaugh, and the many other radio hosts who had me as a guest or covered my work.

To the victims across Noxubee County who made the fight worth fighting and the book worth writing, including Tiny Heard, Ricky Walker, and Mary Allsup. Scott Boyd at the *Macon Beacon* deserves national recognition for his dedication to the First Amendment and reminding us what real news reporting used to be like. Without his reporting and kind permission to use his photography, this book would not be possible.

Thanks to the Noxubee team including Joshua Rogers, Ron Williams, and Joann Sazama who made litigation enjoyable. Thanks to one of the finest court reporters in the country, Ginger Brooks of Brooks Court Reporting in Philadelphia, Mississippi, for making transcripts available to me.

Chris Coates set out decades ago to do justice and ended up doing more for justice, and for America, than he ever dreamed. The nation and the legal profession have been blessed by his professionalism, courtesy, and dedication to the rule of law. I was blessed with the opportunity to practice law with Coates and ponder this story with him.

Thanks to civil rights legend Bartle Bull for reminding America why he and others went to Mississippi in the 1960s, and to Chris Hill, who continues to serve his country. To Robert Popper and Spencer Fisher, excellent lawyers both and great Americans.

Of course, thanks to Jana who put up with the long hours and endless travel for research and interviews for this book, and to Bob and Pat who put up with everything imaginable.

Thanks to those friends from the Voting Section who knew there had to be a book one day. Thanks to Christine Hall at the Alexandria Law Library for creating the quietest place inside the beltway to write it. Thanks to Merritt Green and all the great folks at General Counsel.

Deep gratitude goes to John Driscoll, my old, dear friend who unexpectedly appeared after twenty-five years from the other side of the world on the Fourth of July before my Civil Rights Commission testimony and said just the right things. Our improbable meeting in the back of St. Mary's Church after so many lost decades reminded me there are no coincidences.

Thanks to the hundreds of people I have met along the way. Your hugs, handshakes, letters, and particularly your prayers meant a great deal, particularly to Stuart Mayper and everyone associated with King Street Patriots in Houston. Your continuing warmth and support is deeply humbling.

To the many, many Department of Justice employees, known and anonymous, who provided documents, tips, emails, stories, photographs, names, and materials to me and others in the media, you made this book possible. I, and a grateful nation, thank you.

To Brad Schlozman, without whom the case against Ike Brown would have never been filed and who has endured the roaring lion more than any of us. The folks at Regnery, particularly my editor Jack Langer, deserve thanks for smoothing the edges and doing what I am incapable of doing, which is a lot. Others who had a part to play along the way include Jeff Harr, Corrine Cary, Tabella, Eric Eversole, Kathy Hewston, Terrye Seckinger, Keith McCook, and Kay Butler.

Two people also responsible for this book are Steve Rosenbaum and Loretta King. If not for their preposterous refusal simply to accept a default judgment in the New Black Panther case, I would still be a quiet civil servant in the DOJ Voting Section. If not for them, what you are holding in your hands would not exist.

I apologize to the people I certainly missed. Come work the jib sheets for me and you'll be in the next book.

Notes

Introduction

1. Toni Locy, "D.C. Politics Beckons, Repels Holder; Racial Tensions Have Chilling Effect on Prosecutor's Ambitions," *Washington Post*, December 21, 1996.
2. Ibid.
3. The Department of Justice has many other divisions besides Civil Rights, including the Criminal Division, National Security Division, Civil Division, Environment and Natural Resources Division, and Antitrust Division. Each division is headed by an assistant attorney general, who is a presidential appointee requiring Senate confirmation. An associate attorney general, another presidential appointee, oversees the Civil Rights Division, which is ultimately responsible to the attorney general, who is in charge of the entire DOJ.

   In addition to its litigating components, DOJ also has numerous offices that help the other divisions do their job. These include the

Office of Legal Counsel, which provides binding legal advice to the DOJ; the Office of Legislative Affairs, which serves as the DOJ's liaison with Congress; and the Office of Public Affairs, which handles press relations.

Two components of the Justice Department, meanwhile, exist as internal watchdogs. First, the Office of Professional Responsibility investigates reports of professional misconduct within the DOJ. It answers one way or another to the attorney general. Then there is the Inspector General, who is a political appointee of the president but whose office is supposed to act independently of the rest of the DOJ, thus minimizing his susceptibility to political interference. The IG's jurisdiction, however, is limited to waste, fraud, and abuse.

4.   Eric Holder in "Senate Confirmation Hearings: Eric Holder, Day One," transcript at http://www.nytimes.com/2009/01/16/us/politics/16text-holder.html?_r=1&pagewanted=print.

5.   U.S. Department of Justice, *Settlement Agreement between the United States Department of Justice and Vasquez Funeral Home*, Complaint DJ 202-23-41, revised May 15, 1998, http://www.justice.gov/crt/foia/readingroom/frequent_requests/ada_settlements/il/illvasquez.php.

6.   See *Miller* v. *Johnson*, 515 U. S. 900, 926 (1995) (detailing the "federalism costs exacted by §5"); *Presley* v. *Etowah County Comm'n*, 502 U. S. 491, 500–501 (1992) (describing §5 as "an extraordinary departure from the traditional course of relations between the States and the Federal Government").

7.   *United States* v. *Sheffield Bd. of Comm'rs*, 435 U.S. 100 (1978) (Stevens, J., dissenting).

8.   Specifically, the law prohibits any "voting qualification or prerequisite to voting or standard, practice, or procedure ... which results in a denial or abridgement of the right of any citizen of the United States to vote on account of race or color." See + 42 U.S.C. § 1973(a).

9.   42 U.S.C. § 1973b (f)(2).

10. 42 U.S.C. § 1973gg, et seq.

11. Public Law 107–252; 42 U.S.C. 15301, et seq.

12. Hans A. Von Spakovsky, "Radicalizing Civil Rights," *National Review*, March 9, 2010, http://www.nationalreview.com/articles/229277/radicalizing-civil-rights/hans-von-spakovsky?page=1.

Chapter One

1.   The Estate of Martin Luther King, Jr., *A Call to Conscience: The Land-mark Speeches of Dr. Martin Luther King, Jr.*, http://mlk-kpp01.stanford. edu/kingweb/publications/speeches/address_at_march_on_washing ton.pdf.

2.   Dr. Martin Luther King, Jr., "Loving Your Enemies," Delivered at Dexter Avenue Baptist Church, Montgomery, Alabama, on November 17, 1957. Audio and text available at http://mlk-kpp01.stanford.edu/ index.php/encyclopedia/documentsentry/doc_loving_your_enemies/.

3.   Census reports Tenth census, June 1, 1880, Vol. 5, p. 96.

4.   Michael W. Fitzgerald, *The Union League Movement in the Deep South* (Louisiana State University Press, 1989), 231, and General Stephen D. Lee, *Herman Hattaway* (University Press of Mississippi, 1976), 161.

5.   Simon Wendt, "The Roots of Black Power? Armed Resistance and the Radicalization of the Civil Rights Movement," in Peniel E. Joseph, ed., *The Black Power Movement: Rethinking the Civil Rights Black Power Era* (Routledge, 2006), 155.

6.   Colin Crawford Collection (MUM00093). The Department of Archives and Special Collections, J.D. Williams Library, The University of Mississippi.

7.   Colin Crawford, *Uproar at Dancing Rabbit Creek: Battling Over Race, Class and the Environment* (Perseus Books, 1996).

8.   Colin Crawford Collection (MUM00093). The Department of Archives and Special Collections, J.D. Williams Library, The University of Mississippi.

9.   Ibid.

10. Ibid.

11. Ibid.

12. Ibid.

13. Deposition of Russell Smart, *United States v. Ike Brown, et al.* page 115, ln 6–10.

14. *United States v. Ike Brown, et al*; Proposed Findings of Fact and Conclusions of Law by the United States 26 citing the trial transcript in *United States v. Ike Brown* at 2071-72. All subsequent citations to the trial transcript contained in the Proposed Findings of Fact and Conclusions of Law by the United States will provide the trial transcript

citation included in the Proposed Findings of Fact and Conclusions of Law by the United States.

15. Plaintiff's Exhibit 33, *United States v. Ike Brown*.

16. Trial Transcript Tr. 1749, 2089-90; Plaintiff's Exhibit 174.

17. *United States v. Marengo County Comm'n*, 731 F.2d 1546 (11th Cir. 1984); *Jackson v. Edgefield County S.C. School Dist.*, 650 F. Supp. 1176 (D.S.C. 1986).

18. Trial Transcript at 1884.

19. Trial Transcript at 2395, 2392, 2402, 2413, 2417.

20. Trial Transcript at 939-40.

21. *United States v. Ike Brown*. Deposition of Patsy Roby, pp. 89–90, ln. 11–25, 1–2. Here is the precise exchange: "I did so much, I can't remember. That's how much that I did. I can't remember all of it.... Q. You mean illegal things? A. I stole stuff from people. That's what I was doing, taking, taking, taking money with people. At that time, my mind was so messed up. I was on drugs real bad. That's when it was. Q. When you mean drugs, you mean illegal narcotics? A. Yeah, I was smoking crack. Q. And so your recollection is you didn't work in the 1999 elections because you were in jail? A. I can't remember. I don't know was I in jail or not. I don't know, but I can't remember, because my mind all messed up."

22. Trial Transcript at 960-62.

23. Plaintiff's Exhibits 60 and 61, Trial Transcript at 1557-58.

24. Miss. Code Ann. § 23-15-753 (1991).

25. Trial Transcript at 1792.

26. Plaintiff's Exhibit 68.

27. Trial Transcript at 2269-71.

28. Trial Transcript at 1167.

29. Trial Transcript at 975.

30. Trial Transcript at 980, 2444.

31. Trial Transcript at 1597-98.

32. Trial Transcript at 775, 820-21, 1001-04.

33. Trial Transcript at 2177.

34. *Allsup v. Election of the Office of Election Commissioner for the District 2 of Noxubee County Mississippi*, Noxubee County Cir. Ct. No. 8350 (1993). The court order overturning the election vanished from the circuit clerk's office.

35. Trial Transcript at 910, 913-915.

36. Trial Transcript at 1864, 1870; *United States v. Ike Brown, et al.*, 494 F. Supp.2d 440, 484 n. 71 (S.D.Ms. 2007).

37. Trial Exhibit P-169 at 6-8.

38. Trial Transcript at 2199-2200, 2212.

39. Affidavit of Shawn Slaughter, July 2005, ¶ 7.

40. *Eichelberger v. DEC & Albert Walker*, (No-99-99, Noxubee County Circuit Court).

41. Trial Transcript at 86, 1468, 1537, 1542.

42. "Voting Rights Act pointed in a new direction," *USA Today*, April 3, 2006.

43. Trial Transcript at 1632.

44. "Poll watchers to be on alert," *Clarion Ledger*, August 5, 2003.

45. Interview with Tiny Heard, April 20, 2011.

Chapter Two

1. More information available at http://www.amherstbulletin.com/story/id/81800422005/.

2. Robert A. Kengle, "Declaration of Robert A. Kengle," *Talking Points Memo*, http://talkingpointsmemo.com/documents/2010/10/bob-ken gles-declaration.php?page=1.

3. Daniels now imparts her legal thinking on law students through her professorship at the University of Baltimore School Of Law, where she teaches racialist-infused concepts such as "critical legal theory." Her class syllabus says students will examine "the relationship between law and issues of race, gender, sexual orientation and class. The course will also study more generally the relationship between power and the law, and consider the extent to which law can be considered objective and rational."

4. Chris Coates testimony, http://www.usccr.gov/NBPH/09-24-2010_NBPPhearing.pdf at 16, 83.

5. Ibid., at 16.

6. Ibid., at 83–84.

7. Hans von Spakovsky, "Enough Is Enough, Joe Rich: An Uncivil Man from the Civil Rights Division," http://pajamasmedia.com/blog/enough-is-enough-joe-rich-an-uncivil-man-from-the-civil-rights-division/.

8. See, for example, "Bush's long history of tilting Justice," *Los Angeles Times*, March 29, 2007, http://www.latimes.com/news/opinion/commentary/la-oe-rich29mar29,0,1507657.story, and "In 5-Year Effort, Scant Evidence of Voter Fraud," *New York Times*, April 12, 2007, http://www.nytimes.com/2007/04/12/washington/12fraud.html?pagewanted=print.

9. "U.S. sues black activist on voting act violation," MSNBC, May 2, 2006.

10. "Alleged Voting Rights Violation With a Twist Goes to Trial," *Washington Post*, January 16, 2007.

11. January 17, 2007 exchange between J. Christian Adams and Judge Tom S. Lee in the liability phase trial in *United States v. Ike Brown, et al.* (Case No. Civ. 4:05cv33TSL-LRA) in United States District Court for the Southern District of Mississippi, Jackson Division.

12. Opening Statement of Wilbur Colom in trial of *United States v. Ike Brown*, January 17, 2007.

13. *Spencer v. Sanders*, (No. 98-0113, Noxubee County Circuit Court).

14. *Macon Beacon Shopper*, March 7, 2007.

15. "Colom says he may have to sue Noxubee supes," *Columbus Commercial Dispatch*, March 14, 2007.

16. *United States v. Ike Brown*, 494 F.Supp.2d 440, 486 (S.D. Miss. 2007).

17. *United States v. Ike Brown*, 494 F.Supp.2d 440, 455-6 (S.D. Miss. 2007).

18. *United States v. Ike Brown*, 494 F.Supp.2d 440, 457 (S.D. Miss. 2007).

19. *United States v. Ike Brown*, 494 F.Supp.2d 440, 479 (S.D. Miss. 2007).

20. *United States v. Ike Brown*, Civ. No. 4:05-cv-33 (TSN/AGN), Doc. 225-6, 7.

21. *United States v. Ike Brown*, Civ. No. 4:05-cv-33 (TSN/AGN), Doc. 225-6, 10.

22. *United States v. Ike Brown*, Civ. No. 4:05-cv-33 (TSN/AGN), Doc. 225-6, 35–37.

23. *United States v. Ike Brown*, Civ. No. 4:05-cv-33 (TSN/AGN), Doc. 225-6, 15–27.

24. *United States v. Ike Brown*, Civ. No. 4:05-cv-33 (TSN/AGN), Doc. 225-6, 12, 18, 45–48.

25. Francis J. Grund, *The Americans in Their Moral, Social and Political Relations*, Vol. 1, 1837.

26. *Congressional Globe*, 40th Congress 2d Sess. S.p. 725 (Jan. 1868).

27. *Congressional Globe*, 40th Congress 3d Sess. H.p. 197 (Feb. 8, 1869).

28. *Congressional Globe*, 40th Congress 2d Sess. S.p. 100 (Dec. 5, 10 1867).
29. *Congressional Globe*, 40th Cong. 3d Sess. 1008-09, 1012 (Feb. 8, 1868).
30. Ibid.
31. *Congressional Globe*, 39th Cong. 1st Sess. 1832-33 (April 7, 1866).
32. J. Christian Adams, "Unequal Law Enforcement Reigns at Obama's DOJ," June 28, 2010, http://pajamasmedia.com/blog/j-christian-adams-you-deserve-to-know-%E2%80%94-unequal-law-enforcement-reigns-at-obamas-doj-pjm-exclusive/.
33. Interview with Bill Ready, April 20, 2011.

Chapter Three

1. Paul Kiel, "Obama: Tanner Should Have Been *Fired*, Not Moved," *Talking Points Memorandum*, December 14, 2007, http://tpmmuckraker.talkingpointsmemo.com/archives/004920.php.
2. Letter quoted at the Brad Blog, http://www.bradblog.com/?p=5177.
3. Edward Blum, "Obama Plays the Race Card," American Enterprise for Public Policy Research, November 15, 2007, http://www.aei.org/article/27108.
4. Saul Alinsky, *Rules for Radicals* (New York: Vintage, 1971).
5. Letter of Attorney William H. Jordan, March 23, 2009.
6. "A vindication of interrogation," *Washington Times*, February 24, 2010, http://www.washingtontimes.com/news/2010/feb/24/a-vindication-of-interrogation/print/.
7. "ACLU Announces Historic Fundraising Success, Exceeding Goal And Building Civil Liberties Infrastructure In Battleground States," ACLU Organization News and Highlights, September 15, 2010, http://www.aclu.org/organization-news-and-highlights/aclu-announces-historic-fundraising-success-exceeding-goal-and-buil.
8. Memorandum of Loretta King Acting Assistant Attorney General to Section Chiefs, September 2, 2009, p. 3.
9. Email of Thomas E. Perez, February 3, 2010.
10. Ibid.
11. Eugenia V. Lenvenson, "Conservatives come out; Queer group protests," *Harvard Crimson*, December 2, 1999, http://www.thecrimson.com/article/1999/12/2/conservatives-come-out-queer-group-protests/.

12. Parker R. Conrad, "Vaginal Davis, Holly Hughes Discuss Queer Performance Art in Ribald Evening," *Harvard Crimson*, April 20, 2000, http://www.thecrimson.com/article/2000/4/20/vaginal-davis-holly-hughes-discuss-queer/.

13. "Advancement project senior attorney Elizabeth Westfall offers strategies to protect voters and improve election administration issues in Virginia," Advancement Project, March 6, 2009, http://www.advancementproject.org/news/alerts/2009/03/advancement-project-senior-attorney-elizabeth-westfall-offers-strategies-to-prot.

14. As revealed by a search of Federal Election Commission records on the FEC online database, http://www.fec.gov/finance/disclosure/norindsea.shtml.

15. Ibid.

16. "In shift, Justice Department is hiring lawyers with civil rights backgrounds," *New York Times*, May 31, 2011.

17. Hans A. von Spakovsky, "Amateur Night at the Justice Department," *National Review*, February 2, 2010, http://www.nationalreview.com/corner/194234/amateur-night-justice-department/hans-von-spakovsky.

18. *United States of America v. AIG Federal Savings Bank and Wilmington Finance, Inc.*, http://www.justice.gov/crt/about/hce/documents/aigcomp.pdf.

19. *United States of America v. AIG Federal Savings Bank and Wilmington Finance, Inc.*, No. 10CV178-JJF, http://www.justice.gov/crt/about/hce/documents/aigsettle.pdf.

20. *United States v. Donald Sterling et al.*, Case Nos. 06-4885 DSF, 06-7442 DSF, and 07-7234 DSF, http://www.justice.gov/crt/about/hce/documents/sterlingsettlefinal.pdf.

21. Byron York, "Justice Department steers money to favored groups," *Washington Examiner*, August 5, 2010.

22. *Glasper v. Parish of East Baton Rouge*, Case No. 93-537 (M.D. La.), Document Nos. 183 and 187.

23. Oddly, Glasper has recently been the subject of controversy for purportedly sponsoring a flier against Baton Rouge Mayor-President Kip Holden. Appearing in thousands of mailboxes, the flier accused Holden of having an affair with a woman whose husband later beat up Holden. "D.A. to get case of anti-Holden flyer," *The Advocate*, November 19, 2010.

24. During a March 1, 2011, House Appropriations subcommittee hearing on the Justice Department budget, Chairman Frank Wolf asked Attorney General Holder about a report I wrote for *Pajamas Media* about the DOJ's selective fulfillment of FOIA requests. Holder said he had read my story but claimed it did not account for different complexities in the requests. He was wrong.

Take, for example, what the logs reveal about requests relating to Section 5 of the Voting Rights Act. Stored in a records room, these files are public documents that contain all the information for various submissions made under the preclearance provisions of the Voting Rights Act. The data contained in the files reveal crucial—and controversial—political information on topics ranging from legislative redistricting to voter identification laws.

Contrary to Holder's insinuations, there is no difference in complexity in the requests by liberal and conservative groups for submission files created under Section 5 of the Voting Rights Act—it's a direct "apples to apples" comparison. Holder's testimony is also contradicted by the structure of the files. The Section 5 submission files are already pre-segregated between public and non-public content. The public and non-public content occupy separate portions of the file folder. It takes hardly any effort whatsoever to access a requested Section 5 file, walk to a copier machine, copy the public portion of the file, and mail it to the requestor. The only explanation for why FOIA requests from liberals are fulfilled much faster than those from conservatives is that the DOJ is systematically stonewalling the latter.

25. *Hays v. Louisiana*, 936 F. Supp. 360, 369 (W.D. La. 1996).
26. *Hays v. Louisiana*, 936 F. Supp. 360, 372 (W.D. La. 1996).
27. *United States v. City of Torrance*, (C.D. Cal. 1993, Case No. CV-93-4142 MRP), Doc. no. 336, page 8.
28. *United States v. City of Torrance*, 2000 WL 576422 (9th Cir. May 11, 2000).
29. *Johnson v. Miller*, 864 F. Supp. 1354, 1364 (S.D. Ga. 1994).
30. Ibid.
31. Ibid.
32. *Johnson v. Miller*, 864 F. Supp. 1354, 1368 (S.D. Ga. 1994).
33. *Miller v. Johnson*, 515 U.S. 900, 924 (1995).

34. Hans A. von Spakovsky, "More on Loretta King," *National Review*, December 10, 2009, http://www.nationalreview.com/corner/191485/more-loretta-king/hans-von-spakovsky.

35. *Scott v. Department of Justice*, 920 F. Supp. 1248 (M.D. Fla. 1996).

36. D. Ariz. Nov. 7 1995.

37. *United States v. Jones*, 125 F.3d 1418, 1431 (11th Cir. 1997).

38. Ibid.

39. *United States v. Stacy Sturdevant, et al.*, (D. Kan., Case No. 07-2233-KHV-DJW), February 17, 2010.

40. Hans A. von Spakovsky, "Civil Rights Division Lawyers Slapped With Sanctions," *National Review*, January 6, 2010, http://www.nationalreview.com/corner/192410/civil-rights-division-lawyers-slapped-sanctions/hans-von-spakovsky.

Chapter Four

1. "Candidate Obama's Sense Of Urgency," CBS *60 Minutes*, November 15, 2009, http://www.cbsnews.com/stories/2007/02/09/60minutes/main2456335_page2.shtml?tag=contentMain;contentBody.

2. View video of the event at C-Span, Civil Rights Issues, http://www.c-spanvideo.org/program/CivilRightsIssues21.

3. Ibid.

4. "New Black Panther Party," Southern Poverty Law Center, http://www.splcenter.org/get-informed/intelligence-files/new-black-panther-party.

5. C-Span, Civil Rights Issues, *op cit.*

6. Ibid.

7. Bob Salsberg, "Files Suggest Elder Obama Forced to Leave Harvard," ABC News, April 30, 2011, http://abcnews.go.com/US/wireStory?id=13494373.

8. C-Span, Civil Rights Issues, *op cit.*

9. Ibid.

10. *United States of America v. The Board of Trustees of Southern Illinois University*, Consent Decree, http://www.adversity.net/SIU/SIU-Consent-Decree.pdf.

11. C-Span, Civil Rights Issues, *op cit.*

12. Juan Williams, "Democratic Contenders Put Spotlight on Selma," NPR, March 4, 2007, http://www.wbur.org/npr/7708261/democratic-contenders-put-spotlight-on-selma.

13. One photographer published photos on a flickr account of Obama and Shabazz speaking at the same podium in front of Brown Chapel. After initially granting permission to reproduce the photos for this book, the photographer withdrew his permission. After that, he removed the photos from flickr. To watch the Panthers' "Training Day" video, see New Black Panther Party, "Training Day," video available at http://video.google.com/videoplay?docid=2048551651954219535&ei=ORS CSfLED6ierAKY3bDjCg&q=new+black+panther+party#.

14. Juan Williams, "Democratic Contenders Put Spotlight on Selma," *op cit.*

15. "Racists endorse Obama on candidate's website," WorldNetDaily, March 18, 2008, http://www.wnd.com/index.php?fa=PAGE.printable&pageId=59326.

16. Screenshots of the endorsement can be viewed at http://www.moon battery.com/archives/2008/03/new_black_panth.html, and at http://bobmccarty.com/2008/03/18/new-black-panthers-alive-well-at-obama-site/.

17. Frank Bruni, "Right Wing Baggage Puts Drag on Bush Caravan," *New York Times*, February 24, 2000, http://www.nytimes.com/2000/02/24/us/the-2000-campaign-political-memo-right-wing-baggage-puts-drag-on-bush-caravan.html?ref=bobjonesuniversity.

18. "Democratic Contenders Put Spotlight on Selma," NPR *All Things Considered*, March 4, 2007, http://www.npr.org/templates/transcript/transcript.php?storyId=7708261.

19. Fox News *America Live*, July 14, 2010.

20. Kia Gregory, "The Cats Came Back," *Philadelphia Weekly*, December 17, 2003, http://www.philadelphiaweekly.com/news-and-opinion/cover-story/the_cats_came_back-38373074.html.

21. See Khalid Muhammad's speech at http://www.metacafe.com/watch/456363/khallid_muhammads_speech_kill_the_white_man/.

22. "Black Power," *Washington City Paper*, January 19, 2001.

23. "From boycott to firebomb," *Washington Post*, December 3, 2000.

24. "New Black Panther Party," Southern Poverty Law Center, http://www.splcenter.org/get-informed/intelligence-files/new-black-panther-party.

25. "New Black Panther Party for Self-Defense: Recent Activity," Anti-Defamation League, http://www.adl.org/main_Extremism/new_black_panther_party.htm?Multi_page_sections=sHeading_2.

26. Richard Cohen, "A nasty night at Howard," *Washington Post*, March 1, 1994.

27. Ibid.

28. "New Black Panther Party," Southern Poverty Law Center, http://www.splcenter.org/get-informed/intelligence-files/new-black-panther-party.

29. View the video at http://www.youtube.com/watch?v=En_GRO8DRnc.

30. View the video at http://www.youtube.com/watch?v=SykRrQlpgLs.

31. Greg Chapman, "Going Inside the New Black Panther Party," National Geographic Channel, January 9, 2009, http://ngccommunity.nationalgeographic.com/ngcblogs/inside-ngc/2009/01/going-inside-the-new-black-panther-party.html.

32. A list of his business interests and the hotels can be found at http://www.michaelvroberts.com/robertscompanies/robertshotels.html.

33. See promotional materials for the conference, with Michael Roberts listed as a speaker, here: http://www.prweb.com/releases/2010/05/prweb4040824.htm

34. Ibid.

35. "New Black Panther Party," Southern Poverty Law Center, http://www.splcenter.org/get-informed/intelligence-files/new-black-panther-party.

36. C-Span, Civil Rights Issues, *op cit.*

37. "New Black Panthers' War on Whites," *Philadelphia Daily News*, October 29, 2008.

38. "The Cats Came Back," *Philadelphia Weekly, op cit.*

39. Michelle Malkin, "The New Black Panther Party's teachable moments on race," MichelleMalkin.com, August 2, 2009, http://michellemalkin.com/2009/08/02/the-new-black-panther-partys-teachable-moments-on-race/.

40. Mike Baker, "N.C. GOP lashes out at voting sites near Obama rally," WRAL-TV, October 19, 2008, http://www.wral.com/news/state/story/3769394/.

41. Email from Craig Dosanto, November 4, 2008.

42. OPR Report, "Investigation of Dismissal of Defendants in *United States v. New Black Panther Party for Self-Defense, Inc., et al.*," March 17, 2011 http://democrats.judiciary.house.gov/sites/democrats.judiciary.house.gov/files/OPR%20Report_0.pdf, pp. 11–12.

43. Ibid., p. 16.

44. Ibid., p. 18, n. 16.

45. Testimony of Christopher Hill to the United States Commission on Civil Rights, April 23, 2010, http://www.usccr.gov/NBPH/04-23-2010_ NBPPhearing.pdf, p. 49.

46. Declaration of Bartle Bull, 6, March 30, 2009, http://www.usccr.gov/ NBPH/DeclarationofBartleBull(3-31-09).pdf

47. *United States v. North Carolina Republican Party, et al.*, Civil Action No. 91-161-CIV-5-F (E.D.N.C).

48. Inside NGC, Dominique Christin, http://ngccommunity.nationalgeo graphic.com/ngcblogs/inside-ngc/2009/01/going-inside-the-new-black-panther-party.html.

49. Ibid. Duane Lester, posting at All American Blogger, has posted the entire documentary at his website http://www.allamericanblog ger.com/11155/the-complete-pbs-documentary-on-the-new-black-panther-party/.

50. View the video at http://www.youtube.com/watch?v=oBhzJnJIilI.

51. Dan P. Lee, "Coard v. Coard," *Philadelphia Magazine*, July 2, 2007, http://www.phillymag.com/articles/coard_v_coard/.

52. Declaration of J. Christian Adams, *United States v. New Black Panther Party, et al*, No. 2:09-cv-0065, Document 12-2.

53. OPR report, pp. 31–32.

54. Declaration of Bartle Bull, 6, March 30, 2009, http://www.usccr.gov/ NBPH/DeclarationofBartleBull(3-31-09).pdf.

55. View the video at http://www.youtube.com/watch?v=HVOao5qfAPA &feature=related.

Chapter Five

1. Testimony of Chris Coates before the United States Commission on Civil Rights, September 24, 2010, http://www.usccr.gov/NBPH/09-24-2010_NBPPhearing.pdf, p. 32.

2. Ibid.

3. Ibid., 33.

4. Hans A. von Spakovsky, "They're playing games, literally, in the Justice Department," *Washington Examiner*, February 28, 2011, http://

washingtonexaminer.com/opinion/op-eds/2011/02/theyre-playing-games-literally-justice-department-0.

5. Testimony of Chris Coates before the United States Commission on Civil Rights, September 24, 2010, *op cit.*, p. 80.

6. Steven Rosenfeld, "Is the Justice Department Conducting Latino Outreach on Behalf of the GOP?" Alternet, October 22, 2007, http://www.alternet.org/rights/65749/?page=1.

7. Testimony of Wade Henderson before the House Committee on the Judiciary (Oversight of the Civil Rights Division), March 22, 2007, http://judiciary.house.gov/hearings/March2007/Henderson070322.pdf, p. 6.

8. Testimony of Assistant Attorney General Tom Perez before the United States Commission on Civil Rights, May 12, 2010, http://www.usccr.gov/NBPH/05-14-2010_NBPPhearing.pdf, pp. 46–47.

9. Letter of Ronald Weich to Frank Wolf, July 13, 2009, http://www.usccr.gov/NBPH/CongressionalCorrespondencereNBPP.pdf, p. 11.

10. Ibid.

11. *United States v. Sturdevant*, Case No. 2:07-02233 (D. Kan.), United States' Response to the AIMCO Defendants' Motion for Partial Summary Judgment, pp. 10–12.

12. Letter of Lamar Smith and Frank Wolf to Attorney General Eric Holder, July 17, 2009, http://www.usccr.gov/NBPH/CongressionalCorrespondencereNBPP.pdf, p. 15.

13. Ibid.

14. "No. 3 at Justice OK'd Panther reversal," *Washington Times*, July 30, 2009, http://www.washingtontimes.com/news/2009/jul/30/no-3-at-justice-okd-panther-reversal/.

15. Email of Arthur Goldberg to Christian Adams, November 25, 2009.

16. 42 U.S.C. §1975a(e)(2) and 42 U.S.C. §1975b(e).

17. Letter of Jim Miles to Joseph H. Hunt, November 25, 2009.

18. Hans A. von Spakovsky, "Coates speaks as best he can," *National Review*, January 12, 2010, http://www.nationalreview.com/corner/192685/coates-speaks-best-he-can/hans-von-spakovsky. The article characterizes the quotes of Coates' speech as paraphrases. As someone who heard the speech, I would say the quotes are essentially verbatim.

19. Ibid.

20. Ibid.

21. Letter of Jim Miles to Joseph H. Hunt, January 18, 2010.

22. Ibid.

23. Email of J. Christian Adams to Jody Hunt, May 11, 2010.

24. Ibid.

25. Ibid.

26. Testimony of Assistant Attorney General Tom Perez before the United States Commission on Civil Rights, May 12, 2010, http://www.usccr. gov/NBPH/05-14-2010_NBPPhearing.pdf, p. 17, 27.

27. Ibid., p. 35, ln. 8–9.

28. Ibid., p. 39, ln. 2–6.

29. Ibid., p. 62, ln. 4–5.

30. Ibid., p. 50, ln. 17–22.

31. The full resignation letter is available at http://www.scribd.com/ doc/31574180/J-Christian-Adams-resignation-letter-051910.

32. Letter of Commissioners Abigail Thernstrom and Ashley Taylor to Loretta King, June 22, 2009, http://www.usccr.gov/correspd/ Thernstrom_TaylorLetter2008.pdf.

33. Jennifer Rubin, "New Black Panther Party case: The facts are in," *Washington Post*, January 27, 2011, http://voices.washingtonpost.com/ right-turn/2011/01/the_us_commission_on_civil.html.

34. Jerry Markon and Krissah Thompson, "Dispute over New Black Panthers case causes deep divisions," *Washington Post*, October 22, 2011, http://www.washingtonpost.com/wp-dyn/content/ article/2010/10/22/AR2010102203982.html.

35. Hans A. von Spakovsky, "Bombshell: Defying DOJ Instructions, Chris Coates Will Testify Friday on New Black Panther Case," *Pajamas Media*, September 22, 2010, http://pajamasmedia.com/blog/ bombshell-defying-doj-instructions-christopher-coates-will-testify- on-new-black-panther-case-%e2%80%a6-tomorrow/.

36. Letter of Representative Frank Wolf to Attorney General Eric Holder, September 23, 2010, http://pajamasmedia.com/files/2010/09/Wolf_ letter_to_Holder_9-24-10.pdf.

37. Ibid.

38. Testimony of Chris Coates before the United States Commission on Civil Rights, September 24, 2010, http://www.usccr.gov/NBPH/09-24- 2010_NBPPhearing.pdf, p. 9, ln. 8–18.

39. Ibid., p. 16, ln. 6–7.

40. Ibid., p. 18, ln. 13–14.

41. Ibid., p. 22, ln. 10.

42. Mike M. Ahlers, "Official alleges racially selective enforcement of voting rights cases," CNN, September 24, 2010, http://articles.cnn.com/2010-09-24/politics/civil.rights.black.panther_1_voter-intimidation-case-voting-rights-racial-slurs?_s=PM:POLITICS.

43. Patrik Jonsson, "New Black Panther Party voter intimidation case: 'Bombshell' for Obama?" *The Christian Science Monitor*, September 24, 2010, http://www.csmonitor.com/USA/Politics/2010/0924/New-Black-Panther-Party-voter-intimidation-case-Bombshell-for-Obama.

44. Mary B. Jacoby, "The DOJ's Black Panthers Woes: A Set-Up, With An Assist From Inside," Main Justice, September 26, 2010, http://www.mainjustice.com/2010/09/26/the-dojs-black-panthers-woes-a-set-up-with-an-assist-from-inside/.

45. Hans A. von Spakovsky, "Investigating the Black Panther Case," *National Review*, September 14, 2009, http://www.nationalreview.com/corner/187130/investigating-black-panther-case-hans-von-spakovsky.

46. Holder's comments reprinted in "Eric Holder's 'Made-Up' Defense," *Pajamas Media*, December 31, 2010, http://pajamasmedia.com/blog/eric-holders-made-up-defense/.

47. OPR Report at 75, n. 49.

48. Pamela S. Karlan, "Lessons Learned: Voting Rights and the Bush Administration," 4 Duke J. Const. L. & Pub. Pol'y 17 (2009).

49. OPR Report at 64, n. 38.

50. Ibid.

51. OPR Report at 62.

52. OPR Report at 64.

53. "Justice Lawyers Cleared in Voting Case," *New York Times*, March 29, 2011.

54. OPR Report at 68, n. 40.

55. OPR Report at 61.

56. "Annotated Panther Timeline," *Washington Times*, January 19, 2010, http://www.washingtontimes.com/news/2010/jan/19/annotated-time-line/print/.

57. Hans A. von Spakovsky, "The New Black Panthers and the White House," *National Review*, January 19, 2010, http://www.national review.com/articles/228977/new-black-panthers-and-white-house-hans-von-spakovsky?page=1.

58. "New Black Panther Spotted at Philadelphia Polling Place," FoxNews. com, November 2, 2010, http://www.foxnews.com/politics/2010/11/02/ new-black-panther-spotted-philadelphia-polling-place/.

59. "Breaking Video: New Black Panthers Commit Outrageous Violations of Texas Voting Law," *Pajamas Media*, November 2, 2010, http:// pajamasmedia.com/blog/breaking-video-soon-new-black-panthers-commit-outrageous-violations-of-texas-voting-law/.

Chapter Six

1. "Federal Officials Dispatched to Monitor Primary Elections in New Jersey, New Mexico, and Alabama," Justice Department Dispatch 317, June 5, 2000, http://www.justice.gov/opa/pr/2000/June/317cr.htm.

2. Faye Cochran, telephone conversation with author, April 28, 2011.

3. Ibid.

4. Testimony of Chris Coates before the United States Commission on Civil Rights, September 24, 2010, http://www.usccr.gov/NBPH/09-24-2010_NBPPhearing.pdf, pp. 41–42.

5. Ibid., 42.

6. Dana Beyerle, "Senator says he may be victim of voter fraud," *Tuscaloosa News*, November 7, 2007, http://www.tuscaloosanews.com/ article/20071107/NEWS/71107004?p=all&tc=pgall.

7. Ibid.

8. Faye Cochran, telephone conversation with author, April 28, 2011.

9. Stephanie Taylor, "Two accused of voter fraud in Hale County," *Tuscaloosa News*, August 17, 2007, http://www.tuscaloosanews.com/ article/20070817/LATEST/70817026.

10. Faye Cochran, telephone conversation with author, April 28, 2011.

11. "Two plead not guilty to Hale County election fraud charges," Alabama Public Radio, October 15, 2007, http://www.publicbroadcasting. net/wual/news.newsmain/article/0/0/1165784/Alabama/Two.Plead. Not.Guilty.to.Hale.County.Election.Fraud.Charges.

12. John Shryock, "Court issues decision on Judge Wiggins," WSFA-12, July 30, 2009, http://www.wsfa.com/Global/story.asp?S=10821214.

13. Alabama Court of the Judiciary Case No. 37, In the Matter of Marvin W. Wiggins, Circuit Judge, July 30, 2009, http://wsfa.images.world now.com/images/incoming/linkedwebdocs/SCAN0209_000.pdf.

14. "Former Hale County official sentenced in vote case," Associated Press, August 31, 2010, http://www2.alabamas13.com/m/news/2010/aug/31/former-hale-county-official-sentenced-vote-case-ar-772326/.

15. Jason Morton, "Hale County voter fraud defendant pleads guilty," *Tuscaloosa News*, September 15, 2009, http://www.tuscaloosanews.com/article/20090915/news/909149917?p=all&tc=pgall.

16. "Chapman to Visit Counties with Voter Fraud Allegations," www.sos.alabama.gov, May 24, 2010, http://www.sos.alabama.gov/PR/PR.aspx?ID=3248.

17. Jason Morton, "Hale County officials worry voter fraud is back," *Tuscaloosa News*, May 29, 2010, http://www.tuscaloosanews.com/article/20100528/news/100529584?p=all&tc=pgall.

18. Chris Coates, interview with author.

19. Secretary of State Delbert Hosemann, Report of Election Day Activities in Wilkinson County, June 24, 2008, http://www.sos.ms.gov/links/press_releases/WILKINSON_CO_PRIMARY_REPORT.pdf.

20. Ibid.

21. Ibid.

22. Ibid.

23. Michael Waldman and Justin Levitt, "The Myth of Voter Fraud," *Washington Post*, March 29, 2007, http://www.washingtonpost.com/wp-dyn/content/article/2007/03/28/AR2007032801969.html.

24. Meg Coker, "Sowers guilty on ten voter fraud counts," *The Tunica Times*, April 21, 2011, http://www.tunicatimes.com/index.php?option=com_content&view=article&id=1176:sowers-guilty-on-ten-voter-fraud-counts&catid=2:paid&Itemid=26, and Tunica County NAACP Executive Committee, http://tunicacountynaacp.club.officelive.com/NAACPExecutiveCommittee.aspx. Last checked April 29, 2011.

25. Tunica County NAACP Executive Committee, http://tunicacountynaacp.club.officelive.com/NAACPExecutiveCommittee.aspx. Last checked April 29, 2011.

26. Tova Andrea Wang, "Voting in 2010, Lessons Learned," Demos.org, http://www.demos.org/pubs/2010Election-PostMortem.pdf.

27. Matthew Vadum, "Mississippi NAACP leader sent to prison for 10 counts of voter fraud," *Daily Caller*, July 29, 2011, http://dailycaller.com/2011/07/29/mississippi-naacp-leader-sent-to-prison-for-10-counts-of-voter-fraud/.

28. "Wasserman Schultz: "We've Really Begun To Turn The Economy Around," RealClearPolitics, August 2, 2011, http://realclearpolitics. com/video/2011/08/02/debbie_wasserman_schultz_weve_really_ begun_to_turn_the_economy_around.html.

29. "DNC Chair: How to Stop Voter ID Laws," *The Root*, July 26, 2011, http://www.theroot.com/blogs/dnc/dnc-chair-how-stop-voter-id-laws.

30. 502 U.S. 491 (1992).

31. *The United States of America v. The State of Rhode Island*, http://www. scribd.com/doc/51103523.

32. "Comparison of Colorado Voter Rolls with Department of Revenue Non-Citizen Records," March 8, 2011, http://www.scribd.com/ doc/50308209/Colorado-SOS-report-on-noncitizens.

33. OPR report at 64, n. 38.

34. J. Christian Adams, "Obama's Bumblers Damage Military Voting Rights," *Washington Examiner*, July 13, 2011, http://washingtonex aminer.com/opinion/op-eds/2011/07/obamas-bumblers-damage-military-voting-rights.

35. "Senate Confirmation Hearings: Eric Holder, Day One," *New York Times*, January 16, 2009, http://www.nytimes.com/2009/01/16/us/ politics/16text-holder.html?pagewanted=all.

36. Letter of Loretta King to James P. Cauley III, Esq., August 17, 2009, http://www.justice.gov/crt/about/vot/sec_5/ltr/l_081709.php.

37. Ibid.

38. Ibid.

39. *United States of America v. Waller County, Texas; and Ellen C. Shel-burne, Waller County Registrar*, http://www.justice.gov/crt/about/vot/ sec_5/waller_comp.pdf/.

40. *United States of America v. City of Calera, Alabama*, http://www.justice. gov/crt/about/vot/sec_5/calera_comp.pdf.

41. Dan Eggen, "Gonzales Defends Approval of Texas Redistricting by Justice," *Washington Post*, December 3, 2005, http://www.washington post.com/wp-dyn/content/article/2005/12/02/AR2005120201802.html.

42. Ibid.

43. "Hoyer Statement on New Revelations About Republicans Redistrict-ing Tactics in Texas," Democratic Whip Steny Hoyer, December 2, 2005, http://www.democraticwhip.gov/content/hoyer-statement-new-revelations-about-republicans-redistricting-tactics-texas.

44. "Hoyer, Conyers, Pelosi, Waxman & Clay on Texas Redistricting," DCCC, December 2, 2005, http://dccc.org/blog/entry/hoyer_conyers_pelosi_waxman_clay_on_texas_redistricting/.

45. Ibid.

46. *League of United Latin American Citizens, et al. v. Perry*, 548 U. S. 399 (2006), http://www.law.cornell.edu/supct/html/05-204.ZS.html.

Chapter Seven

1. Mellon Auditorium, Architectural Overview, http://www.mellonauditorium.com/history.htm.

2. Cameron W. Barr, "Council Chief Builds a Base In the New Montgomery," *Washington Post*, April 3, 2005, http://www.washingtonpost.com/wp-dyn/articles/A22074-2005Apr2.html.

3. Title IX is codified at 20 U.S.C. § 1681, *et seq.*

4. Byron York, "Why did feds claim Kindle violates civil rights?" *Washington Examiner*, August 3, 2010, http://washingtonexaminer.com/news/science-and-technology/why-did-feds-claim-kindle-violates-civil-rights#ixzz1KOiOXCVY.

5. "Attorney General Eric Holder Speaks About the Department of Justice's Priorities and Mission," April 25, 2011, http://www.justice.gov/iso/opa/ag/speeches/2011/ag-speech-110425.html. Holder quotes Attorney General Edward Levi. Holder uses the comment to describe "where we must go from here."

6. Ibid.

7. Randal C. Archibold, "Ranchers Alarmed by Killing Near Border," *New York Times*, April 4, 2010, http://www.nytimes.com/2010/04/05/us/05arizona.html.

8. Letter of Loretta King to Sheriff Joseph Arpaio, March 10, 2009, http://www.azcentral.com/ic/pdf/0310justice.pdf.

9. Jackie Mahendra, "Success: Justice Department Sends Monitors to Maricopa, AZ, Arpaio Breaks Ties with Extreme Group," Reform Immigration for America, http://reformimmigrationforamerica.org/blog/blog/success-justice-department-sends-monitors-to-maricopa-az-arpaio-breaks-ties-with-extreme-group/.

10. Letter of David N. Kelley to Omar Jadwat, ACLU Immigrants' Rights Project, July 22, 2006, http://www.scribd.com/doc/31610036/Jay-Bybee-Inherent-Authority-Immigration-Memo.

11.   Jerry Markon, "Memo from 2002 could complicate challenge of Arizona immigration law," *Washington Post*, May 18, 2010, http://www.washingtonpost.com/wp-dyn/content/article/2010/05/17/AR2010051702175.html?wprss=rss_nation.

12.   *United States v. County of Kane, Illinois*, http://www.justice.gov/crt/about/vot/sec_203/documents/kane_comp.php.

13.   *United States v. City of Los Angeles, California, Board of Police Commissioners*, http://www.lapdonline.org/assets/pdf/final_consent_decree.pdf.

14.   Joel Rubin, "Justice Department warns LAPD to take a stronger stance against racial profiling," *Los Angeles Times*, November 14, 2010, http://articles.latimes.com/2010/nov/14/local/la-me-lapd-bias-20101114.

15.   Heather MacDonald, "Targeting the Police," *Weekly Standard*, January 31, 2011.

16.   Jerry Markon, "Justice Department's Civil Rights Division steps up enforcement," *Washington Post*, June 4, 2010, http://www.washingtonpost.com/wp-dyn/content/article/2010/06/03/AR2010060304938.html.

17.   About IRJ: Sponsors, Institute on Race and Justice, http://www.irj.neu.edu/about_irj/sponsors/.

18.   "Remarks as Prepared for Delivery by Assistant Attorney General for Civil Rights Thomas E. Perez at the Civil Rights and School Discipline: Addressing Disparities to Ensure Equal Educational Opportunities Conference," September 27, 2010, http://www.justice.gov/crt/speeches/perez_eosconf_speech.php.

19.   Tracy Russo, "Civil Rights and School Discipline," The Justice Blog, October 1, 2010, http://blogs.usdoj.gov/blog/archives/997.

20.   "Remarks as Prepared for Delivery by Assistant Attorney General for Civil Rights Thomas E. Perez," *op. cit.*

21.   *Frank Ricci, et al., v. John DeStegano, et al.*, http://www.americanbar.org/content/dam/aba/publishing/preview/publiced_preview_briefs_pdfs_07_08_08_328_VacaturandRemandAmCuUSA.authcheckdam.pdf.

22.   *United States v. State of New Jersey and New Jersey Civil Service Commission*, http://media.nj.com/ledgerupdates_impact/other/cops.pdf.

23.   "Civil Service Board Announces Police Recruit Scores," Dayton News Source, March 11, 2011, video available at http://abc.daytonsnews

source.com/shared/newsroom/top_stories/videos/wkef_vid_6103. shtml.

24. Andrew C. McCarthy, "Why the al-Qaeda Seven Matter," *National Review*, March 9, 2010, http://www.nationalreview.com/articles/ print/229281.

25. "Muslim Women: Past and Present," Women's Islamic Initiative in Spirituality and Equality, http://www.wisemuslimwomen.org/muslim women/bio/raheemah_abdulaleem/.

26. Jerry Markon, "Justice Department sues on behalf of Muslim teacher, triggering debate," *Washington Post*, March 22, 2011, http://www. washingtonpost.com/politics/justice-department-sues-on-behalf-of- muslim-teacher-triggering-debate/2010/07/28/ABfSPtEB_story.html.

Chapter Eight

1. "Justice and Vote Fraud," *Wall Street Journal*, October 27, 2008.

2. Judy Harrison, "District judge clears Tobin," *Bangor Daily News*, February 18, 2009.

3. Thomas B. Edsall, "GOP Official Faces Sentence in Phone-Jamming," *Washington Post*, May 17, 2006, http://www.washingtonpost.com/ wp-dyn/content/article/2006/05/16/AR2006051601712.html.

4. See, Deborah White, "Obama Campaign Promises: Civil Liberties & Rights," About.com, which captures Obama Campaign website infor- mation at http://usliberals.about.com/od/patriotactcivilrights/a/ ObamaCivRghts.htm.

5. Opinion at *United States v. Son Ja Cha; In Han Cha*, http://www.ca9. uscourts.gov/datastore/opinions/2010/03/09/09-10147.pdf.

6. Dana M. Perino and Bill Burck, "Friday Night Hack Attack," *National Review*, February 22, 2010, .

7. See the letter here: http://judiciary.house.gov/hearings/pdf/Mukasey- Filip090119.pdf.

8. Jennifer Rubin, "The Decline of the Justice Department," *Weekly Standard*, January 31, 2011, http://www.weeklystandard.com/articles/ decline-justice-department_536871.html.

9. Hans A. von Spakovsky, "They're playing games, literally, in the Jus- tice Department," *Washington Examiner*, February 28, 2011.

10. Mark Niesse, "Charges dropped in Hawaii for forced labor trial," *Kansas City Star*, August 5, 2011, http://www.kansascity. com/2011/08/05/3058113/charges-dropped-in-hawaii-forced.html.

11. "New Low: 17% Say U.S. Government Has Consent of the Governed," Rasmussen Reports, August 7, 2011, http://www.rasmussenreports. com/public_content/politics/general_politics/august_2011/new_ low_17_say_u_s_government_has_consent_of_the_governed.

12. "Only 17% Say Government Has Consent of the Public," naked capitalism, August 8, 2011, http://www.nakedcapitalism.com/2011/08/ only-17-say-government-has-consent-of-the-public.html.

Index

FROM REGNERY PUBLISHING
COMES A NEW IMPRINT

History is full of heroes and villains, stories and back stories.
But too often, only one side of the story reaches the public.
That's why Regnery Publishing is proud to announce the launch
of its new imprint **Regnery History**! Introducing a line-up of
fascinating and captivating titles within the history, biography,
and military categories, **Regnery History** titles will offer you:

★ A new perspective on historical figures and topics
   that deserve attention, but may have been ignored,
   overlooked, or even covered up in the past

★ Compelling and comprehensive biographies

★ An entertaining and educating journey into our past
   that will change the way you see history forever

To learn more, go to
RegneryHistory.com